Making Science
Laboratory Equipment

Making Science Laboratory Equipment

A manual for students and teachers in developing countries

Xavier F. Carelse
Department of Physics
University of Zimbabwe

JOHN WILEY & SONS LIMITED

Chichester · New York · Brisbane · Toronto · Singapore

Library of Congress Cataloging in Publication Data:

Carelse, Xavier F.
  Making science laboratory equipment.

  Bibliography: p.
  Includes index.
  1. Laboratories—Apparatus and supplies—Handbooks,
manuals, etc. I. Title.
0185.C324 1983   507′.8   82–8589

ISBN 0 471 10353 5

British Library Cataloguing in Publication Data:

Carelse, Xavier Francis
  Making science laboratory equipment.
  1. Laboratories—Underdeveloped areas—
  Furniture, equipment, etc.
  2. Schools—Underdeveloped areas—Furniture,
  equipments, etc.
  I. Title
  371.6′234   LB332/5.L/

ISBN 0 471 10353 5

Photosetting by Thomson Press (India) Limited, New Delhi and
Printed in Great Britain by Page Bros (Norwich) Ltd.

Contents

Preface

Science teaching in developing countries suffers from the lack of adequate laboratory equipment, aggravated in the last eight years by the very high rate of inflation in the industrial countries from which it is usually ordered. The phenomenal increase in the school-going population, which was encouraged in the post-colonial years and which was an attestation of heightened aspirations, became, almost overnight, an insupportable burden on resources. A rapid deterioration in facilities is being experienced in all but a few private or select government-favoured institutions. This is particularly alarming as the hopes of economic progress are closely tied to the rate at which scientists, engineers, and medical practitioners may be trained.

This problem has been checked, to some extent, by the use of multipurpose kits, which cost very little but with which most of the important principles could be demonstrated or tested. Overseas manufacturers have already turned out such kits for chemistry, mechanics, electricity, electronics, etc. Many Third World countries are now also producing their own versions through such groups as the Science Education Project Unit (SEPU) in Kenya, the Zimbabwe Secondary School Science Project (Zim-Sci) in Zimbabwe and similar ones at many universities in Nigeria.

This approach is particularly useful for the first two or three years at secondary school where the classes are large. But at higher levels, the pupils are expected to acquire hands-on experience of working with certain classical apparatus. They need to handle a metre bridge that looks like a metre bridge, an optical bench that can be identified as such. Furthermore the teacher must be equipped to demonstrate, in a visually effective manner, such important topics as the vernier scale, among other things.

Such single-purpose equipment is expensive. Because of erratic demand, problems of distribution, and the uncertain availability of large quantities of raw materials, it is unlikely that it can be mass-produced in a local factory at a cost which would be less than that of the imported article.

This impasse could be overcome if the teachers were to construct such equipment themselves. In fact, a recent list of basic equipment, specified by the Nigerian Federal Ministry of Education, included 'equipment that should be manufactured'. Various teachers' training colleges and the faculties of education of many universities have introduced courses into their curriculum in which teachers were given training in the construction of some equipment. Unfortunately, many of the problems, encountered when the teacher in rural areas tries to implement this knowledge, are not tackled. The main one, that of lack of money, is usually not dealt with at all. A fatalistic sink-or-swim attitude is often adopted.

The primary thesis of this book is that the subject of improvisation has become of such economic importance to the developing world that it is no longer sufficient to treat it with the hit-or-miss amateurism of the past. It must now be approached with a dedicated overall philosophy by which teachers are trained to fend for themselves continuously, mobilizing all the recources available to them. These resources are considerable, if used effectively. It includes the school's woodwork master, the village blacksmiths and carpenters, the pupils and their parents and, most important, their traditional enthusiasm for handicrafts. All pupils, whether in the academic stream or not, should be required to follow a handicrafts, woodwork or metalwork course to prepare them for the new needs of their country.

This book attempts to bridge the many gaps which exist between the use of the multipurpose kits and the requirements of university entrance. The approach is wholeheartedly and unreservedly directed towards the problems encountered by the teacher in underprivileged, usually rural, schools. It is assumed that:

1. The teacher and the headmaster are positively motivated towards a programme of improvisation;
2. there is not much money available but that sufficient may be found to get the programme started;
3. the school is, perhaps by commuting taxi transport, within a distance of, say, 50 kilometres from a town with a population of not less than 20,000 people.

It is believed, in the last point, that the building activity in a town of this size should be able to sustain at least one well-stocked supplier of tools and building materials.

Nowhere is it assumed that this book is written only for the male teacher. At home, I make it a point to encourage my two daughters to construct for themselves the toy furniture they want for their doll's house.

Part I is entitled 'Techniques' and consists of four chapters. Chapters 1 and 2 deal with various tools and materials. The number of tools is kept to a minimum and is divided into kits of which the basic kit A is used in almost all the construction projects. The supplementary kits B, C and D need only be purchased as required or afforded. Chapter 3 is concerned with electrical tools and apparatus and covers, certain aspects of fault tracing, and repairs. Chapter 4, in many respects, may be the most valuable in the book. It shows in, it is hoped, a realistic way, how the task of equipping a laboratory may be undertaken with a minimum of funds.

Part II, entitled 'Projects', contains five chapters, including an Appendix. Chapters 5 and 6 include 28 physics and 18 chemistry projects respectively, while Chapter 7 embodies 5 of biology and 5 of geography. Chapter 8 describes the construction of 6 pieces of equipment which may be required in the workshop. Because of limitations to the size of the book, the projects have had to be carefully selected. Most are essential items for a laboratory catering for the fourth and higher years of secondary school. A few have been included because they illustrate the way in which certain scrap or building materials may be used. Also, techniques, not mentioned in Part I but specific to a project, are described in detail when the project is dealt with. By mastering all the techniques presented in both parts of the book, the readers may themselves be able to enlarge the repertoire of the book. Wherever necessary, technical or near-technical drawings have been prepared for the benefit of artisans who may be called upon to assist the teacher.

Chapter 9, the Appendix, contains the stock lists as well as certains bits of information which, in some cases, are relevant to the book as a whole while others are supplementary to particular projects. Supplementary information such as the description of the corona experiment or the comparison of local and standard time have been removed to the Appendix so that the description of the project with which they are concerned is not obscured by their inclusion.

May I say finally that this book is the culmination of 17 years of teaching in schools and universities in 5 different African countries and 8 years of working in industrial research and development in the United Kingdom. A lifetime of experience is tied up in it. Please make the best use of it.

Part I

Techniques

CHAPTER 1

The elements of woodwork

1.1 INTRODUCTION

The tools and materials in this course have been carefully chosen to avoid complicated and tedious work. Those which are essential for basic woodwork construction, and which must definitely be purchased, have been grouped together and are referred to as kit A. Almost all projects require some tool or other from the basic kit A. How soon you acquire each individual item in this kit will depend on the projects that you undertake. In general, you will be well advised to purchase all the items as soon as you are able to. More expensive power tools and accessories may also be bought but these do not have a high priority. They have been grouped into the supplementary kit B (see Section 1.3).

For our working materials, we will rely, to a large extent, on man-made boards. They are ideal for our purposes, being easy to use, readily available, and usually not very much more expensive than planed timber. If they are, you will soon find that their ease of use justifies the extra expense. Most countries do already have factories producing various types from hardboards and softboards to the more expensive plywoods and blockboards.

Where it will be necessary to use natural timbers, the sawing and planing can usually be done for you. A visit to the timber section of the market will reveal at least one shed where an enterprising young man has acquired a heavy-duty planing machine and circular ripsaw. You can buy rough-sawn timber of almost any size and he will cut it into strips or boards and plane them on all surfaces to the thickness that you require. If you fail to find such a person, a carpenter or joiner may be prepared to provide you with this service. In a few towns near timber-producing areas, you may find facilities such as a power planer at the local sawmill. The cost of this service usually doubles the cost of the timber but, again, it is worth the extra money.

If you have planned your project carefully you could also get the machinist to cut your man-made boards to the widths and lengths that you require; but it is only worth saving labour and time in this way if you intend to mass-produce an article. For single items, do your own cutting but, while doing so, choose your dimensions in such a way that you can eventually mass-produce it with the minimum of wastage. It is advisable to cut your timber to exact fractions of the two dimensions of the board. The fact that boards are still supplied in imperial standard sizes, such as 8 feet by 4 feet, leads many carpenters in anglophone countries to continue using inches, instead of millimetres, for their measurements. It is interesting to note that even in staunchly metricized countries like France, one standard board size, 2442 mm by 1221 mm, is really the 8 feet by 4 feet size in disguise.

We will now discuss in detail the tools, the materials and the methods of joining and fixing which will be needed for this course. How wooden structures are put together and the types of structures that form the basic frames for laboratory equipment will, at the end of this chapter, be dealt with in such a way that it will be shown that the construction of laboratory equipment may be undertaken with very little trepidation indeed.

For your convenience, a glossary of woodworking and other terms appears in Section 9.7.

1.2   BASIC KIT A: HANDTOOLS

This kit, shown in Fig. 1.1, consists of the following tools:
    various saws: panel saw, hacksaw and fretsaw;

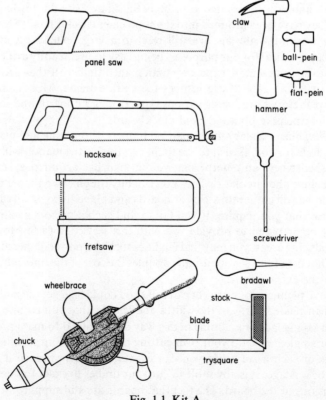

Fig. 1.1 Kit A

a claw hammer;
a cabinet screwdriver; a bradawl;
a wheelbrace and accessories;
a trysquare.

1.2.1 Saws

A saw has a cutting edge consisting of a succession of sharp points or teeth, of which the shape, size, and pitch make a particular saw suitable for one job but not for others. A coarse-cutting saw has a few points per inch (p.p.i.) of its length; a fine saw has more.

The pitch of a saw is the spacing between the teeth, that is, it is the reciprocal of the p.p.i. For convenience, it may be expressed in millimetres. Therefore an 18 p.p.i. saw will have a pitch of 1.4 mm. Generally the thickness of the material to be cut determines the pitch required, a useful rule being that the thickness should be between two and six times the spacing between the teeth. It is possible to cut timber thicker than six times the spacing but this is tedious and time-consuming. Boards thinner than twice the pitch may also be tackled if the saw-cut is made at a very acute angle to the work. This increases the effective thickness of the board (see Fig. 1.2).

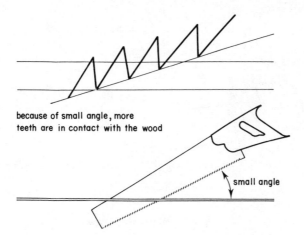

Fig. 1.2 Cutting through thin boards

The panel saw

This saw has a blade about half a metre long and will cope adequately with most of our jobs. As the name implies, it is especially designed for cutting large boards. A panel saw has 10 p.p.i. (or 2.5 mm pitch) and so can cut quite easily through boards of 5 mm to 15 mm thickness, while hardboard and plywood of 3 mm thickness can be managed just as well.

6

If, on the other hand, you want to make very accurate joints, you may also invest in a tenon saw but many carpenters, at least in West Africa, make their half-lap joints and tenons by using only a panel saw.

Hints

1. Your stance (how you stand or bend in relation to the job) should be well-balanced and firm.
2. Your sawing arm should be free to move in a direct line with the intended cut. You should be able to apply a light-to-medium pressure on the downward stroke without affecting your balance (Fig. 1.3(a)).

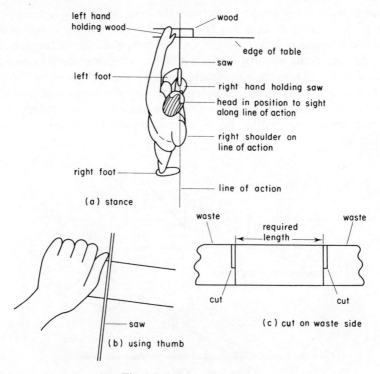

Fig. 1.3 Using a panel saw

3. Point your index finger along the blade for better control.
4. Position the cut by using your thumb as a guide (Fig. 1.3(b)).
5. Always make cuts on the waste side of the line to which you are working. If you cut on the line, you will find that the piece will be slightly undersize (Fig. 1.3(c)).
6. When cutting a large sheet of hardboard or thin plywood, support it on two other stouter boards and saw between them (Fig. 1.4). Use the saw at a very low angle to increase the number of teeth in contact with the material (Fig. 1.4).
7. Use a bench hook when cutting across the grain. A bench hook is easily constructed by screwing two short strips of wood, 120 mm long by 40 mm wide by 20 mm thick, along the edges, top and bottom, of a rectangular piece of wood, 200 mm by 150 mm by

20 mm thick (Fig. 1.5(a)). The piece to be cut is gripped against the upper strip while the lower strip butts against the edge of the workbench (Fig. 1.5(b)). In this way the work is held very steady for accurate cutting.

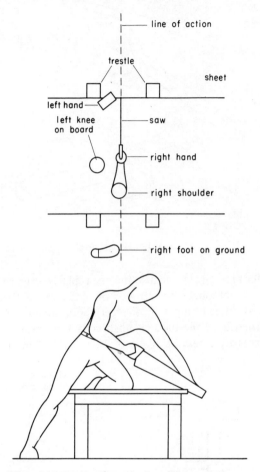

Fig. 1.4 Sawing large sheets of thin wood

Hacksaw

This tool is primarily intended for cutting metal but, as it may also be used for hardboard and plastic, it has been included in this chapter. A junior hacksaw is a useful tool with a fine blade and is only a fraction of the price of the standard version (Fig. 1.6). Cheaper still is the mini-hacksaw which is really just a plastic handle with a slot into which the standard hacksaw blade is fitted. It can be fitted with broken pieces of blade, only 70 mm long, and is tough enough to be used on steel. However, the standard hacksaw is the preferred tool and is the one that we will consider for our work.

Unlike the panel saw, it has a detachable blade which may be changed to suit

8

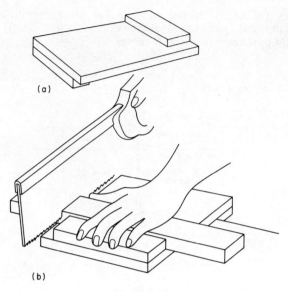

(a)

(b)

Fig. 1.5 Bench hook

the type of material to be cut and also may be replaced if worn or broken. Most hacksaws can accommodate two lengths of blade, viz. 250 mm (10 inch) and 300 mm (12 inch). After fitting, with the teeth pointing away from the handle, a wing nut is turned until the blade is absolutely taut without the frame being subjected to excessive stress. A blade of 18 p.p.i. (1.4 mm pitch) is the most

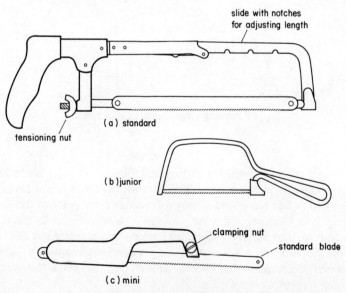

slide with notches
for adjusting length

(a) standard

tensioning nut

(b) junior

clamping nut

standard blade

(c) mini

Fig. 1.6 Types of hacksaw

generally useful and can also be used for cutting hardboard or thin plywood.

The handle may be of the pistol-grip type or the less expensive straight type. Choose whichever is comfortable for you.

Hints

1. Use you thumb as a guide to start the cut, then transfer both hands to the saw (Fig. 1.7). With both hands thus occupied, it is important that the workpiece be clamped tightly or held firmly in a vice.

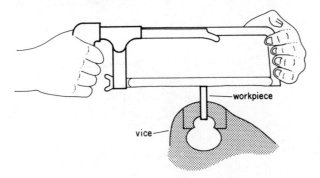

Fig. 1.7 Cutting with a hacksaw

2. Stand slightly closer to the workpiece than you do when using the panel saw. In this way, an even pressure will be applied throughout the stroke and the entire length of the blade will be brought into play. About 40 strokes per minute are adequate with pressure being applied only in the forward stroke.
3. A spot of oil on the blade will make the sawing easier and will also protect the blade.
4. A hacksaw may also be used for cutting fairly thin sheet. The blade is then held at a very small angle to the sheet. Use a light, almost caressing downstroke and no pressure at all in the upstroke.
5. If the sheet is too thin, or made of soft materials such as lead, support it on hardboard and cut through both materials simultaneously.

Fretsaw

This tool resembles a hacksaw in construction, but the frame has a deeper reach and it uses a thinner, more flexible blade. The blade is only 2 or 3 mm wide and is mounted between clamps with the teeth pointing *towards* the handle. It can be used to cut holes and intricate curves and is required in the construction of certain chemistry and optics equipment.

Hints

1. To start an enclosed cut, drill a hole in the waste part of the timber. Detach the blade and pass it through the hole before fixing the blade back on the frame. Hold the work flat on the table with sufficient overhang to allow you to use the saw or, better still, hold it on a special fretwork platform into which a V-notch has been cut (Fig. 1.8). The saw

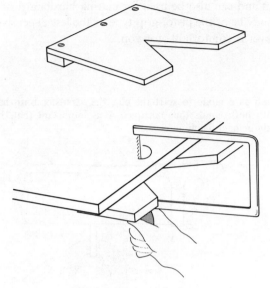

Fig. 1.8 Fretsaw platform

is held with the handle below the piece to be cut. Use only light pressure with slow even strokes. Do not allow the blade to bend under the force of the cut.
2. The fretsaw provides a very simple way of making wooden frames. It is possible to make these using half-lap joints, but unless you are a skilled carpenter, it is unlikely that the resulting frame will be perfectly flat. With a fretsaw all that you need to do, is to cut a rectangular hole in a rectangular piece of blockboard or plywood. This method is used in the construction of the duplicating machine (Project 8.2).

1.2.2   Trysquare

This is a vital tool for accurate marking out and for setting right angles. An all-metal trysquare is preferred to the traditional type with a wooden stock and metal blade. The wide variation of humidity in the tropics affects the moisture content of the wood causing it alternately to swell and contract, thereby reducing the accuracy of the tool.

Hints

1. Keep a thin film of oil or grease on the blade to reduce friction and wear during use and to prevent rust from obliterating the graduations.
2. Learner carpenters are often tempted to use a trysquare as a hammer. This is the worst thing you can do to it.
3. The use of the try-square is discussed fully in Appendix 9.8.

1.2.3 Hammer

A 16 to 20 ounce (about 500 gram) claw hammer is the recommended buy as it drives *and* pulls out nails. If you wish, you may also buy a flat-pein hammer which

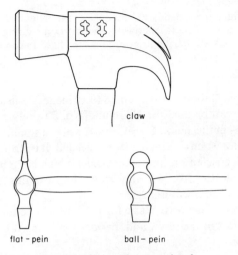

claw

flat – pein   ball – pein

Fig. 1.9 Various hammer heads

is suitable for small nails, pins, and tacks. Choose a hammer with a forged head and a hardwood handle—preferably hickory. Cheap, cast heads tend to shatter and rubber grips on metal handles become slippery in the tropical heat. Various types of hammer heads are shown in Fig. 1.9.

Hints

1. Grip the hammer near the end of the handle, not in the middle (Fig. 1.10).
2. Start the nail by tapping, then hit squarely, such that the handle is at right angles to the nail at the moment of impact.
3. Use a firm stroke, pivoting from the elbow with no wrist movement.
4. Occasionally rub the hammer face lightly on a flat sheet of fine sandpaper. This keeps the face clean and free of grease. A slippery face often causes nails to bend.

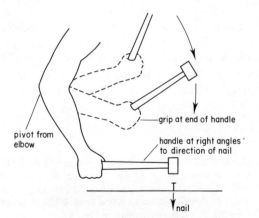

grip at end of handle

pivot from elbow

handle at right angles to direction of nail

nail

Fig. 1.10 Using a hammer

5. Rub raw linseed oil into the handle at least once a year preferably just at the beginning of the dry season. This reduces the shrinkage that can occur during this time and which, if severe, could crack the handle or even cause the head to come off.

1.2.4. Screwdriver

A cabinet screwdriver, about 20 to 25 cm (8 to 10 inches) long and having a blade about 5 mm wide, can be used for No. 6 and No. 8 woodscrews which are the recommended sizes in this book. For electrical work, a smaller one, about 10 cm (4 inches) long with a 3 mm (1/8 inch) blade is needed. It is strongly recommended that you get the electrician's testing screwdriver which has a built-in neon lamp and can be used for testing live 240 volt wiring. The use of this type of screwdriver is explained in detail in Section 3.2.3.

Use a screwdriver of the correct size for the screw to be turned. An ill-fitting tool damages the slot in the screw and, besides rendering it unsightly, makes it difficult to remove.

1.2.5 Bradawl

The bradawl closely resembles a small screwdriver. It has a pin with a flattened point embedded in a wooden handle (See Fig. 1.1). It is used for marking points in timber into which holes are to be drilled. This mark, if sufficiently deep, can serve as a starting hole for woodscrews of No. 6 gauge and less.

Hints

1. The cutting edge is held at right angles to the grain and the hole is made by pushing hard into the wood. Twist the point slightly to and fro before withdrawing it.
2. Do not use this tool as a screwdriver as the pin will loosen and render it useless.
3. Keep the point sharp by rubbing it gently on very fine sandpaper.

1.2.6 Wheelbrace

This tool is cheaper than the electrical drill discussed in Section 1.3. It does not require a supply of electricity and it can be used in much more confined places. The side-handle, which is removable, allows more pressure and firmer control to be applied when needed. The chuck has three self-centering jaws which takes the same bits that are used with an electrical power tool. Holes with diameters up to 8 mm may be drilled into wood, metal, and plastics.

Hints

1. For accurate drilling, sight the bit against a trysquare (Fig. 1.11) or get someone, standing away from the work, to advise you if you are drilling at an incorrect angle.
2. A depth-stop should be used when drilling to a fixed depth. Depth-stops can be bought or made from a piece of drilled-out scrap wood (Fig. 1.12). A short length of rubber tubing fitted over the bit, or a piece of insulation tape wrapped around the bit, will help to prevent it from going deeper than intended.

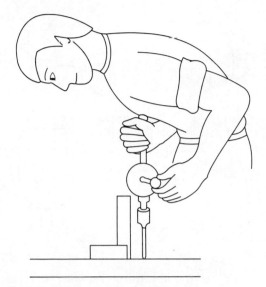

Fig. 1.11 Sighting a brace against a trysquare

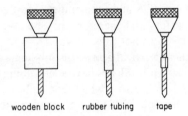

wooden block   rubber tubing   tape

Fig. 1.12 Depth-stops

3. Oil the brace frequently at the chuck, the handle, and the wheel.
4. The most frequent use of the brace will be to drill starter and clearance holes into wood for screws and bolts. This aspect is covered in more detail in Section 1.5.2.

1.3 SUPPLEMENTARY KIT B: POWER TOOLS

Although not included in the basic kit, these tools may become your most satisfying investment. They could cut down your work to such an extent that woodwork becomes a pleasure. The main tool is a hand-held electric drill for which there are a number of accessories. The drill and some of the most important accessories are shown in Figs. 1.13 to 1.16. Sometimes, for a little extra money, it is possible to buy the drill complete with some of these items.

Remember that most of the effort in carpentry goes into sawing, screwing, and sanding. A power tool makes very light work of these.

14

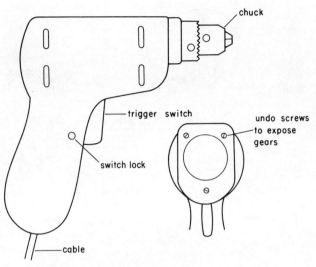

chuck

trigger switch

undo screws
to expose
gears

switch lock

cable

Fig. 1.13 Power drill

1.3.1 Electric drill

Purchase a two-speed drill with a chuck capable of taking bits with diameters of
8 mm (5/16 inch) or 9 mm (3/8 inch) maximum. Most power tools are double-
insulated for electrical safety and therefore may be used with a two-core cable
and a two-pin plug. This does not prevent you from using a three-pin plug for
uniformity with the other electrical apparatus in your workshop or laboratory.
In this case the longer earth-pin will not have a lead going to it (see Section 3.5.3).
Whichever plug you fit, choose one which is tough, resilient and will not get
damaged if you store the drill with other tools. A rubber or soft plastic plug
would be ideal.

Select the correct speed for the job according to Table 1.1. This reduces
overloading, prevents overheating and so increases the life of the accessories. The
bits, in particular, are easily blunted by using the wrong speed. A drill with a

Table 1.1 Drilling speeds

Speed	Function	Limits
Fast: 2500 rpm to 3000 rpm	Drilling into wood	Bits up to 10 mm
	Drilling into steel	Bits up to 6 mm
	Sanding and polishing	—
	Circular saw or jigsaw	Wood up to 6 mm thick
Slow: up to 1000 rpm	Drilling into wood	Bits 10 to 25 mm
	Drilling into steel	Bits 6 to 10 mm
	Drilling into masonry	Bits up to 8 mm
	Circular saw	Wood up to 25 mm thick

hammer action is more expensive but is very useful for drilling holes into masonry when you are required to mount equipment on a wall.

A decrease in speed during use is caused by overloading and can result in overheating of the armature and the bit. To avoid damage, withdraw the tool from the work and run it freely for a few seconds before using it again. This enables the built-in fan to cool the armature down. Make sure that the air vents on the drill are clear and unobstructed.

Occasionally apply a drop of oil on the chuck and annually clean and repack the gearbox with car grease. The gearbox may be removed by undoing three screws in the head of the drill, just behind the chuck.

1.3.2 Bits and other chuck-inserts

Buy a good quality set of high-speed twist bits in sizes ranging from 1 mm to 6.5 mm in steps of 0.5 mm (Fig. 1.14). The set which is given away free with the

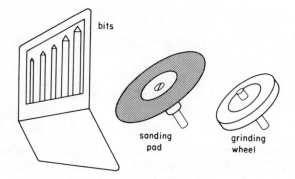

Fig. 1.14 Chuck-insert accessories

drill is usually not of a good quality unless it bears the name of the manufacturer of the drill itself. Tempered molybdenum steel sets are a good buy and should have a blue-black (almost black) oxidized surface. Do not be fooled by unscrupulous manufacturers who paint the bits black to fool the buyer. As a test of quality, try scratching the shank of the bit with the point of a woodscrew. You should not be able to make an impression.

Other accessories which fit into the chuck include a sanding disc, a grinding wheel, a wire brush and a paint stirrer. These are inexpensive, easy to fit, and useful for small but vital jobs.

1.3.3 Circular saw attachment

A circular saw is the most useful of the drill attachments (Fig. 1.15). With it you may cut softwood, including plywood, up to 35 mm thick with very little effort. The blade can be set at an angle, if necessary. The depth of cut can be controlled so making it useful for cutting grooves, slots, and rebates.

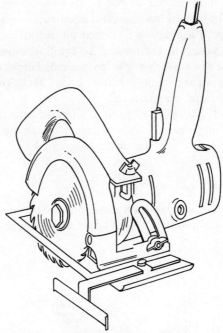

Fig. 1.15 Circular saw attachment

1.3.4 Vertical stand

For accurate drilling the drill should be mounted in a vertical stand bolted to a workbench (Fig. 1.16). It is particularly useful when an identical pattern of holes has to be drilled in many similar pieces. Simply stack the pieces, one on top of the other, secure in a cramp and drill through them all simultaneously.

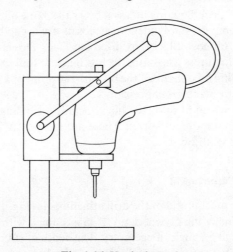

Fig. 1.16 Vertical stand

General hints

The instructions for the assembly, use and care of these tools are usually supplied by the manufacturers. Read them very carefully. Pin them up on your wall for easy reference and as a reminder for a maintenance schedule. As they are fairly expensive, regular maintenance will safeguard your investment by prolonging the useful life of the tools.

You may find that in spite of financial considerations, you are forced to buy an expensive tool because it is indispensable for constructing a piece of equipment that you need desperately. Let your own requirements guide you in your final decision.

Broadly speaking, specialized tools should only be purchased if

1. no local handyman has the necessary tool,
2. the handyman's charges are so high that the purchase of the tool becomes an economical investment,
3. there is the possibility that the tool could be used for other jobs or that the apparatus is to be produced in quantities of four or more.

1.4   STRUCTURAL MATERIALS

1.4.1   Natural timbers

Timbers are placed in two groups: softwoods and hardwoods. Softwoods are obtained from coniferous trees such as pine, podocarpus, cypress, etc.

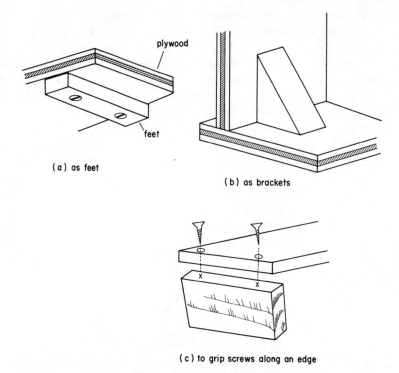

(a) as feet

(b) as brackets

(c) to grip screws along an edge

Fig. 1.17 Uses of timber

18

Hardwoods come from broad-leaved deciduous trees. The distinction is therefore generic so that some softwoods may, in fact, be harder than some hardwoods.

In this course, timber is used for the following purposes:

1. as feet for certain equipment. These are strips of hard-wearing timber fixed under the equipment (Fig. 1.17(a)).
2. as brackets. Triangular pieces are used to support two boards at right angles to each other (Fig. 1.17(b)).
3. plywood cannot hold screws which are driven into its edge. Natural timber is therefore used whenever this is necessary. It will provide a good grip, but only if the screw is driven at right angles to the grain (Fig. 1.17(c)).
4. thin strips of timber may be used as an edging for plywood to improve the appearance of the finished product.

As a rough but fairly reliable guide, you will find that those timbers which are used, in your area, for the construction of the solid, outer doors of dwellings (not flush inner doors) are best-suited to our purposes especially if they are used in the making of front doors. These timbers are durable and straight-grained with very little tendency to warp. Because of their water-resistant properties many of these are also used for laboratory furniture. Table 1.2 gives a lists of timbers which are available in various countries.

Having decided on the type of timber you want it will then be necessary to choose a particular board from the stacks in the timber yard. Fresh timber has a high moisture content and should be allowed to season, i.e. to dry out, before being put to use. The drying process causes shrinking, often by as much as 10 per cent, most of which takes place along the direction of the ring markings on the timber. If the curvature of the growth-ring markings on the timber is pronounced, warping should be expected (Fig. 1.18).

By touch and smell, you can tell if a board has been freshly cut and should therefore be rejected. Choose only the oldest, driest boards which would already have seasoned and would show signs of warping if the grain pattern was wrong.

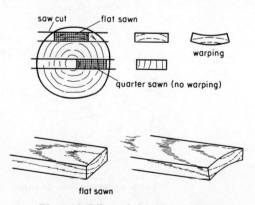

Fig. 1.18 Effect of rings on warping

Fig. 1.19 Checking for distortion

Raise one end of the board to eye level and look down its length (Fig. 1.19). Any distortion will be clearly visible. Select old boards which have retained their straightness. Occasionally only fresh timber may be available. It may, of course, be left to dry out by laying the boards horizontally with bricks or strips of wood placed at intervals to raise it off the floor and so allow the free circulation of air around it.

The growth-ring patterns are more visible after the boards have been planed. An examination of a 3.6 metre board will certainly reveal lengths of 0.6 metres or so which show very little likelihood of possible future warping. It is seldom that we will be requiring pieces longer than this. Saw off these straight-grained lengths and have them planed to 40 mm by 20 mm, 75 mm by 12 mm or 100 mm by 12 mm sections as specified in Stock List 1 (Appendix 9.1). The rest of the timber should be cut up and planed to the 25 mm by 12 mm pieces used as feet for benches and boxes.

1.4.2 Plywood and blockboard

Plywood is made from a number of thin wood veneers (plies) peeled from a log. For strength and rigidity the plies are bound to each other with their grains running at right angles in alternate layers (Fig. 1.20). Most plywoods are marked as interior grade, i.e. the plies have been bonded with a non-waterproof adhesive. Exterior grade or marine-ply is bonded with a water-resistant phenolic resin adhesive and is fairly difficult to obtain. As much of the equipment used in laboratories is liable to be splashed with water, it is recommended that plywood-based apparatus should be varnished.

Plywood and blockboard are the ideal woodworking materials for do-it-

Table 1.2 Suitable timbers

Name	Other names	Where grown	Remarks
Aini		West India	For laboratory furniture water resistant
Apamate	Pink poui, May flower	Trinidad, Tobago	
Camphorwood		Kenya, Tanzania	
Cedar, Burmese	Toon	South and Southeast Asia	
Cedar, Mexican	Spanish cedar	West Indies	Water resistant
Cedar, white	Deodar	West Indies	Water resistant
Crabwood	Guyana mahogany	Guyana	
Cypress		Himalayas	
Eucalyptus		World wide	
Gmelina	Yamani, Gambari, Gumbar Gomari	India and Burma, West Africa and Southern Africa	
Guarea	West Africa, Zaire		
Idigbo	Emeri	West Africa to Equatorial Guinea	Water resistant
Iroko	Odum, Mvule, Kambala Moreira, Tule	Throughout tropical Africa	Used for laboratory furniture; water resistant, similar to teak
Katon	Sentul, Thitto	Southeast Asia	
Mahogany, African	Acajou, Khaya, Ngollon Krala, Mangona, Munyama, Mkamgazi, Imbuia	West Africa to Gabon, Uganda, Tanzania, Sudan, Mozambique	
Mahogany, Honduras		West Indies, most tropical countries	
Makore	Agamokwe, Baku, Cherry Mahogany	West Africa	For laboratory furniture; water resistant
Meranti		Southeast Asia	
Mora		Guyana	Low cost, laboratory furniture; water resistant
Muninga	Mukwa, Mninga, Kiaat	South Africa, East Africa	For laboratory furniture; water resistant

Name	Alternative names	Growing areas	Properties
Nyatch	Padong	Southeast Asia	Low-cost, water resistant
Pali		West India	
Purple heart		Guyana (British)	
Sapele	Aboudikro	West Africa, Uganda, Tanzania	Similar to Mahogany
Teak		Almost all tropical countries	For laboratory furniture; water resistant
Tembusu	Anan, Yellow heart, Pemesu	Southeast Asia	Water resistant
Utile	Sipo, Assie	West Africa, Liberia to Gabon, Uganda	
Walnut		Himalayas, North Burma	

Guide to Timber growing areas:
West Africa—Ivory coast, Ghana, Nigeria, Cameroun;
South Asia—India, Bangladesh, Ceylon, Burma;
Southeast Asia—Malaysia, Indonesia;
West Indies—Jamaica, Belize, Trinidad, Tobago, Caribbean islands, Puerto Rico.

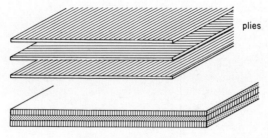

Fig. 1.20 Plywood

yourselfers. Consider the following properties:

1. it has considerable strength,
2. it has a high resistance to impact and shock, to splitting (even when nailed, screwed, or bolted near the edges), to racking and distortion,
3. thinner pieces may be curved with no loss of strength,
4. it is available in a wide variety of sizes and thicknesses.

Thin plywood can be cut cleanly with a fine-pitch saw such as a tenon saw or hacksaw. Thin plywood is more easily drilled and sawed if backed with a piece of softwood. A panel saw can be used effectively on blockboard and thicker plywood. Curved shapes can be cut with a fretsaw. A hacksaw may also be used for this purpose provided the curvature is not excessive. As with all sawing, the finished or decorated surface of the material should face upward to confine, to the undersurface, the splintering that may occur.

Blockboard resembles plywood somewhat. It is made of rectangular strips of

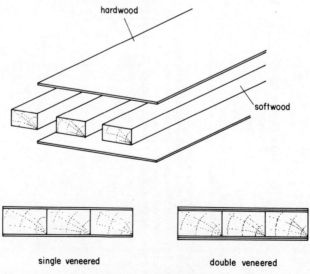

single veneered   double veneered

Fig. 1.21 Blockboard

softwood bonded edge-to-edge and sandwiched between single or double veneers of harder, close-grained wood (Fig. 1.21). It is cheaper than plywood and can be used as an alternative whenever the latter is specified in our course. The length of the cut piece should follow the direction of the core strips which is, in fact, the direction of greater strength. When applying paint or varnish, both upper and lower surfaces should be covered. This prevents warping caused by uneven drying when only one face is covered.

The edge of a piece of plywood has a rough appearance which may be unsightly. Sand the edge until it is quite smooth: then paint or varnish it. Pinning a strip of hardwood to it is a good idea if there is a chance that the edge would be subjected to knocks (Fig. 1.22).

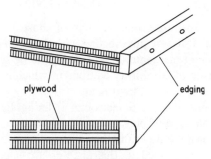

plywood   edging

Fig. 1.22 Edging

1.4.3   Hardboard

Hardboard is made from softwood pulp which has been compressed into sheets under high pressure. There are two types which are commonly available and are described as standard and medium grade respectively. Both have a hard glossy finished surface on one side and a rough-weave texture on the other. The most common thickness is 3 mm (1/8 inch) and is obtainable in sheets of 2442 mm by 1221 mm (8 feet by 4 feet). Medium hardboard, the softer of the two, has a light-straw colour and can be used as a surfacing material for walls and ceilings. It takes drawing pins quite easily and can be used for notice boards. Standard hardboard is dark brown in colour and is more rigid than plywood of the same thickness. It is often an economical substitute for plywood of up to 5 mm thickness.

Use a tenon saw or a hacksaw and always cut with the face side uppermost. Use gentle pressure when sawing; do not force the saw or it will either tear the sheet or jump out and score the surface. To prevent any tearaway when nearing the end of the cut, support both ends of the sheet.

When fixing, drive screws and nails through hardboard and not into it.

Perforated hardboard has a regular pattern of holes drilled into it and is useful for display and other purposes. In Section 1.7, a tool rack, made from perforated board, is described.

1.4.4 Storing timbers

It is not expected that large quantities of timber will be stored for long periods. Nevertheless, timber should be laid horizontally and raised on bricks especially if the storage area is damp or if there is a possibility of water seeping in. Ideally, the storage area should be dry and well ventilated to assist the timber to season and to prevent mould and mildew from rotting it.

If storage space is limited, the timber may be stored absolutely vertically. If timber is leaned at an angle against the wall, it will tend to sag and so acquire a curve or warp.

1.5 FIXINGS AND FASTENINGS

Few things are more frustrating than an item of construction coming apart as soon as it is put to use. If it were put together with the appreciation that it will be mishandled, then much time, material and effort will be saved later in repairs. This is particularly true of laboratory equipment which is in constant use and may be subjected to quite rough treatment.

In this course the general idea is to insist that all fixings be done using adhesive and screws although nails, panel pins, etc., will be used for economy whenever the strength of the fixing is not critical and the construction will not be weakened by using it. The fixings mentioned in this chapter are usually easily available although in some small towns you may have to search around a bit.

1.5.1 Nails

Nails are a cheap fixing aid which, if properly used, can be almost as effective as screws. However, the holding strength is much less and so nails cannot be recommended for equipment which is intended to stand up to rough handling. We will consider only a few of the many varieties of nails. These are: round nails, oval nails, clout nails, pins, and tacks.

Round nails (also known as French nails) are the least expensive and are the most readily obtainable (Fig. 1.23(a)). They are used for general purpose fixing but have large, perhaps unattractive, heads. They are suitable as a temporary fixing in the development of prototype equipment (see Section 4.4, on mass-production techniques). Very often they may be the only type of nail which you can get in the market or hardware stores and you will have to learn to live with them. For large immovable structures such as notice boards they are probably the most efficient form of fixing.

Oval nails are ideal for joinery work (Fig. 1.23(b)). They are less likely to split the wood if driven with the long head-axis following the grain. The smaller sizes (half- to one-inch) are the most useful for our purposes. They cost about 50 per cent more than round nails.

Panel or hardboard pins (Fig. 1.23 (c) and (d)) are used for light joinery and for fixing hardboard, cardboard, or thin plywood. The price may be five to eight

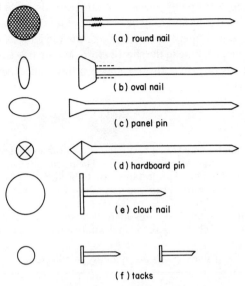

Fig. 1.23 Types of nails

times that of round nails but as you will only be requiring the half-inch size, of which there are almost a thousand in 100 grams, it may be acceptable. Small 3/4-inch round nails, with their heads cut off just before punching them into the surface, are a good substitute for panel pins. They are inconspicuous and, if punching is done at a slight angle, will hold just as well (Fig. 1.24).

Clout nails (Fig. 1.23 (e)) are used for fixing roofing felt or softboard (fibreboard). They have a limited use for the jobs with which we will be dealing, but as they are very easily obtainable and also quite inexpensive, it is worth keeping a supply for use whenever they appear to be suitable. They are usually zinc-coated and this encourages their use in equipment which may be wetted during an experiment.

Tacks (Fig. 1.23(f)) are commonly used for shoe repairs and, if not available at hardware stores, may be obtained, in small quantities from shoe repairers. They are useful for fixing cloth and plastic sheeting to wooden frames and could

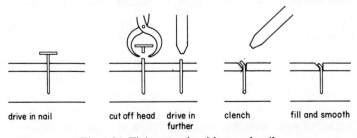

Fig. 1.24 Fixing panels with round nails

be used as a substitute for panel pins if their larger heads could be tolerated. They are made of hardened steel and may be used for pinning soft metal sheets such as aluminium, lead, and copper thinner than 0.5 mm (26 gauge). For thicker sheets it is advisable to punch a hole in the sheet before pinning (see Section 2.2.3, for the use of the punch). A large woodscrew makes a fairly effective punch if the real thing is not available.

Hints

1. As nails can be manufactured fairly easily and are seldom sold under brand names, you may find that the quality varies considerably. The points or heads may not be formed properly and sometimes small projections have to be filed away before the nails can be used. As nails are generally cheap you can afford to pay more for a better quality product when you find it.
2. When purchasing nails, the dealer will often allow you to select an assortment of sizes at the same weigh-in. Table 1.3 gives an indication of the approximate number of nails

Table 1.3   Nails, quantity in 500 grams

Length							
in mm	12	20	25	38	50	75	100
in inches	0.5	0.75	1	1.5	2	3	4
Description							
round	—	1940	880	390	180	77	50
oval	3700	2200	740	470	230	61	—
clout	1190	550	375	350	275	—	—
panel pin	4630	2310	1420	740	390	—	—

you will obtain in 500 grams. If you want an assortment, a good initial selection will consist of ten each of 4-inch and 3-inch nails (160 grams), plus twenty each of 2-inch and 1.5-inch nails (80 grams) and, the remainder, about equal weights of 1-inch and 3/4-inch nails. For further purchases, just top up those sizes that you use most frequently.
3. Nails have to be driven through the lighter into the heavier wood, the length of the nail being 2.5 to 3 times the thickness of the piece to be held (Fig. 1.25(a)). If the nail passes through both pieces, clench it by bending the protruding point and hammering it flat (Fig. 1.25(b)). Avoid driving into end-grain as this gives a fairly weak grip but, if you have to, the grip may be improved by dovetailing the direction of the nails. This is done by driving alternate nails at opposing angles into the wood (Fig. 1.25(c)).

1.5.2   Woodscrews

Screws (or screw-nails, as they are called in West Africa) are, weight for weight, about ten times more expensive than nails but their greater holding strength and the subsequent saving in repair time and expense justify the additional cost.

Various types of screws (Fig. 1.26) are available, the most popular being the countersunk, flat-head woodscrew. Other types such as raised head, roundhead, cross-slot head, are often available in a few sizes in large towns or cities.

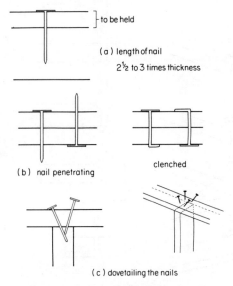

Fig. 1.25 Improving the grip of nails

Countersunk screws are used for general woodwork, for fixing hinges, plates, and miscellaneous hardware to wood. The general procedure for using these screws is shown in Fig. 1.27.

Raised head screws are for fixing metal plates especially if a decorative effect is sought. They are usually nickel or chrome plated.

Roundhead screws are ideal for fixing metal plate to wood. The head protrudes above the work and the flat undersurface holds the plate firmly. Screws 3/4-inch by No. 6 or 5/8-inch by No. 6 are worth keeping in stock for fixing strips and brackets made of metal.

When constructing equipment to be used in a chemistry laboratory, or other corrosive environment, use screws of brass instead of steel because of their resistance to corrosion. The 1-inch by No. 8 size in probably the most useful.

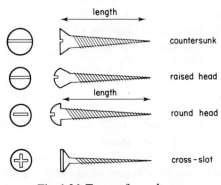

Fig. 1.26 Types of woodscrews

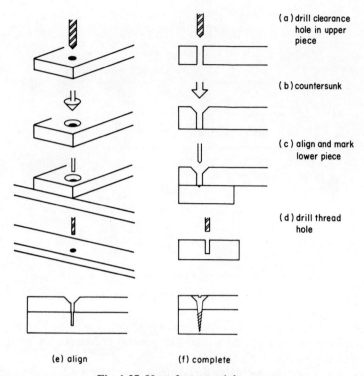

(a) drill clearance hole in upper piece

(b) countersunk

(c) align and mark lower piece

(d) drill thread hole

(e) align

(f) complete

Fig. 1.27 Use of countersink screws

Brass screws are also recommended for use as terminals for electrical apparatus because of their low contact resistance. They make good contact with copper wire and will take ordinary soldering for permanent electrical joints. If the heads are left protruding about 5 mm above the work, crocodile clips could be attached to them for much of the temporary connections that are used in experimental work. Further reference will be made to this aspect of the use of screws in Projects 5.2.1 to 5.2.5.

The gauge of the screw may be calculated as follows: measure the diameter of the screw head in thirty-seconds of an inch, then subtract 2 to obtain the gauge. For example, a screw has a head diameter of 5/16 inch, which is equal to 10 thirty-seconds (10/32), subtract 2 to give 8. Therefore a No. 8 screw has a head diameter of 5/16 inch (see Table 1.4).

1.5.3 Nuts and bolts

For our purposes the machine bolt (7 to 12 mm diameter) and the machine screw (3 to 6 mm diameter) are the most useful.

Machine bolts (Fig. 1.28(a)) are used for fixing wooden or metal framing such as workbenches. They may be obtained at car spares dealers but are cheaply available from car breakers or 'motor butchers'. It is advisable to use them with

Table 1.4 Starter holes for woodscrews

Gauge	4	6	8	10
Most useful lengths (inches)	$\frac{1}{2}$	$\frac{3}{4}$, 1	$\frac{3}{4}$, 1, $1\frac{1}{2}$	$1\frac{1}{2}$
Head diameter (inches)	3/16(5 mm)	$\frac{1}{4}$(6.5 mm)	5/16(8 mm)	3/8(9.5 mm)
Hardwood: clearance hole	1/8(3 mm)	5/32(4 mm)	3/16(5 mm)	7/32(5.5 mm)
thread hole	5/64(2 mm)	5/64(2 mm)	3/32(2.5 mm)	1/8(3 mm)
Softwood: clearance hole	Use bradawl		5/32(4 mm)	5/32(4 mm)
thread hole	Use bradawl		5/64(2 mm)	5/64(2 mm)

washers. Motor dealers and scrap dealers stock bolts up to 1/2 inch diameter and length of up to 4 inches (100 mm). If you require heavier bolts you may have to collect them yourself. Bolts of up to 3/4 inch diameter are used in the assembly of the rear axle and the differential gearbox of trucks and lorries. Scrap dealers do not usually take these apart but they would be prepared to let you have them for a nominal price. The casings of these heavy gearboxes provide fairly good make-shift anvils.

Machine screws (Fig. 1.28(b) and (c)) are obtained from hardware stores but care must be taken when purchasing these. Test the tightness of the nut on the screw thread. A very slack fit means the nut will soon work loose especially if the fixture is subjected to vibration or stress. These cheap versions usually have a large, flat-dome, slotted head and a square nut (Fig. 1.28(b)). Roundhead screws with hexagonal nuts are a better quality (Fig. 1.28(c)). The thickness of the nut should be greater than the diameter of the hole. If not, the screw may only be useful for holding together joints which are not stressed, e.g. in electrical bench

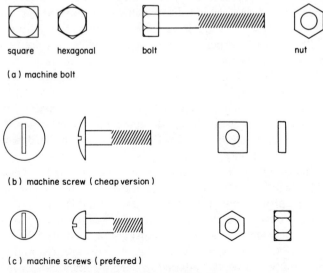

square   hexagonal   bolt   nut

(a) machine bolt

(b) machine screw (cheap version)

(c) machine screws (preferred)

Fig. 1.28 Types of bolts

apparatus. Although bolts may be made from hardened steel or stainless steel, the most commonly available mild steel types are used in our projects.

1.5.4 Adhesives

There are many adhesives and glues available today. The general purpose office or household types can be obtained from supermarkets and are useful for repairing light, paper-based articles, but for constructional work you have to choose the correct adhesive for the work at hand. Most laboratory equipment may require a waterproof adhesive. Strength and rigidity are important although it may sometimes be necessary to specify a flexible adhesive. Only a few of these, sold under various brand names, are mentioned here. In recent years new types have proliferated and it is to be expected that newer ones are in the pipeline. The rule to observe for all of them is to read the maker's instructions very carefully before use. Table 1.5 compares some of the properties of the more easily available adhesives.

The most important use to which we will put adhesives is to strengthen the joints in the construction of wooden apparatus. As these will usually be butt joints and not the more sophisticated types, which experienced carpenters will use, it is even more important that they should be strengthened.

PVA adhesives are recommended for most of our construction work. It is sold in small tubes under the brand name Uhu and in larger quantities of 2 kilograms or so as Super Extra Diamond, Evostik W Resin, Unibond, etc. They are fairly waterproof and easy to use. Setting takes place 20 minutes after application and is complete in 24 hours. Cramping is essential and this is provided in our joints by the screw fixings.

The second most important adhesive in our course is polystyrene cement which can be obtained commercially but which you are advised to make yourself by dissolving polystyrene, available as styrofoam or as the outer transparent tubes of ballpoint pens, in petrol. Some of its applications are explained in Section 2.5.3. It can also be used as a varnish to give a waterproof coat to wood and paper. It is probably the most interesting material which can be derived from what is just scrap.

As an alternative to PVA adhesives, urea glues are inexpensive and much more waterproof. One brand, Cascamite, is sold in most hardware stores. They come in powder form and have to be mixed with water to start the hardening process. To avoid wastage, mix only as much as you need.

Epoxy resins are among the strongest adhesives you will find and usually come in twin packs: the resin and the hardener. Setting only starts when these are mixed together in equal proportions. The mixture stays workable for about 10 minutes but hardening is only complete after 24 hours (12 hours if the temperature is above 30 °C), during which time the joint must be cramped. A high speed variety can set hard in 10 to 15 minutes. This product is very expensive and not always available but you would be well advised to keep a small quantity in stock for repairing equipment made from glass, ceramic or plastic. For reasons of

Table 1.5 Adhesives

Type of adhesive	Brand or trade name(s)	Adhesion, stress resistance	Waterproof	Moisture resistance	Cost
Epoxy resins	Araldite	Excellent	Excellent	Excellent	Expensive
Ureas	Cascamite	Excellent	Good	Good	Average
Fish glue	Wood glue	Excellent	Poor	Poor	Inexpensive
PVA adhesives	Uhu, Evostik W Resin, Super Extra Diamond	Good	Poor	Fair	Average
Contact cements	Evostick, 358, Bostik	Good	Good	Good	Average
Polystyrene cement	(Make this yourself)	Good	Good	Good	Inexpensive
Pastes and gums	Gloy, Grip-fix	Fair	Poor	Poor	Inexpensive

economy only, it is not worth using this material to repair wooden items. Furthermore, it will not adhere to polythene—in fact, very few adhesives do.

Animal and fish glues (made by boiling down hides, bones, and sinews) have been with us for centuries and are still used by furniture makers. They are available as toffee-like slabs which are melted and applied hot. The material is very commonly used for sticking the labels on food cans and jars. Unfortunately it is water soluble and not very moisture resistant. In hot, humid tropical lands it is next to useless but in drier desert or savannah parts it can be recommended for economy provided it is not in direct contact with water. It has one advantage over most other adhesives: if you realize that you have made a mistake in positioning two pieces which you have stuck together, you need only to moisten the joint to separate the pieces and try again.

1.6 THE BASIC FRAMES

General guidelines

The foregoing pages have dealt in some detail with the tools and techniques which we will require. We will now consider the types of structures which form the basis of laboratory apparatus. Surprisingly, there are only four frames which you need to know about. They are very simple and, either individually or in combination, they may be adapted to form the basis of all the wood-and-glass or wood-and-metal structures we need.

The instructions are very simple and require a minimum of expertise. However, it is expected that you pay great care and attention to every aspect of the work. Marking out should be done carefully to the exact millimetre where possible. Saw-cuts should follow the lines drawn with the cut being displaced to the waste side of the timber. The cuts should also be square with the timber; that is, the blade of the saw should be exactly perpendicular to the surface of the timber especially when cutting wedge shapes such as brackets.

Joints should be fixed firmly, using both glue and screws. Nails should be avoided except for temporary pinning or for fixing panel boards to frames. Fairly hard wood, chosen from Table 1.2, or man-made boards such as plywood and hardboard will be specified. If you have to deviate from these instructions, do so only under the following conditions:

1. you do not have the proper materials for the job either because you cannot afford them or they are not available;
2. you cannot yet afford to buy the proper tools or your tools are old and you have not been able to service or replace them;
3. you are convinced that the change you are contemplating will improve the quality of the final product.

If you follow the instructions, you should produce a serviceable, robust piece of equipment, with very little effort, expense, or expertise. A reduction in either effort or expense will very likely have an adverse effect on the work. If, on the other hand, your knowledge of carpentry is better than has been assumed in this book, you and the school are indeed fortunate and you are given every encouragement to improve on the suggestions. In fact you may find that, by bringing this additional experience to bear on the construction, you may even be able to use cheaper materials without degrading your work.

1.6.1 The bench

This is the basic structure for optical benches, metre bridges, potentiometers, etc. It is the simplest of the frames and consists of a long narrow strip of 12 mm plywood resting on two or more feet made from strips of hardwood (Fig. 1.29).

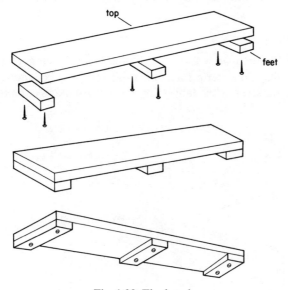

Fig. 1.29 The bench

These strips are about 10 to 15 mm thick. One is placed across each end of the board with others in between to prevent sagging. The spacing between these supports depends on the thickness of the board.

The following guidelines may be of use:

Thickness	Spacing
10 mm	200 mm on average or 150 to 250 mm apart
15 mm	400 mm on average or 300 to 400 mm apart
20 mm	800 mm on average or 600 to 800 mm apart

For optical benches on which the lens holders, etc. have to be accurately aligned, choose the closer spacing because even very slight sagging could create some frustrating problems, especially in those experiments which involve image location by parallax methods.

The strips are fixed to the board with 1-inch by No. 8 woodscrews which, for concealment, are driven through the strips into the board.

It is advisable that the board should be fitted with hardwood edging of about 1/8 inch thickness which may be glued and pinned on by using 1/2 inch panel pins or headless nails (see Section 1.5.1, Fig. 1.24). Coat the bench with a wood seal (if available) and varnish. A polyurethane varnish (e.g. Ronseal) is expensive but fairly widely obtainable. It is probably the best finish which can be given to laboratory equipment—and furniture—and is strongly recommended if you can afford it. However its shelf-life is very short as it tends to set solid in the can after a few months. Therefore only buy small quantities at a time when you need it.

1.6.2 The platform

The platform is used as a chassis or 'breadboard' (temporary chassis) for electrical circuits and experiments. It is raised on pieces of timber about 35 to 50 mm above the level of the table (Fig. 1.30). This allows components such as

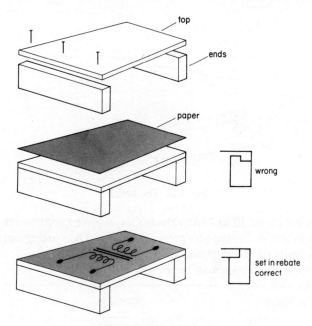

Fig. 1.30 The platform

toggle switches and terminals to protrude under the top. Interconnections between the components may therefore be concealed while the top surface could be covered with white paper on which a schematic drawing of the circuit could be neatly depicted.

The feet or uprights must be squarely and accurately planed so that the platform does not wobble when placed on a flat surface. The thicker the material of which the uprights are made the more rigid will be the structure.

The fixing can be done using 1-inch nails at 20 mm intervals. This is usually adequate but, if the equipment is going to be in continuous use by large numbers of students, use 1-inch by No. 8 countersunk screws at 50 to 80 mm spacing. In any case, the joints may be further strengthened by gluing a triangular moulding into the angle between the top and the uprights.

Chamfer the top edges of the plywood and rub down all surfaces with fine sandpaper.

A sheet of paper such as is used in duplicating machines could now be glued to the top surface of the plywood. The drawings or inscriptions describing the circuit, experiment, etc., for which the platform is to be used, may be done before or after all the connections are made. There is a danger that the paper will be soiled while the work of mounting the components is being carried out. Before you start this stage of the work, draw or write whatever would finally appear on the paper. This is best done with a black felt-tipped pen although a combination of colours may also be used for effect. When this is done, apply two or three coats of clean polystyrene solution over the entire sheet (see Section 1.5.4, for making polystyrene cement). This has the effect of rendering the paper waterproof.

You may then, very lightly, mark out the fixing holes through which screws, wires, switches, and the shafts of potentiometers will pass when the components of the circuits are being mounted. After they have mounted and the wiring is completed, the pencil marks can be erased and the waterproofed paper gently wiped with a damp soapy cloth to remove all dirty marks. Follow this by wringing the cloth thoroughly and then wiping off all traces of the soap and drying thoroughly.

1.6.3   The box

The box is useful as an enclosure, for lamps, etc., and as low-cost instrument cases and may be made in different sizes.

The two ends, designated A (Fig. 1.31), should be made of timber of at least 12 mm thickness. It must be planed quite squarely and uniformly with the grain running in the longer dimension, that is, along the direction of the width of the box. The two sides, B, are made of 6 mm plywood, while the top and the bottom are made either of hardboard or 3 mm plywood.

As the box is usually completely closed, the structure is intrinsically quite strong and robust. In this case the fixing may be done only with nails, driven at staggered angles to improve the holding strength. The lid should be fastened with screws so that it could be removed when necessary to afford access to the interior of the box.

1.6.4   The stand

Very often a vertical stand (Fig. 1.32) is required for mounting equipment. This is usually the same for demonstration equipment, but it is also useful for equipment

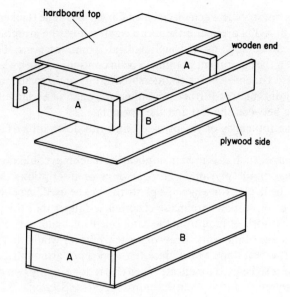

Fig. 1.31 The box

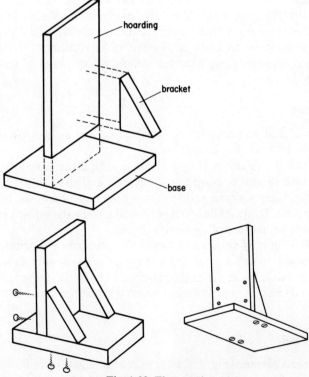

Fig. 1.32 The stand

in which liquid levels have to be monitored, e.g. Hare's apparatus, Boyle's law apparatus, the manometer, etc. In essence we require a stout board, called the hoarding, to be held in a vertical position. This is done by fixing it to a smaller horizontal base for stability. Both the hoarding and the base are made from plywood. The thickness of the base and of the vertical board depends on the height according to Table 1.6.

Table 1.6 Optimum thickness of materials

Height of stand (cm)	Thickness of hoarding (mm)	Thickness of base (mm)
20 to 40	6	12
40 to 60	9	12
60 to 90	12	20

The width of the base is equal to that of the hoarding. The length of the base should not be less than one-third of the vertical height. The size of the brackets is also related to the height. Roughly speaking, they should measure about $0.3h \times 0.2h$ where h is the vertical height. Two brackets placed behind the hoarding are usually sufficient but if the width of the hoarding is greater than its height then additional brackets could be used. The base should be provided with feet or pads which could be screwed to its undersurface.

For large hoardings, with linear dimensions exceeding one metre, it may be cheaper and simpler to use shelf brackets which are made of steel or wrought iron. These are easily available at the hardware stores.

1.7 SOME USEFUL PROJECTS

Having described the fundamentals of what you will require for the wooden structures in this course, you should now practise constructing each of the frames. This will ensure that you master the techniques involved. For the purpose of economy, construct frames which will be useful in your laboratory. In Chapter 5 you will find described various types of apparatus derived from each basic frame. The projects listed below could be ideal for a start. This involves articles which are always in demand but are fairly simple to make.

1. Optical bench   Project 5.1.1 (bench)
2. Optical screen   Project 5.1.3 (stand)
3. Lamp-box   Project 5.1.2 (box)
4. Test-tube rack   Project 6.1.1 (platform)

These projects will require only the knowledge which you should have acquired up to this point. Other items to start with are the bench hook and the fretsaw platform mentioned in Section 1.2.1.

A larger and equally useful project would be the construction of a tool rack from perforated hardboard. Start with a piece measuring about 1000 mm by

700 mm. Using one-inch round nails fix two strips of softwood measuring 1000 mm by 40 mm by 20 mm along the edges. Space the nails at 100 mm intervals. Now cut two more strips of wood of the same cross-section (40 mm by 20 mm), making them just long enough to fit snugly into position along the end of the board between the other two strips (Fig. 1.33). Nail them in place. The

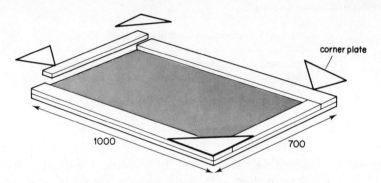

Fig. 1.33 Assembling the tool rack

corners may then be strengthened with angle plates made from triangular pieces of 3 mm plywood or hardboard. These reinforcing pieces may be fixed with vinyl adhesive and panel pins.

The rack is fixed in a vertical position against a wall. You will probably require some assistance for this part of the job. The tools are suspended from hooks inserted into the holes in the board. Make a supply of such hooks from stout iron wire of 3 mm diameter. The ideal shape for these hooks is shown in Fig.1.34.

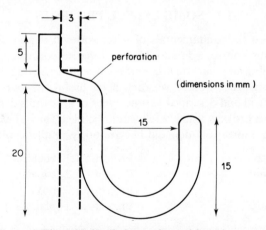

Fig. 1.34 Hook for perforated board

Once inserted, they will hold the tools quite securely. The advantage of using perforated board is that these hooks may be moved about so that the rack can be used for many storage and display purposes.

CHAPTER 2

Metal, glass, and plastics

2.1 INTRODUCTION

None of the techniques examined in this chapter is very difficult or complicated. Most are specific to particular projects and should only be studied and implemented when the need arises.

2.2 SUPPLEMENTARY KIT C

Although the tools of the basic kit (i.e. kit A) will continue to be essential in this course, you may now have to acquire additional tools in kit C, the second of our supplementary kits. This contains the following items:

bunsen burner,
half-round, second-cut file, 200 mm (8 inches) long,
triangular, medium-cut file, 150 mm (6 inches) long,
centre-punch,
knife,
G-cramp, with 100 mm opening,
machinist's vice with 75 mm jaw width.

As with supplementary kit B, these tools may be purchased as required. With the exception of the vice, none of the tools in this list is very expensive and you should be able to purchase them all at the same time.

2.2.1 Bunsen burner

It should be safe to assume that, being a science teacher, you have access to a bunsen burner (Fig.2.1). If not, you will almost certainly have to place an overseas order to acquire this item. Ensure that you specify the type of fuel which is available to you, i.e. bottled, town or petrol gas or methylated spirits. You may also try making one (see Project 8.6). The use of the bunsen burner is dealt with in detail in Section 2.4.1.

2.2.2 Files

Files are obtained in a variety of lengths and cross-sections, some of which are shown in Fig. 2.2. Various grades of cutting surface, known as rough, bastard,

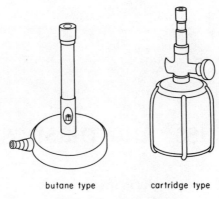

butane type   cartridge type

Fig. 2.1 Bunsen burners

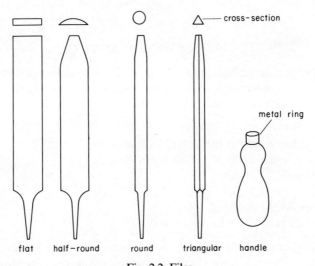

flat   half—round   round   triangular   handle

Fig. 2.2 Files

second-cut, smooth, and dead-smooth, are also available. For our purposes, we suggest that you use a 200 mm long half-round file of bastard or second-cut grade. It can be used for deburring, chamfering and smoothing edges, enlarging holes and also, edge-wise, for cutting through thin sheet for which the hacksaw may be too coarse. In addition, keep a flat or a triangular second-cut file, 150 mm long, for scoring glass tubes and rods prior to snapping them. They are also useful for giving a final light smoothing to corners and edges.

Hints

1. Ensure that the wooden handle fits tightly as some nasty accidents can occur if it comes off during a job.
2. When using a file, assume the stance and the two-handed hold which has been described for the hacksaw (Fig. 2.3).

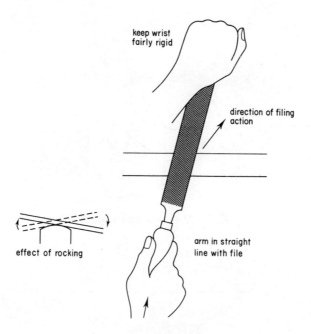

keep wrist
fairly rigid

direction of filing
action

effect of rocking

arm in straight
line with file

Fig. 2.3 Using a file

3. When filing large areas, avoid rocking the file as this causes rounding of the surface.
4. The files in kit C may be used for cutting duplicate keys and for sharpening saws.
5. If a really smooth finish is required after a filing job, sanding with fine emery paper is suggested.

2.2.3 The centre-punch

Whenever a hole is to be drilled in metal, the centre of the hole must be marked. If this is not done the drill will wander over the surface and the hole will be displaced. The required mark is an indentation made by using a hammer and a centre-punch.

Hints

1. The punch is held in the left hand with the tip of the third finger guiding the point (Fig. 2.4).
2. A light tap to locate the point, followed by a harder blow will leave a full dot into which the point of the bit may be inserted before the drill is switched on.

2.2.4 Knife

A knife with a sharp, stubby, replaceable blade (Fig. 2.5(b)) is very useful for trimming or whittling wood and plastics. Low-cost versions have wooden handles and are just as useful as the more expensive ones with shaped metal

42

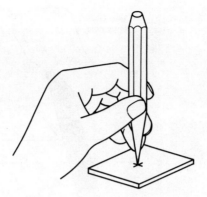

Fig. 2.4 Using the centre-punch

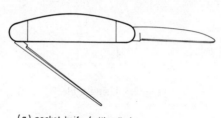

(a) pocket knife (with spike)

(b) utility knife with replaceable blades

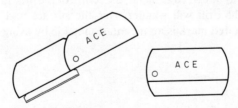

(c) razor blade holder

(d) a simple holder

Fig. 2.5 Knives

handles and retractable blades. However, the latter may be equipped with blades of a variety of shapes and purposes or even with a key-hole saw or a hacksaw. These are expensive. For many of our purposes, a sturdy pocket knife with a blade about 50 mm in length may suffice (Fig. 2.5(a)).

Hints

1. A soft sheet or thin metal foil can be cut with a knife, especially if the sheet is quite flat. Lay it on a sheet of hardboard and, without using excessive pressure, guide the knife along a straight edge to make a series of light scores along the full length of the intended cut. The same method may be used with cardboard and softboard.
2. Many pocket knives come equipped with a sharp pointed spike as one of the 'blades' (Fig. 2.5(a)). This can be used in the same way as a bradawl (see Section 1.2.5).
3. Discarded razor blades, especially the two-edged type, are safer to use when inserted in a holder designed for this purpose (Fig. 2.5(c)). These holders are used by dressmakers and are sold by shops dealing in haberdashery and other dressmaking accessories.
4. A simple razor blade holder may be improvised by holding the blade in several layers of paper folded over the topmost edge (Fig. 2.5(d)).

2.2.5   G-cramp

A G-cramp (Fig. 2.6) with an opening of at least 100 mm (4 inches) will be required. It must be of very good quality otherwise it is next to useless. Choose

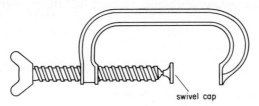
swivel cap

Fig. 2.6 The G-cramp

one with a cast-iron frame and a screw thread with a solid square section such as is seen in the jacks used for lifting motor cars. The point of the screw should be fitted with a swivel cap (not just a washer) so that irregular objects may be held firmly.

Regularly lubricate both the cap and the screw thread. This makes the cramp easier to tighten and also increases its useful life.

2.2.6   Machinist's vice

In recent years, the cost of a good vice has short up alarmingly relative to the other lighter tools and so you will have to consider carefully whether it should be purchased. We have, as far as possible, designed the projects so that you do not often require a vice, but it is very handy to have if you can afford it. In priority it should rank below the power drill and some of its attachments. For most purposes the G-cramp will suffice.

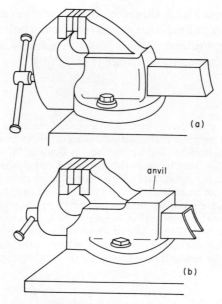

Fig. 2.7 Machinist's vice

The preferred size is one with a 75 mm (3 inch) jaw but you could get a 50 mm (2 inch) unit for economy as this usually costs half the price (Fig. 2.7(a)).

Hints

1. You may find that some relatively cheap but inferior makes of vice are available. I do not think that you should be afraid to purchase any of these. For the purposes for which you will be using it, any vice is better than a G-cramp and certainly better than nothing at all.
2. If you do buy a cheap make, do not subject it to excessive hammering. There is very often a strong temptation to use the jaws of the vice as an anvil. For a good vice this may be allowed but not encouraged. Some low-cost vices are designed with a platform on the fixed section. This is intended to be used as an anvil (Fig. 2.7(b)).

2.3 WORKING WITH METAL

Much of what has been learnt in the last chapter will be found to be useful.

There is no harm, in fact, in viewing metal work as an extension of woodwork. After all, it is unusual to find a metalworker who did not work with wood before he turned to metal.

2.3.1 Marking

Make all your measurements to the nearest millimetre. Ideally, a steel rule should be used, but the transparent plastic ruler used in schools is adequate. Lines drawn on metal surfaces should be executed with a scribe, which is a pen-like instrument with a hard, sharp point. The points of a pair of compasses or dividers found in mathematic sets will serve in this respect. If neither of these is available, a ballpoint pen will do.

2.3.2 Bending

We will discuss this technique in two parts: first of all, the bending of sheets, which can be done without heating the materials; then we will consider rods and strips which may require more force, and, perhaps, the application of heat. (It is assumed that you do not have access to a bending machine.)

Sheet (up to 1 mm thickness only)

A flat surface with a straight hard edge is required. A table will do, provided that the edge has not been radiused (i.e. not rounded). The line along which the sheet is to be bent should be clearly marked. Place the sheet with the mark lined up exactly along the edge of the table. The sheet is firmly clamped in this position preferably with a length of flat timber on it and secured with cramps.

The position of the hands depend to some extent on the width of that part of the sheet which overhangs the table. If the width of this part is more than 100 mm, the fingers should point away from the table, spreading as widely as possible over the part to be bent. If the width of the overhang is less than 100 mm, rest the fingers on the fixed part of the sheet. In both cases the little finger and the fleshy base of the thumb should rest exactly on the line. Both of these positions are shown in Fig. 2.8.

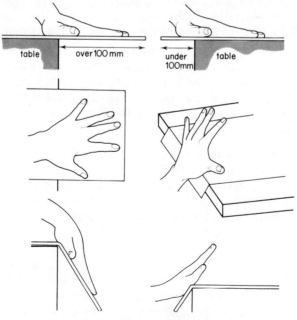

Fig. 2.8 Bending thin sheet

To start the bend, press firmly and simultaneously with both hands, the maximum pressure being applied by the palms to the edge of the table where the bend is to take place. The sheet should then bend sharply over the full length of the mark. If not, transfer pressure momentarily to those parts which have not started to bend. In this way, gradually increase the angle of the bend until the desired angle is achieved.

At all times the parts of the sheet at either side of the mark should be kept as flat as possible. Do not let the sheet curve by applying pressure away from the mark.

Rods and strips

The procedure for bending rods and strips depends on the thickness of the material and on the radius of the bend. We will consider two categories:

1. rods of less than 3 mm diameter and strips less than 3 mm thickness and less than 80 mm wide. These can be bent in almost any radius while cold, if the bend is made around a hard edge of the desired radius. In our work the radius is usually very small, very often being equal to the thickness. For sections less than 3 mm thick, this should not present much trouble. Again use the base of your thumb to provide firm pressure to start the bend. The bend can then be completed by hammering.

   For cold bending, a vice is almost a necessity. Alternatively, the piece could be gripped between two thick strips of steel held in one or two G-cramps.

2. rods of 3 to 12 mm diameter or strips from 3 to 6 mm thick and less than 50 mm wide. These pieces must be heated especially if the bending radius is less than twice the thickness of the material. Use a punch to mark the point at which bending is to be done. Rest the piece between two bricks and heat the mark with the hottest flame of a bunsen burner concentrated on the mark. Rotate the burner around the piece till all sides are evenly heated. When the piece has a red glow, it can be bent manually to the desired angle. Protect your hands by using gloves or by wrapping a cloth around the piece. If the bend is to be made quite close to the end, so that a firm grip is impossible, use a hammer and tap firmly in the desired direction.

These bends may be made without any mechanical grip or cramp as bending will take place only at the hot spot.

If a good, heavy-duty vice is available, then bending of material of this thickness may be attempted without heating. You may, however, have to use a heavy club-hammer. Bending will then take place at the inside edge of the jaws of the vice.

2.3.3 Drilling

When drilling holes through an object made of metal, the bit will have a tendency to grab the metal. This can be quite dangerous as the object could start to spin with the bit. The work must be fixed in a vice or clamped to a worktop. Use a low speed and apply oil to the spot to be drilled. When a large hole is to be made, start with a smaller drill and gradually increase the size.

When drilling into thin sheet, the hole will become misshaped if the bit grabs. To avoid this happening, place a piece of cloth between the work and the bit, and drill through it. The cloth will reduce the bit's tendency to grab and a neat hole will be produced.

2.3.4 Riveting

Suitable rivets for joining metal plates are sometimes available at hardware stores. As a substitute you could use 3- or 4-inch nails which will have diameters of $3\frac{1}{2}$ and 4 mm respectively. These may be used for joining plates and strips.

The two pieces to be joined are held in position and a hole of the required diameter is drilled through both. Insert the nail through the holes (Fig. 2.9(a))

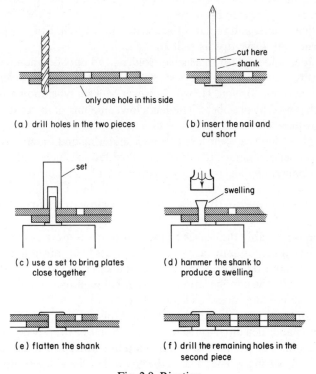

(a) drill holes in the two pieces

(b) insert the nail and cut short

(c) use a set to bring plates close together

(d) hammer the shank to produce a swelling

(e) flatten the shank

(f) drill the remaining holes in the second piece

Fig. 2.9 Riveting

and using a hacksaw, cut off the sharp end, leaving a tail about 4 mm long protruding above the plates (Fig. 2.9(b)). Place the assembly with the nail, head downward, resting on a hard flat surface such as an anvil. The surfaces which are brought into contact must fit snugly against each other and so should be free of burrs and dents. Bring the plates firmly together by using a rivet set which can be improvised from a piece of metal tubing (Fig. 2.9(c)) or a block of hardwood with a 6 mm hole drilled into it. Use a hammer to spread the rivet tail by driving squarely onto it (Fig. 2.9(d)). Finish off with a series of taps until the tail is quite flat. The reverse pein-end of a ball-pein or even a flat-pein hammer could be used to finish it off (Fig. 2.9(e)).

If more than one rivet is to be used, drill all the required holes into one of the plates and only one hole to match in the other. Fix the rivet that goes through the matched holes before drilling the remaining holes in the second plate (Fig. 2.9(f)).

2.3.5 Joining

This is done by the techniques of either soldering or brazing which describes the process for joining metals by means of a lower-melting metal or alloy known as solder. Soldering is done between temperatures of 60° and 300 °C and is discussed fully in Chapter 3. Brazing produces a stronger joint, uses harder solders with higher melting points, and requires the use of a blowtorch. For our purposes, a bunsen burner will serve just as well.

These harder solders, known as silver solders, can only be obtained from the main hardware suppliers but if you place an order with your local dealer he will be prepared to get some for you. He will, however, stock a type known as tinman's solder which is used by plumbers. This has a lower melting point, costs less, and is quite an adequate substitute.

Because of the high temperature at which soldering and brazing is done, the surface will undergo an increase in the rate of oxidation which could prevent the solder from bounding. The oxide layer is removed by combination with a flux and rises as a slag to the surface of the molten solder. The simplest fluxes are (a) dilute hydrochloric acid, (b) borax (sodium pyroborate), and (c) boracic acid (boric acid).

Boric acid is probably the easiest to use, but borax is more easily obtainable, usually from chemists or hardware stores. The pieces to be joined must be kept in position throughout the operation, care being taken that the two parts are held together in exactly the configuration that you will require of the finished work. The surfaces in contact must be clean.

Heat the join strongly using the blowtorch. Moisten the end of a rod of silver solder in water and then dip it in the borax flux. Some of the powder will cling to the rod. Press this against the hot metal at a point where it is to be applied and continue heating strongly. The rod and the flux will melt and flow onto the metal. With more flux on the rod, continue to apply the solder to the joint. The solder will flow between the surfaces to be joined. If it carries sufficient flux with it, a clean uniform bond should result.

When you are satisfied with the joint, allow it to cool. The braze will set immediately, especially if you pour some water over it.

Inspect the hidden underside of the join. The solder should have flowed through but if you are not quite satisfied you could turn over and repeat some of the work on this side. Before you start heating, it may be advisable to place the joint in a G-cramp to prevent it coming apart if too much heat is applied.

When you are satisfied, cool thoroughly. If necessary you could hold the joint under a water tap. Scrape off any surplus flux and smooth out the solder using a file.

2.4 WORKING WITH GLASS

Anyone who has had the pleasure of seeing a skilled glassblower at work will seriously doubt if such an art can be learnt by reading a book—let alone part of a chapter! Let me put you straight right now. It is not possible.

What we hope to do in this section is to learn the absolute minimum which should be known to get on with the task of equipping a laboratory. Insofar as working with glass is concerned this means only:

1. snapping glass rods and tubes;
2. drawing tubes into capillaries and loops;
3. sealing a tube;
4. blowing a small bulb;
5. making bends in rods and tubes.

These are the only techniques about which you will need to know and, in any case, the only tasks which you can perform with the simple equipment at your disposal. For this you will need a flat hand-file and a bunsen burner. You will be working with tubing of 6.5, 12, and 24 mm outside diameter (o.d.) and capillary tubing of 6 mm o.d. and 0.5 mm bore. All of these will be of soda-lime glass which has a softening point of 710 °C and can therefore be worked in the flame of the bunsen burner.

2.4.1 Using a bunsen burner

The temperature of the flame is controlled by adjusting the size of the air vent near the base of the burner. The flame consists of three regions viz. a, a blue conical zone; b, a clear zone; c, a yellow luminous zone. Zones a and c increase in size as the air is cut off while zone b increases as the air supply is increased. Fig. 2.10 shows the manner in which these regions vary in size as the air vent is adjusted. A glass tube, if held in the flame, will attain a temperature in the range indicated. To simplify the discussion of the use of the bunsen burner, we will describe the flame produced by these adjustments as type I, type II, etc.

The procedure for working soda-lime glass in a bunsen burner flame is as follows.

Stage one: warming the glass

Using flame type I and, holding the tube as described in Section 2.4.3, move it in and out of region b of the flame, gradually reducing the time that it spends out of the flame. Heat a large part of the glass, extending about 30 mm on either side of

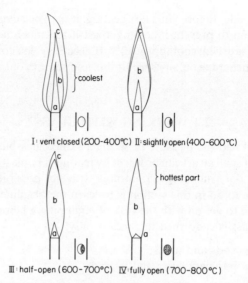

I: vent closed (200-400°C) II: slightly open (400-600°C)

III: half-open (600-700°C) IV: fully open (700-800°C)

Fig. 2.10 Bunsen burner flame

the point to be worked. Open the vent (flame type II) while continuing to move the glass so that the hot area is kept large. Do not take the glass out of the flame but rather move the flame to different parts of the hot area of the glass. Throughout this period the work is kept in zone c.

Stage two: softening the glass

Open the vent about half way (flame type III) and move the glass to the upper part of zone b. The hot area should not extend more than 20 mm on either side of the working point. Rotate the glass so that it is uniformly heated and unwanted asymmetries are thereby avoided. When the flame starts to turn orange, open the vent fully (flame type IV) and gradually move the work up to the top reaches of zone b. Zone c at this time should be hardly noticeable. Concentrate the flame on the part to be worked while continuing any necessary rotary and lateral motion. Soon the flame will become bright orange and the part of the glass in the flame will glow noticeably.

At this stage the glass may be bent, drawn, blown and otherwise manipulated. Do not rush the work. Plan carefully the amount of shaping you want to execute in each step. The glass must be glowing and must be rotated fairly rapidly to prevent it from sagging and becoming distorted.

Remember that the upper and outer reaches of zone b are the hottest parts of the flame; zone c is cooler; zone a, the coolest, is not used in glass work.

Stage three: annealing

When you have completed the manipulation you will want to cool the glass. If cooling takes place too rapidly and unevenly, stresses will be set up in the glass.

The work will become very fragile and even slight impacts, vibrations, or pressure could cause it to shatter. It must therefore be annealed, i.e. kept at a fairly high temperature (515 °C) just below the softening point until all the stresses are relieved (after 15 minutes). Then very slow cooling (about 200 °C per hour) should take place until a temperature of about 180 °C is reached. After this it can be allowed to cool in air.

For soda-lime glass, special annealing enclosures are not needed especially if only very simple work has been undertaken. The procedure that we will adopt is to keep the work in a type II flame for about 15 minutes after which the air is shut off completely. The glass is then held for a further 15 minutes in the type I flame.

The remainder of the cooling cycle may be completed in a domestic oven set at 250 °C (very hot). The work is left at this temperature for about 30 minutes and then the oven may be turned off. Leave the work in the oven, preferably overnight, or until it is cool enough to be touched.

2.4.2 Cutting tubes and rods

Tubes up to 15 mm in diameter and rods up to 8 mm can be snapped manually after a single transverse scratch has been made about a third of the distance along a circumference. The edge of a flat, single-cut hand file can be used for this purpose (Fig. 2.11(a)). Ensure that the scratch is well marked and uniform at the

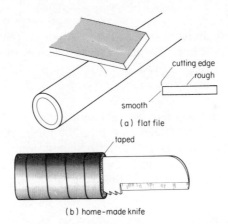

(a) flat file

(b) home-made knife

Fig. 2.11 Glass-cutting tools

first attempt. Avoid going over it a second time. The cutting edge must therefore be kept in good condition. The advantage of a flat file is that the edge can be restored by grinding off the smooth narrow face. A triangular file may also be used but this cannot be restored. If you can afford to buy a proper glass-cutting knife, by all means, do so. An adequate knife can be made from a discarded hacksaw blade (Fig. 2.11(b)).

After the scratch has been made, grasp the tube in both hands with the mark visible between the hands and facing away from you. Hold the tube at shoulder

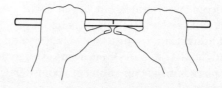

(a) breaking by hand

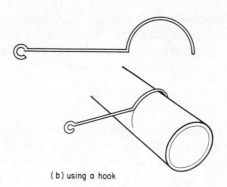

(b) using a hook

Fig. 2.12 Snapping glass tubes

height with your arms quite straight and rigid. Apply the thumbs exactly behind the mark (Fig. 2.12(a)). Bend the tube by pressing hard with your thumbs and at the same time forcing back the two halves of the tube in an apparent attempt to bring your wrists together. The tube should snap quite cleanly. (Practise the grip with a pencil.)

Tubes of 24 mm diameter require a different technique. A scratch should be made right around the circumference. Bend a 200 mm length of 1 mm diameter iron wire into the form of a hook which fits snugly around the tube. Heat the hook to red heat and apply directly to the scratch (Fig. 2.12(b)). A crack should appear almost immediately and will divide the tube along the mark.

2.4.3 Heating glass tubes

The cut edges should always be smoothed by heating. In all cases where glass tubes are heated, the unheated end should be closed with a stopper. This prevents the flame from travelling along the inside and so confines the heat to one end. It also prevents water, formed during combustion, from condensing inside the tube. This water could run down to the hot end and cause it to crack and shatter.

Hold the tube in the left hand, and rotate by rolling it between the index and forefinger while the other three fingers hold it lightly in a horizontal position (Fig. 2.13). Practise the execution of this movement with either hand. Try to prevent the tube from wobbling up or down or sideways while you are doing so.

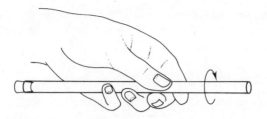

Fig. 2.13 Holding in the left hand

Each roll should take the tube through 180° or so, always in the same direction. Although this movement is intermittent, the point of the tube should remain steadily in the flame, otherwise uneven heating will result.

To smoothe the end, hold it in the flame of type II (very little air) until the flame turns orange. Increase the air supply till the flame is of type III. As soon as the glass starts to soften, remove it from the flame and set it aside to cool. Further heating can be used to strengthen the end. The heat will cause the walls to thicken with the tube becoming slightly constricted (Fig. 2.14(a)). The original diameter of the tube may be restored by using a brass rod as a reamer before the glass cools (Fig. 2.14(b)).

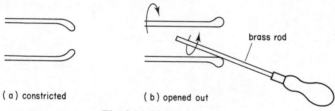

brass rod

(a) constricted   (b) opened out

Fig. 2.14 Using a reamer

If the tube has to be heated at a point near the middle, it may be held in two hands. The left hand, palm downward as before, holds the stoppered half and the right hand, palm upward, has the open end (Fig. 2.15). Rotation must be simultaneous and uniform so that when the glass has softened, the two halves of the tube are kept in line and no twisting takes place. To ensure that this is the

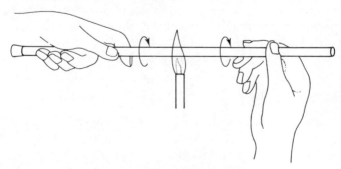

Fig. 2.15 Two-handed hold

case, three alignment marks may be scratched along the length of the glass at 10 mm spacing centred at the part to be softened. Continued rotation after softening should not displace the marks.

2.4.4 Sealing a glass tube

This is a technique which could be used for making test-tubes although it should be pointed out that it is only 25% cheaper than buying the ready-made article. However, it is important to know how to seal off a tube correctly whether making your own test-tubes or not.

Hold the tube in both hands, the left palm down, the right facing up. Rotating as before, heat a section along a distance twice as much as the diameter. When it has softened draw out this section to a length of about 300 mm. Cut at the midpoint of the thin portion and seal the points by heating momentarily in the flame (Fig. 2.16(a)).

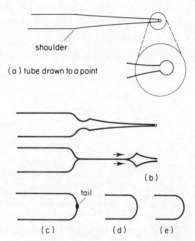

Fig. 2.16 Making a test-tube end

Adjust the burner to give a very narrow type IV flame and heat the tube just below the shoulder of the point, i.e. just where the narrowing commences. With rotation this area should soften and constrict (Fig. 2.16(b)). Draw this constriction out to a fine capillary, break off close to the shoulder and seal (Fig. 2.16(c)). Heat the sealed end in a type III flame to absorb any tails (Fig. 2.16(d)) then blow out until a hemispherical bowl is obtained (Fig. 2.16(e)).

2.4.5 Blowing a small bulb

Close the tube, as before, by making a hemispherical end. Then heat along a length *l* from the sealed end. If we assume that the bulb will have a wall thickness equal to that of the tube, then *l* is calculated from the equation

$$l = D^2/d$$

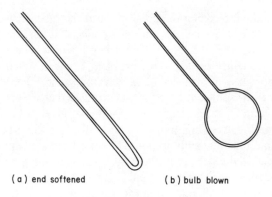

(a) end softened   (b) bulb blown

Fig. 2.17 Forming a bulb

where D and d are the diameters of the bulb and tube respectively. For a bulb of diameter 20 mm, blown from 6.5 mm tube, heat a length of 60 mm.

The tube is held at an angle of 45° and rotated, as usual, to prevent the softened glass from sagging. When sufficient glass has gathered the bulb is blown out to the desired diameter (Fig. 2.17).

This technique is used in Project 6.2.6 to construct a thermometer from capillary tubing.

2.4.6 Bending a glass tube

The following technique may be used to make sharp L-bends in tubes of up to 15 mm diameter. Stopper one end as usual and make a small mark with a file or glass knife at the point where the bending will take place. While rotating, heat a length equal to twice the diameter of the tube centred about the mark until the wall thickens and constricts (Fig. 2.18(a)). Remove from the flame and pull slightly (Fig. 2.18(b)) before bending to the desired angle (Fig. 2.18(c)). Blow into the

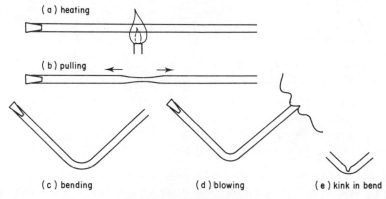

(a) heating

(b) pulling

(c) bending   (d) blowing   (e) kink in bend

Fig. 2.18 Making a sharp bend

open end, gradually increasing the pressure until the tube recovers its original diameter (Fig. 2.18(d)). Sometimes you may notice that the inner corner of the bend may have kinked (Fig. 2.18(e)). This is a fault which occurs when the glass has not been sufficiently heated. This problem is encountered when using a bunsen burner for glass-blowing as the temperatures reached are sometimes not high enough to allow sufficient time for executing all the necessary work on the glass. The apparently simple task of bending a glass tube requires three manoeuvres—pulling, bending, and blowing—all to be done before the glass sets. Therefore pulling and bending should be completed almost before the glass is out of the flame. In the same movement the open end should be brought to the mouth ready for blowing. This movement is more easily executed if, as has been already advised, the right hand, palm uppermost, is holding the open end.

The ideal bend should have a constant diameter and uniform wall thickness. This is not only aesthetically desirable but will also be mechanically stronger.

Fortunately we need not put very strict demands on the perfection of these bends as they will only be needed in shaping delivery tubes for a few chemistry experiments involving gas collection, etc.

2.5 WORKING WITH PLASTICS

Most of the plastics which are commonly in use nowadays are inexpensive petroleum-based polymers. They can be produced with such an amazing variety of properties that hardly any manufactured article today does not consist partly or wholly of these materials.

There is not enough space in this book to discuss all the plastics which could be of use in the construction of laboratory equipment. It has been decided that our discussions will be confined to:

1. acrylic sheet,
2. polystyrene,
3. polyethylene,
4. polyvinyl chloride.

2.5.1 Acrylic sheet

This transparent glass-like plastic is sold under such brand names as Perspex (UK) and Plexiglas (Germany). It has two main uses:

1. as an electrical insulating material which can be cut, drilled and machined using ordinary workshop tools; and,
2. as a glass substitute which, while it is completely transparent and colourless, is also flexible, unbreakable, and lightweight.

It is much more expensive than glass if purchased under the brand names but there are unbranded varieties which are comparable in price to glass. In recent years it has found a market as a substitute for glass in make-shift window panes and windscreens for automobiles especially in countries where these items cannot otherwise be replaced or are very expensive.

It is much softer than glass and is quite easily scratched. This is partly overcome by the fact that it can be polished. A brisk rubdown with a metal polish such as Brasso will produce an incredibly glass-like finish even on a rough-sawn surface. Very deep scratches can be filled with acrylic cement. This cement is made by dissolving pieces of acrylic sheet (usually chips and shavings left over after drilling or machining) in chloroform. Apply very thin coats of cement to the scratched surface and allow each coat to dry thoroughly. Avoid getting air bubbles trapped in the cement. Polish thoroughly to restore the original surface.

Acrylic cement is used to join together pieces of sheet to form enclosures. Very strong bonding can be achieved and, if the surfaces are machined to fit snugly against each other, these joints can be perfectly watertight.

All the methods for joining wood can also be used for acrylic sheet. This includes screwing and bolting. It may also be tapped to accept machine screws. Self-tapping screws may be used but in this case do not force the screw into the starter hole. Instead, turn it in and out of the hole while progressively going deeper at each cycle and, every so often, remove the screw completely to blow acrylic particles out of the hole. In this way the screw gradually cuts a thread in the plastic.

2.5.2 Expanded polystyrene

Polystyrene is available in a variety of forms:

1. as a brittle, glass-like plastic used in making disposable drinking tumblers and the outer tubes of ball point pens;
2. as the white, light-weight, cork-like material, used for packing electrical and other equipment, and known as expanded polystyrene or styrofoam;
3. as thin flexible film used in making high quality capacitors; and
4. as a fibre which is woven into the synthetic cloth known as terylene.

It is soluble in a variety of organic solvents, including petrol. It is fairly easy to make a cement by dissolving pieces of styrofoam in petrol.

There is a very wide range of applications of polystyrene in the expanded and the compact forms.

Styrofoam, in common with all polymeric foams, is a crumbly material but can be cut neatly with a very sharp blade. However, the easiest method to adopt is to use a hot-wire cutter such as is described in Project 8.4. An electric current is passed through the wire and causes it to heat up. At a temperature of about 120 °C the polystyrene will melt and thus the wire will cut into it. The material will seal again as soon as the wire has moved on so that a smooth cut surface results. A variety of shapes, even three-dimensional models, can be produced quite easily, hence its importance as a teaching aid. Fig. 2.19 shows a model of a river bed made by cutting slabs of foam to fit the contour lines of a map.

In the absence of a hot-wire cutter, any heated metallic object can be used to

58

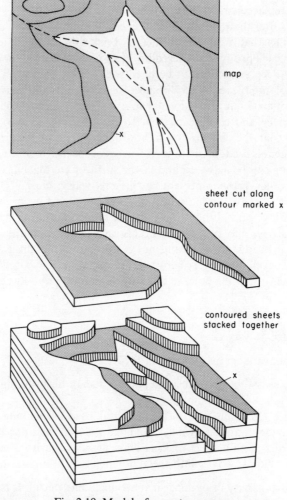

map

sheet cut along
contour marked x

contoured sheets
stacked together

x

Fig. 2.19 Model of a contour map

cut or shape the foam. In Project 5.5.1, the insulation for a set of calorimeters is
cut out using tin cans. A heated knife or soldering iron can be used for detailed
shaping. Some suppliers of science education equipment produce spheres of
various sizes. These are used for modelling crystal lattices. Try to make your
own spheres. Experimenting with styrofoam shapes costs virtually nothing
because you can get it as scrap outside most electrical shops.

To remove polystyrene clinging to the cutter after it has cooled, wash it in
petrol. This operation must be done in the open or in a well-ventilated room. Be
sure to shut off all burners and other sources of heat that you may have been
using.

Polystyrene cement (see Section 1.5.4) cannot be used with styrofoam as the petrol will dissolve it or distort it. If you wish to bond bits of foam together, use a vinyl adhesive such as Uhu. It does not dissolve styrofoam and it is waterproof.

A word about polyurethane foam: this is the spongy rubbery material used in mattresses and chair cushions. It is also found in upholstered furniture and in car seats. Do not be tempted to use a hot-wire cutter on this substance. Besides being very inflammable, it also gives off poisonous cyanide fumes when heated. In an enclosed space it can kill you in seconds. If you have to cut it, use a very sharp knife instead.

2.5.3 Extruded polystyrene

Our main interest in compact polystyrene concerns the outer tubes of ballpoint pens, as we have mentioned earlier. These make an excellent substitute for glass tubing and, using woodworking tools and cement, you can even make elbow bends and T-tubes.

Lengthening the tubes

These tubes are only about 130 mm long and often have a small hole drilled into the wall, half-way along its length. Your first step is to stop up this hole using polystyrene cement.

One end of the tube is generally tapered and, in the pen, contains the writing tip. This taper is useful in lengthening the tube as it can fit quite snugly into the blunt end of a second tube. First immerse the ends to be joined in petrol for two or three minutes. This will soften the surfaces so that when the ends are brought together (Fig. 2.20(a)) they will bed in each other quite firmly, forming their own adhesive. To strengthen the joint, dab on some polystyrene cement.

Lay the joined tubes on sheets of polythene (from plastic bags) and leave for a day or so to harden and set. Polythene has the property that almost no adhesive can stick to it. After the adhesive is set, the sheets can be pulled away quite easily. Ensure, however, that the polythene sheet does not have any creases which could be enfolded and gripped by the adhesive.

Making L-bends

If a right-angle bend is required, the tube should be cut, using a hacksaw, at 45°. For non-rectangular bends, the tube is cut at an angle which is half the required angle of the bend. Rotate one of the two cut pieces through 180° around the longitudinal axis and then rejoin at the desired angle (Fig. 2.20(b)).

The ends should be immersed in petrol for two or three minutes, before being fitted together. The bend should be held in place in a clamp. Two pieces of wood, lined with polythene sheet, and weighted with a heavy object could make a suitable clamp if not disturbed.

60

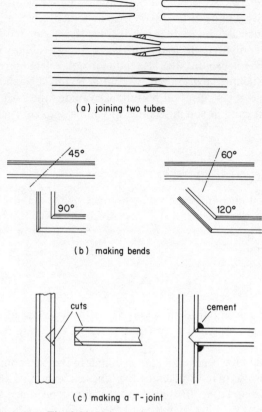

(a) joining two tubes

(b) making bends

(c) making a T-joint

Fig. 2.20 Using polystyrene tubes

Making a T-tube

Two tubes are required—one to be the leg of the T and the other the cross-piece.
Use a hacksaw to cut a vee-shaped notch halfway along the length of the cross-piece (Fig. 2.20(c)). Then cut one end of the leg to a wedge that would fit exactly into the notch. Clean off any rough edges from the cuts in petrol or, better still, just brush some petrol onto it and leave to stand for a while. Press the two pieces together to form the T. Dab some polystyrene cement on the join, clamp in position and leave to set.

Care should be taken that the bore is not obstructed by the cement when the tubes are pushed together.

2.5.4 Polyethylene

Polyethylene is commercially available as polythene and alkathene and is the cheapest plastic material. It is used for very low-cost packaging or containers and is the most abundant form of scrap with the exception of wastepaper. It is important for us to investigate the ways in which it can be incorporated into our programme of scrap recycling.

Polyethylene can be cut with a sharp knife. Even quite thick sheets may be cut this way but a hacksaw or a panel saw can also be used.

It is not easy to find an adhesive that will stick to polyethylene. It is therefore not feasible even to attempt to use an adhesive. Fortunately we do have an alternative way of joining this plastic.

Polyethylene melts very easily when heated above 120 °C although some grades have a higher melting point. At higher temperatures it retains its composition and thus solidifies back into its original form when it is cooled. These properties make it the ideal material to join by using welding techniques.

Welding is a process for joining two pieces by causing their surfaces in contact to melt and merge so that on cooling they adhere to each other. In the case of metals, heating would have to be done with a powerful blow lamp or by using an electric arc. For polyethylene, an ordinary soldering iron or a domestic flat iron (used for pressing clothes) is used.

Joining thin sheets

A flat iron is allowed to get hot enough for ironing cotton but too hot for synthetic materials. The two sheets to be joined are laid on the smooth surface of a piece of hardboard. The point of the iron is then, with very slight pressure, slowly drawn along the line where the materials are to be joined (Fig. 2.21). With practice, the optimum pressure and speed, for best results, will be discovered. It varies somewhat with the grade and thickness of the material to be joined.

The technique can be used for sealing plastic bags or for joining small pieces

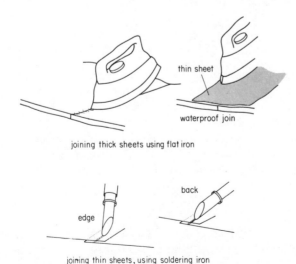

joining thick sheets using flat iron

joining thin sheets, using soldering iron

Fig. 2.21 Welding polythene

together to form a large sheet. This may be necessary if you have collected a number of plastic shopping bags and wish to join them together to form a dust cover, say, for expensive equipment.

A soldering iron may also be used for welding polythene.

Repairing containers

Polyethylene buckets sometimes crack along the bottom after long use. The crack can easily be mended by welding the two edges of the crack together. To ensure that the join is watertight, a strip of polythene sheet can be laid over the crack and welded in place.

2.5.5   Polyvinyl chloride (PVC)

PVC is resistant to most of the laboratory hazards such as water, acids, alkalis and oxidizing agents. Because of its almost leatherlike toughness, it has completely ousted rubber as a flexible electrical insulator and, as vinyl flooring, it has all but removed cork from the household scene.

There are three sources of PVC which are widespread and on which we will concentrate.

Electric cables

In many of the projects we will be using the $1.5\,mm^2$ and $2.5\,mm^2$ copper wire found in domestic PVC covered cable. If the casing and the sleeves are carefully removed—usually this can only be done in lengths of 300 to 500 mm—then we have a supply of PVC tubes which can be used whenever we require flexible tubing.

Vinyl flooring

This is obtainable as sheet or as tiles and can be purchased locally. The sheet is good for protecting the worktops of laboratory benches and is much cheaper than melamine (Formica) which is often recommended. It is therefore not necessary to have an expensive teak worktop.

The tiles and off-cuts of sheeting can be used as templates and stencils. If a map outline is drawn on and cut out of a vinyl tile (Project 6.3.2) it can be used as a stencil for reproducing the map into the students' exercise books.

Expanded PVC

The imitation leather which is used extensively in the manufacture of shoes, suitcases, briefcases, and car seats is another form of PVC. A metre or so of this material can be used to make an apron for your own use when you are handling solutions and corrosive chemicals.

2.6   USEFUL PROJECTS

A number of simple projects, described in Chapter 6, may serve to test the skills developed in this chapter. These are:

Project 6.1.2   Tripod
Project 6.2.1   Glass loop
Project 6.2.3   Droppers
Project 6.3.1   Dishes and scoops

A knife made from a discarded hacksaw blade was described in Section 2.2.4. You could try your hand at making this. You may also wish to fashion the tools mentioned below. They will make useful additions to your kits.

2.6.1   Using can-opening keys

A bradawl

Choose the long keys that are used for opening sardine cans. Cut off the eye and file that end to a sharp, flat point, like that of a screwdriver (Fig. 2.22(a)).

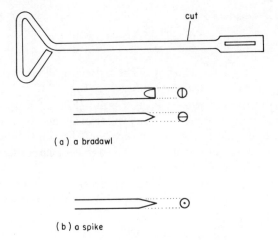

(a) a bradawl

(b) a spike

Fig. 2.22 Simple tools from can openers

A shoemaker's 'last'

If a rounded point was imparted to the above key (Fig. 2.22(b)), you would end up with a 'last' which may be used for piercing tough materials such as leather and PVC.

Making a large needle

The keys with which cans of sardines and corned beef are opened already have a convenient eye (Fig. 2.23(a)). Straighten the key and then, using a hammer,

64

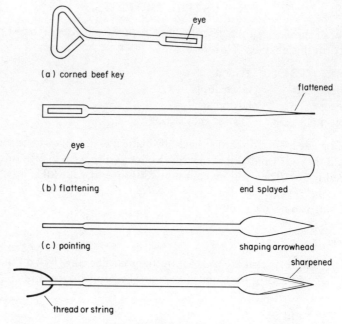

(a) corned beef key

(b) flattening

(c) pointing

Fig. 2.23 Making a needle

flatten the end furthest from the eye. The flattening should take place in the direction perpendicular to the plane of the eye (Fig. 2.23(b)). Turn it sideways and hammer the splayed end to form a point (Fig. 2.23(c)). By alternately flattening and pointing, the end of the key will take on the shape of an arrowhead (Fig. 2.23(c)). Use a file to sharpen the edges of the point. When the point is pressed into the material to be stitched, the edges will cut a slit which makes it easier to pull the thread through.

This needle may be used for stitching jute sacks and for repairing leather and canvas goods. It may be required in Project 6.3.3 in which lifeguards are made for protecting measuring cylinders.

2.6.2 Making a spanner

A simple open-ended spanner may be made from steel plate of about 3 mm thickness or more. A very good quality steel may be obtained as scrap from old cars. The leaves of the rear suspension springs may be separated by cutting away the brackets that hold them together (Fig. 2.24(a)).

From one of the leaves cut a strip measuring 200 mm by 30 to 35 mm. This is large enough to make a spanner with a jaw opening of 15 to 20 mm. Using a hacksaw, cut the ends at an angle of 60° (Fig. 2.24(b)). This angle allows the spanner to be used in a confined space.

Measure the distance x between opposite faces of the nut, for which the spanner is intended. Into the angled edge of the piece, cut two parallel slits

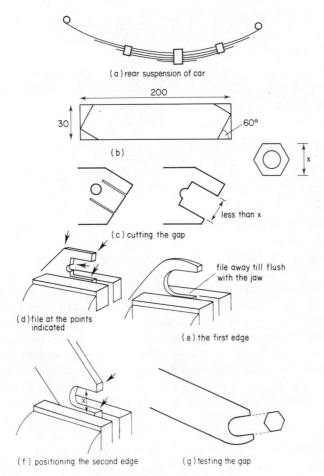

(a) rear suspension of car

200

30

60°

x

(b)

less than x

(c) cutting the gap

file away till flush
with the jaw

(d) file at the points
indicated

(e) the first edge

x

(f) positioning the second edge

(g) testing the gap

Fig. 2.24 Making a spanner

separated by a distance of at least 3 mm less than x. Between these slits, and at a distance x from the angled edge, drill a hole of 6 mm diameter (Fig. 2.24(c)). Insert a junior hacksaw blade in this hole and make cuts to meet the previous cuts at right angles. This produces an open-ended gap in the metal as shown.

The following steps are necessary to shape this gap to the correct width. Place the piece in a vice as shown in (Fig. 2.24(d)). One edge of the gap is held parallel to, and less than 1 mm above, the top of the vice jaws. Apply a half-round bastard file to the parts indicated. The edge of the gap should be filed until it is flush with the vice jaws (Fig. 2.24(e)). In this way a completely straight edge is obtained.

Turn the piece around so that the second edge is now gripped in the jaw. Carefully adjust the position of the spanner so that the previously filed edge is a distance x above the top of the vice jaws, and exactly parallel to it (Fig. 2.24(f)). The second edge may now be filed until it is flush with the jaws.

Test the fit of the spanner on the nut (Fig. 2.24(g)) and carefully adjust the width if it is too tight.

CHAPTER 3

Electricity

3.1 INTRODUCTION

It is not easy, some would say impossible, to run a science laboratory without electricity. Even if mains electricity is not available, some form of stored electricity, obtained perhaps from an accumulator or from dry cells, should be at hand.

Electrical experiments can be the most fascinating and rewarding in your work, but there is a tendency to think of electrical equipment as being expensive, if not actually a luxury. This is not so. Because of the ease with which electricity may be applied to almost every task, the components used in electrical equipment have, relative to the cost of many others, become quite cheap. Anyone who has bought a packet of candles recently will soon realize that electrical lighting costs less, besides being more effective than that outmoded form of illumination. Often the belief that electrical components are expensive encourages some dealers to charge four or five times more that the current price in the country of manufacture.

The construction or improvisation of electrical equipment is quite simple. It is not necessary to adhere absolutely to all of the instructions given for electrical equipment in Chapter 5. Neither the materials nor the dimentions, as we have stipulated them, are critical. In this chapter the broad outlines of the design and construction for such equipment will be discussed. One of the joys of constructing electrical apparatus is that, if you make a mistake it is usually very easy to rectify it. Modifications can be made to existing equipment without much difficulty provided only that, in the original construction, enough extra space was allowed on the chassis (the board to which the components are attached).

The tools with which, as usual, we will deal first should not present any problem either in cost or in their implementation.

3.2 SUPPLEMENTARY KIT D: ELECTRICAL TOOLS

This kit consists of the following items:

long-nosed pliers, 180 mm long,
wire stripper,
testing screwdriver,

continuity tester,
soldering iron,
desoldering tool,
multimeter.

The first five items are inexpensive and essential for any electrical work and so it will be assumed that you possess all of these. The desoldering tool is useful but may not be easily obtainable. The multimeter is usually very expensive but, like the electrical drill of kit B and the vice of kit C, it can simplify many of the tasks that you may encounter in this course.

3.2.1 Pliers

A pair of pliers allow a tight grip to be applied by hand to small objects. Long-nosed pliers (Fig. 3.1(a)) with thick rubber or plastic insulation on the handles are required for holding nuts while you tighten a screw, for wrapping wire around a terminal and for making tight radius bends and kinks in component leads prior to soldering. They are also useful for holding wires and components which may heat up during soldering.

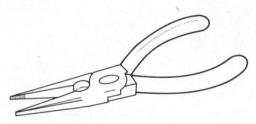

(a) long-nosed pliers

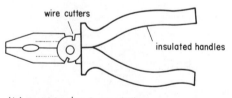

(b) electricians' snub-nosed pliers

Fig. 3.1 Pliers

Hints

1. The pliers should come with recessed side-cutters which are used for cutting, stripping, and cleaning wires.
2. It is not good practice to subject the jaws to excessive twisting as this could cause them to become permanently misaligned.
3. The electrician's pliers, if you get these, are equipped with a set of wire-cutting shears which are strong enough to cut quite thick iron wire. This may be purchased in addition to the above (Fig. 3.1(b)).

68

3.2.2 Wire stripper

The simple type known as the Bib cutter is shown in Fig. 3.2. This is quite cheap and effective, especially if the jaws can be set by means of a cam clamped with a screw. The newer model which has a stepped adjustment becomes difficult to use after a while as it tends to become too loose.

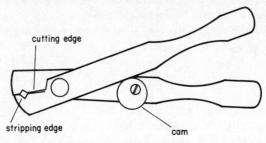

Fig. 3.2 Wire stripper

3.2.3 Mains-testing screwdriver

A current as low as 50 microamperes can make a neon lamp glow visibly, provided the potential appearing across it is more than 70 volts. This fact is used in the mains-testing screwdriver (Fig. 3.3(a)). It contains a neon discharge lamp

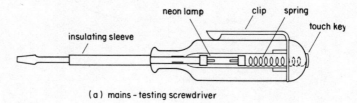

(a) mains - testing screwdriver

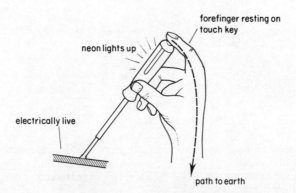

(b) using a testing screwdriver

Fig. 3.3 Mains-testing screwdriver

about the size of a glass fuse. One terminal of the lamp makes contact with the shaft of the screwdriver. A retaining spring pushes down on the lamp and also presses against a touch-pad in the top of the handle. If you wish to test a point, hold the screwdriver with its handle gripped between your thumb and middle finger with the forefinger resting lightly on the touch-pad (Fig. 3.3(b)). Bring the blade of the screwdriver into contact with the point to be tested. If the point is 'live', the neon will light up when your forefinger touches the pad. This happens because your body acts as a conductor to complete the circuit from the live point, through the lamp and pad, to earth.

Of course, this tool can be used as a regular screwdriver.

3.2.4 Continuity tester

This is a simple instrument (Fig. 3.4) in which a battery is connected in series with a lamp and two floating leads ending in crocodile clips. When the clips are brought together, the circuit is completed and the lamp lights up.

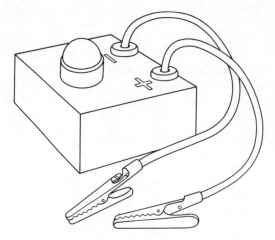

Fig. 3.4 A continuity tester

If the clips are connected to opposite ends of a lead, connector, or switch, continuity of the circuit through these devices will also be indicated by the lamp lighting up.

Project 8.5 describes the construction of a continuity tester.

Hint

1. Do not use the tester on a circuit which is 'live', i.e. switched on.
2. The tester may be used for testing the polarity of semiconductor diodes and rectifiers. If the lamp lights up, the positive lead is connected to the anode.

3.2.5 Soldering iron

The soldering iron with which most people are familiar is the electrically heated type (Fig. 3.5). This may have a power consumption of 15 to 100 watts depending on the size and thermal capacity of the components to be joined. Personally, I prefer one with a 25 or 30 watt element which can be used both for transistor work (if you do not allow the iron to be in contact with the joint for more than two or three seconds) and medium-sized electrical joints.

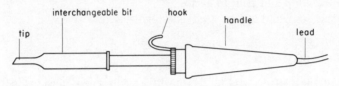

Fig. 3.5 Soldering iron

Occasionally you may need to solder some fairly heavy pieces but the joint conducts away the heat so quickly that the temperature of the tip cannot be maintained at the melting point of the solder. You then employ what is known as impact soldering whereby the iron is kept in an enclosed, draught-free box or cup until a high temperature is obtained. The point is then quickly brought into contact with the joint and the solder and, hopefully, enough heat would have been stored up in the iron to allow for the soldering operation to be performed. You may find, however, that a succession of impact passes may be required to complete the job.

3.2.6 Desoldering tool

The tool, sometimes referred to as a solder-sucker, is a suction device which looks and works like a pump in reverse (Fig. 3.6). The plunger is pushed in until it locks in position. When the release button is depressed, the plunger is released.

If you wish to remove solder from a point, heat it with a soldering iron until it melts. Bring the nozzle of the solder-sucker close to the solder and press the release button. A powerful spring will rapidly push up the plunger and create a vacuum in the cylinder. This sucks the liquid solder up into the cylinder. The solidified solder is then pushed out by depressing the plunger. When it locks the desoldering tool is ready for use again.

Hints

1. It is desirable to have a guard around the head of the plunger because there is a real danger of getting hit in the eye or face when the plunger shoots up.
2. Use the desoldering tool to dismantle electronic equipment such as old discarded radios. This becomes a cheap source of components.

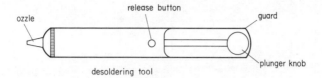

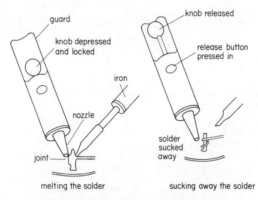

Fig. 3.6 Using the desoldering tool

3.2.7 Multimeter

The multirange meter (Fig. 3.7) to give the full name, can be used for measuring current, voltage, and resistance (Fig. 3.8). The basic instrument is a microammeter on which the full scale deflection (f.s.d.) determines the sensitivity and accuracy of the measurements. The multimeters which are in most common use have a basic movement of 50 microamperes at f.s.d. but are expensive. Instruments of 100 microamperes are available at about a quarter of the price and are generally just as useful. The only drawback is that you will not be able to measure resistances below 10 ohms with accuracy.

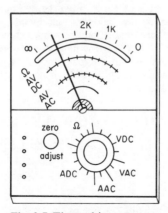

Fig. 3.7 The multirange meter

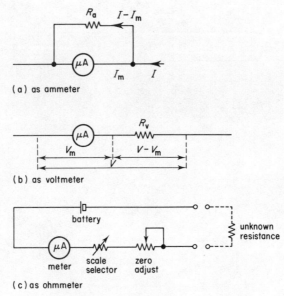

(a) as ammeter

(b) as voltmeter

(c) as ohmmeter

Fig. 3.8 Using the multirange meter

The multimeter can be used for a.c. and d.c. measurements. The most useful ranges are these:

d.c.: Current 1 mA, 100 mA, and (not always present) 10 A;
     Voltage 10 V;
     Resistance 2 kilohm (mid-scale).
a.c.: Current 1 A
     Voltage 250 V

Hints

1. Before taking resistance measurements, bring the two probes into contact with each other and adjust the zero on the scale that you intend to use.
2. With the unknown resistance in position the pointer should come to rest between 10 per cent and 90 per cent of f.s.d. for the most accurate readings.
3. When the meter is set for resistance measurement, a battery is connected into the circuit. After taking a reading, do not leave the instrument at the ohmmeter settings as this shortens the life of the battery.

3.3 THE ELECTRICAL CIRCUIT

An electrical circuit as seen in Fig. 3.9 consists basically, of four parts, namely:

    the power source,
    the switch or control,
    the fuse or protection device,
    the load or appliance to be energized.

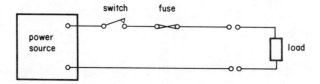

Fig. 3.9 The electrical circuit

We will discuss each in some detail to examine points which will enable you to be confident in the handling of electrical equipment.

3.3.1 The power source

There are two classes of power sources available to us. These are direct current (d.c.) and alternating current (a.c.). The former is usually obtained from batteries and the latter from the socket outlet of the electrical mains supply in your home or place of work (Fig. 3.10).

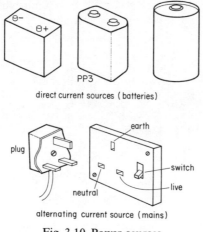

direct current sources (batteries)

alternating current source (mains)

Fig. 3.10 Power sources

The word 'circuit' is used advisedly because electricity circulates continuously from the source and must have a line of return to the source. Every power source must therefore have at least two terminals or outlets. In d.c. circuits the terminals are described as the positive and the negative respectively; in a.c. circuits they are called the live and the neutral.

Electrical potential is a rather arbitrary quantity that has to be measured with respect to some reference. For reasons of safety this reference is usually the earth. It is a fairly straightforward business to earth one of the terminals of a d.c. supply. Usually it does not matter which one but, by convention, preference is given to earthing the negative terminal. A.c. circuits, on the other hand, are slightly more complicated.

Direct grounding of an a.c. supply can only be done through a transformer,

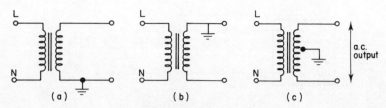

Fig. 3.11 Earthing of a.c. sources

the secondary winding of which is electrically isolated from the mains. Earthing can then be made at any of the terminals of the secondary, at a centre tap or at any intermediate point (Fig. 3.11).

3.3.2 The switch

In its simplest form, a switch is a manually operated device which either completes (makes) or interrupts (breaks) the flow of current through the circuit. In its two functions it is said to be either closed or open respectively. As seen from Fig. 3.12 the closed switch carriers the full current current in the circuit; when open, it withstands the full voltage of the source.

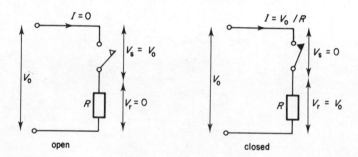

Fig. 3.12 Effect of switching

It is not possible for current to stop flowing at the instant the contact is broken. For a fraction of a second after the circuit is broken, an electric arc is formed between the two contacts. A voltage of 10 to 20 volts appears across the switch and we have, for a very short space of time, both current and voltage existing at the contacts. The power dissipation shoots up and some damage occurs to the contact surfaces. This happens every time the switch is opened and, because of contact-bounce, when the switch is closed.

The damage is less severe in a.c. circuits because the oscillations of the voltage could shut off the arc. Therefore you cannot always take a switch intended for a.c. and use it for d.c. without taking this into consideration. As a rough guide, the d.c. voltage should be less than one-third of the rated a.c. voltage.

It is not possible to increase the current rating just because the working voltage has been reduced. Generally the current rating remains unchanged until the voltage has been reduced to one-third of the specified maximum value. After that

Table 3.1 Adjustment of switch ratings

Nominal rating:	1 A at 240 Va.c.		
a.c.		d.c.	
Volts	Current	Volts	Current
240	1	75	1
160	1	50	1
80	1	25	1
40	2	12	2
20	4	6	4
10	8	3	8

the current may be increased in reverse proportion to the voltage (Table 3.1).

The plug-key (Fig. 3.13(a)) often used in school laboratories, is intended for low voltage, high current work. It has a disadvantage in that students tend to leave the plug in position for long periods and so discharge the batteries unnecessarily. This cannot happen with contact switches (Fig. 3.13(b)) which have to be held down manually while measurements are taken. It is clearly advisable to use this type of switch when dry cells are used as the power source.

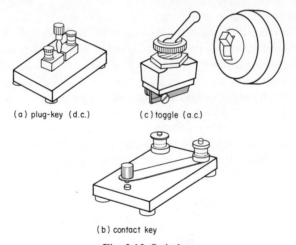

(a) plug-key (d.c.)   (c) toggle (a.c.)

(b) contact key

Fig. 3.13 Switches

The toggle switch (Fig. 3.13(c)) is designed for mains operation but, with proper derating, may be used for battery-operated circuits. For example, a switch rated at 240 V a.c. and 1 ampere may be used for 12 V d.c. and 2 amperes.

3.3.3 The fuse

A fuse is a short length of metal wire or strip which will melt and break a circuit if the current through it exceeds a specified value.

Keep a stock of 1, 5, and 15 A fuse wire. You will require this for repairing the

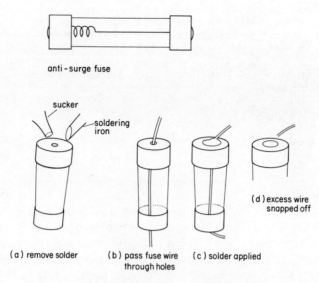

anti-surge fuse

sucker
soldering
iron

(d) excess wire
snapped off

(a) remove solder   (b) pass fuse wire   (c) solder applied
                          through holes

Fig. 3.14 Repairing a glass fuse

plug-in fuses in the mains distribution boxes. It is also possible to repair the ordinary glass or ceramic enclosed cartridge fuses (Fig. 3.14). It is useful to note that the 36G (0.193 mm diameter) copper wire used in the strands of flexible twin lighting cable will fuse at 8 amperes. Two strands fuse at 15 amperes. This wire is therefore a useful substitute for standard fuse wire of the same rating.

Use a soldering iron to remove the solder from both ends of the fuse cartridge. This can be done by melting the solder and sucking it away with a desoldering tool or blowing it away with a sudden puff. Remove the two ends of the fuse wire and ensure that the holes are quite clear. Thread the replacement wire through the two holes. Draw it tightly at an angle to the hole and fix in place with a spot of solder. As soon as the solder is set you can snap off the ends of the wire simply by wiggling it.

3.3.4   The load

In laboratory work, the appliance or load is usually some experimental equipment such as a metre bridge or potentiometer. The current for this is supplied from a battery or a power pack. Most experiments at secondary school level are conducted at low potentials (1 to 12 volts) and medium currents (1 to 5 amperes).

The current which is drawn by the load determines how often the accumulators will have to be recharged. A metre bridge, in series with a low-resistance rheostat, may draw 0.5 ampere from a 2-volt battery. Thus during a 3-hour practical session, 1.5 ampere-hours (Ah) of charge will be lost. As there may be two or three such sessions per week an accumulator with a capacity of 5 Ah may appear to be adequate if it were not for the fact that the e.m.f. tends to fall when half the charge has been used. Laboratory batteries should therefore have a minimum capacity of 10 (preferably more). The charger described in Project 8.3 will be capable of recharging two sets of six accumulators a day: one set at 2 amperes during the working day and another at 0.5 ampere overnight.

3.4 DEVELOPING ELECTRICAL APPARATUS

This is done in five stages, viz.:

1. draw the circuit;
2. choose the principle of operation;
3. choose the components;
4. decide on the layout;
5. construct it.

3.4.1 Diagrams

Two circuit diagrams are required:

1. the overall circuit which includes not only the basic circuit but also all the peripheral and external components and devices which are necessary for its operation;
2. the basic circuit only, with the peripherals replaced by clearly marked terminals to which they are to be attached. This highlights the essential constituents of the intended apparatus.

3.4.2 Principle of operation

We may now decide on the manner in which the apparatus will be operated and acted on by the student. This will depend on the operating skills which the equipment is intended to teach. For example, if a variable resistance is required, should it be a plug-in type, a switched type, a continuously variable type or should the student manually connect and disconnect the component at a set of terminals? Will the power supply be alternating current (a.c.) or direct current (d.c.)? How will the experiment be monitored: with a galvanometer or a multimeter?

With extra equipment it is surprising how many different interpretations can be given to the same basic circuit. Consider, for example, the Wheatstone bridge, as used for measuring an unknown resistance. Figs. 3.15(a) and (b) show the overall and the basic circuit diagrams respectively. The decision to use direct current, possibly in the form of an accumulator, can be taken immediately but how will the resistances be varied? An inspection of the illustrated catalogues of a few manufacturers of science teaching equipment will give you some indication of the variety of approaches that can be adopted. Besides using individual variable resistance boxes, there are also available the post office box, the metre bridge and other types which use a combination of switched and sliding-contact resistances (Fig. 3.16).

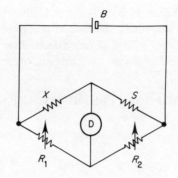

(a) overall circuit

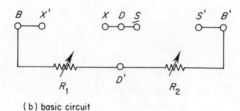

(b) basic circuit

Fig. 3.15 Wheatstone bridge

3.4.3. Components

An experiment in physics may have one or a combination of two objectives: to make an absolute or comparative measurement of a physical quantity, or to make simultaneous measurements of two or more quantities with the intention of establishing a relationship between them. Usually a range of measurements has to be taken: the wider the range, the more useful the experiment will be.

Equipment must be designed to cope with a range of readings. Consequently the components in the equipment should cover a wide range of values and, in the

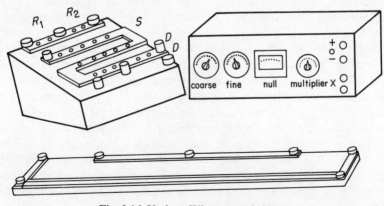

Fig. 3.16 Various Wheatstone bridges

case of electrical experiments, must be able to withstand the variation of voltage, current, power dissipation, temperature, etc., which such a range produces.

Reasonable accuracy is expected of the component values but this need not be insisted upon. The 2 to 5% accuracy of mass-produced components is adequate for our purposes. Carbon resistors used in electronic equipment may substitute for the precise but expensive resistors usually supplied to schools. Both resistors and capacitors are manufactured cheaply in enormous quantities.

They are produced in values which increase geometrically in jumps of approximately 20%. This produces the E.12 series of values, so-called because it takes twelve steps to increase by a factor of ten, e.g. between 1 and 10 the values are:

$$1, 1.2, 1.5, 1.8, 2.2, 2.7, 3.3, 3.9, 4.7, 5.6, 6.8, 8.2, 10;$$

between 10 and 100 they are:

$$10, 12, 15, 18, 22, 27, 33, 39, 47, 56, 68, 82, 100;$$

and between 100 and 1000 they are:

$$100, 120, 150, 180, 220, 270, 330, 390, 470, 560, 680, 820, 1000, \text{etc.}$$

Components with these values are, nowadays, made with a tolerance of 5%, i.e. a resistance of 100 ohms could, in fact, have a value anywhere between 95 and 105 ohms. The usual carbon resistances with a power rating of 0.5 watts used in radios are available in values ranging from 10 ohms to megohms and are the cheapest electronic components that you could buy. All of these can be used with supplies of 2 volts. If you intend to use them with supplies of 12 volts or so then all resistances below 270 ohms should be rated at one watt or more.

Standard resistors may be combined in series or parallel to produce non-standard values. This method also increases the power and voltage ratings. Most half-watt resistors will only withstand a potential of 300 volts maximum: two half-watt resistors of 100 ohms each will produce a one-watt resistance of 200 ohms capable of withstanding 600 volts. This technique is most effective when the resistors have closely similar values. If you combined a 22 ohm resistor in series with one of 180 ohms you will obtain a 202 ohm resistance with ratings of 0.56 watts and 340 volts maximum.

One disadvantage of these carbon resistances is that their values tend to alter or drift with age especially when operated near their maximum power ratings. It is suggested that you do not allow them to dissipate more than a quarter of their maximum allowed power rating.

Components that are sealed in the same packet are usually from the same batch of manufacture. Such components have closely identical values and are ideal for applications where the ratio of their values is more important than their actual values. It is also important to use these common-batch components whenever you wish to produce a number of identical units of the same equipment.

The values of electronic components, you will find, are sometimes not printed on them. Instead they are marked with a series of coloured stripes or dots. This colour coding is discussed in Section 9.6 of the appendix.

The choice of terminals determines the ease with which some components and

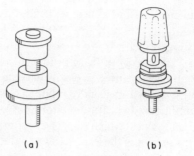

(a)   (b)

Fig. 3.17 Terminals

peripheral devices may be changed. The all-brass terminal (Fig. 3.17(a)) which still appears in older equipment has largely been replaced by a cheaper version which combines a 4 mm ('banana') socket with a screw-down clamp (Fig. 3.17(b)). The shaft of the screw has a transverse hole through which a lead may be passed.

These terminals come in at least eight colours which help identification in equipment. For d.c. power supplies, the positive terminal is usually red while the negative is black. The earth connector may be green but there is a tendency nowadays to use white or yellow for this purpose. The reason for this change, is that the most common form of colour blindness is an inability to distinguish between red and green. This has led many nations to adopt colour codes which avoid the use of both red and green in the same set.

3.4.4 Layout

The pupil should encounter little difficulty in understanding the operation of the equipment. Preferably there should be some similarity between the layout and the diagrams which were presented during the lessons. As this is more readily accomplished with an open construction, i.e. the equipment is not enclosed in a case, nothing in the basic design should constitute a hazard to the user. Generally, only voltages below 12 volts should be used. Currents should be kept to such a level that no component heats up beyond 60° C. Remember that at 65° C an object is just too hot to hold; at 70° C contact with it could be painful.

On the other hand, variable resistances, in which rotary switches and soldered joints are used, should be enclosed in a box. This protects it from damage and prevents dust particles from getting between the switch contacts.

Terminals and controls should be easily accessible. In enclosed equipment, the panel on which these components are mounted is referred to as the control panel. It is usually either the top panel, e.g. for resistance boxes, or the front panel, e.g. power supplies. Terminals are placed as follows (see Fig. 3.18):

1. on open-type equipment (e.g. metre bridges) to the rear edge;
2. on closed-type equipment on which the control panel faces upward (e.g. resistance boxes) to the rear or side edges;

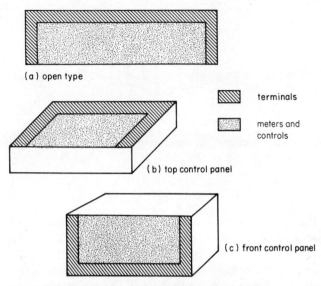

(a) open type

terminals

meters and controls

(b) top control panel

(c) front control panel

Fig. 3.18 Position of terminals and controls

3. on closed-type equipment on which the control panel faces forward (e.g. power supplies) along the lower edge of the front panel or, sometimes, on the rear panel.

Controls are placed as follows:

1. on open-type equipment along the front edge;
2. on closed-type equipment centrally on the control or front panel.

The Wheatstone bridges shown in Fig. 3.16 are good examples of the above criteria.

3.4.5 Mounting the components

The reliability, ruggedness and serviceability of the circuit depends on the way in which the components are mounted and wired. They should be rigidly attached to prevent their being displaced from their positions and should be accessible to allow for testing *in situ*, removal, and replacement without unnecessary difficulty. Do not crowd them together when they are dissipating more than 25% of their maximum power ratings but allow a free circulation of air around them.

The tag board

This consists of a double row of tinned tags fixed to a laminated board (Fig. 3.19). The tags which may be arranged singly or in pairs are provided with a hook to which the component leads are attached. The tag board is useful for mounting arrays of components which are intended to be switched in and out of the circuit.

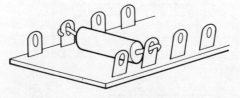

Fig. 3.19 Tag board

It is therefore recommended in the construction of resistance and capacitance boxes.

The strip board

A layer of copper is bonded to a laminated board after which it is scored leaving parallel strips of metal running the length of the board (Fig. 3.20(a)). Holes are drilled into the strips at fixed intervals (Fig. 3.20(b)). In the most popular make, the holes and strips have the same spacing which may be 2.5, 3.8, and 5 mm respectively. The 3.8 mm and 5 mm spacings are easier to work with as there is less risk of stray splashes of solder forming short-circuits between the strips, but

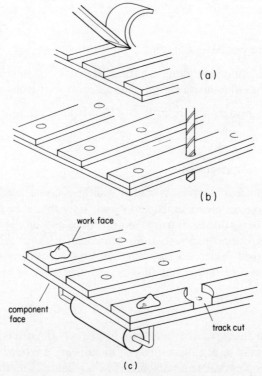

(a)

(b)

work face

component face

track cut

(c)

Fig. 3.20 Making and using a strip board

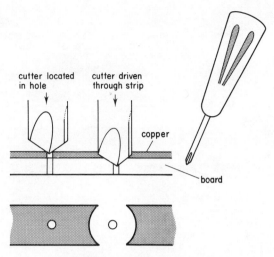

cutter located
in hole

cutter driven
through strip

copper

board

Fig. 3.21 Using a spot face cutter

it should be mentioned that the 2.5 mm spacing has become the standard for use with integrated circuit modules for electronic applications. This size may therefore be more readily obtained.

The components are usually placed at right angles to the strips (Fig. 3.20(c)) with the body of the component being placed on the side of the board which does not have the strips. This is the component face of the board. The leads pass through the holes and the solder joints are made directly onto the strip in the opposite side, which is the work face. When components on the same strip are to be isolated, the strip may be cut with a knife or with a special tool known as a spot face cutter (Fig. 3.21).

An improvised component board

This can be made from 3 mm plywood and copper wire. Plywood is chosen in preference to hardboard because it is more rigid and much stronger. Tags are made of wire obtained from single core twin-and-earth cable used for domestic electrical wiring. Both the 1.5 mm^2 (15 A) or 2.5 mm^2 (20 A) wire are suitable.

Two types of mounting fixtures are used and these are described simply as being either tags or strips. Tags are needed when only two components are to be joined at a common point. When more than two components are involved, a strip must be used.

A hole of 2 or 2.5 mm is drilled about 8 mm from the edge of the board. A tag can be made by passing a 25 mm length of wire through the hole and bringing the ends together in a tight loop. For extra security the ends could be soldered together but usually this is not necessary (Fig. 3.22(a)). Tags can also be placed in the middle of the board by drilling a pair of holes about 8 mm apart, passing one end of the wire through each hole and bringing the ends together (Fig. 3.22(b)).

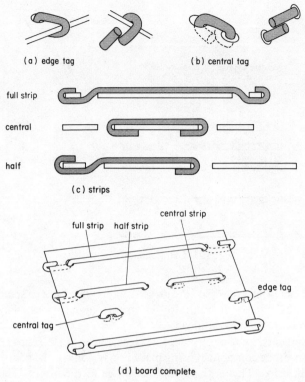

(a) edge tag   (b) central tag

full strip

central

half

(c) strips

central strip

full strip   half strip

edge tag

central tag

(d) board complete

Fig. 3.22 Improvised wire board

Strips can either cover the full width of the board or only a section of it. In the former case the holes are drilled at the edges and the wire looped back over the top as in (Fig. 3.22(c)). Centrally placed strips are looped as in the same figure. The half-strip which originates at an edge but does not cover the entire length of the board has a combination of both types of loops.

Tin the pieces when they are all in position. Tinning increases the rigidity of the wire and also makes easier the task of attaching the components.

Each board with its arrangement of tags and strips can be designed for the particular circuit you have in mind (see Fig. 3.22(d)). To give you an idea of how these can be made we have chosen Project 5.2.5 which contains a circuit for a decade capacitance box. This circuit consists of polyester and electrolytic capacitors in both parallel and series combinations. We have assumed that the dimensions for the capacitors are as shown in (Fig. 3.23(a)).

The leads of the electrolytic capacitors are axial, i.e. they point along the direction of the longest dimension (Fig. 3.23(a)). The polyester capacitors have radial leads, which lie perpendicular to the length, and are intended for use with printed-circuit boards. The leads are bent so that they are almost axial (Fig. 3.23(b)), or bits of copper wire could be attached to provide axial leads.

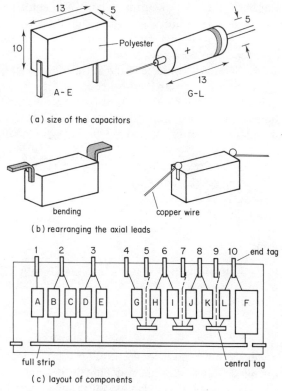

(a) size of the capacitors

bending   copper wire

(b) rearranging the axial leads

full strip   central tag

(c) layout of components

Fig. 3.23 Use of the wire board

The layout which is shown in (Fig. 3.23(c)) uses a combination of edge and central tags and a full strip. It is not easy to wrap the leads around the copper wire but it has been found that suitable joints can be made by positioning the leads flat against the wire.

3.5 ELECTRICAL PRACTICE

3.5.1 Safety first

1. Never turn on or work with an electric appliance while you are standing on a wet floor or leaning on a wet workbench.
2. Before you start any repairs on electrical equipment, unplug it from the mains. Switching off is not enough.
3. Never poke anything except a plug into any socket.
4. Never use water to extinguish a fire in an item that is plugged in. First unplug it and then use a chemical fire extinguisher. You should have at least one extinguisher in the laboratory. The low-cost type sold by automobile dealers and spares shops are adequate for most small fires.

5. Do not unplug equipment by pulling on the cord. This could damage the cord, give you a shock or start a fire. Pull on the plug itself.
6. Unplug ALL electrical equipment at the end of a laboratory session. Disconnect the leads from all batteries.
7. No inflammable materials should be found in the room in which batteries are left on charge overnight or over the weekend.
8. Do not run cables across the floor. Either run them across the ceiling or along the walls. Better still, your laboratory should have sufficient socket outlets spaced not more than 5 metres apart along the walls or placed on every work bench.
9. Lighting equipment and certain double insulated portable equipment may be operated without an earth connection. Nevertheless it is more sensible to insist that all socket outlets in the laboratory must have an earthed connection.

3.5.2 Fault tracing

For this purpose, a mains-testing screwdriver and a continuity tester are required. We will assume you are working either with a d.c. supply of less than 24 volts or an a.c. mains supply of more than 100 volts.

1. *Low-voltage d.c. supply*

The fault is more likely to be a poor connection. This may be located by wiggling each connection, plug, and switch while watching the galvanometers, ammeters, etc. which are in the circuit. If this has no effect, check the batteries. If the batteries are all right, use a continuity tester on every component in the circuit.

A.c. equipment with supplies of less than 24 volts may be handled in the same way.

2. *Mains supply, equipment switched on but not functioning*

Do the following checks.
(a) Have you switched the equipment on? If not, do so.
(b) Have you plugged it into the mains? If not, do so.
(c) Is the plug making good contact with the mains socket? Try wiggling it about or move it in and out of the socket a few times. If, while you are doing this, the equipment turns on and off, the socket or the pins on the plug are faulty.
(d) Do the pins show signs of oxidation? If so, clean the pins and try again. If the pins are sound, check the wiring inside the plug. Rewire if necessary (see Section 3.5.3).

If the socket is faulty, have it replaced by a competent electrician.

3. *Mains supply, equipment disconnected*

Using a testing screwdriver, test the live (right-hand) hole in the socket. If this lights up, plug in another electrical device such as a lamp. If the lamp lights up, power is reaching the socket. Proceed with 5. If the lamp does not light up even though the screwdriver indication was positive, call in an electrician.

If neither the screwdriver nor the lamp lights up, power is not reaching the socket. At this stage, unplug all the electrical equipment in the laboratory, especially if it is found that none of the sockets has any power.

4. *Mains supply, power not reaching socket*

Your attention should now turn to the mains distribution box. This is a metal or rigid plastic box from which wires lead through conduits in the wall to the various sockets in the room or building. Find out where it is located. It is usually fitted with an isolation switch, which you should turn off, and a door or cover which, when removèd, reveals an array of fuses or switch-like circuit breakers.

Inspect the fuses. If any have blown or ruptured, replace with a new fuse of the same current rating.

Inspect the circuit breakers, if any. They should all be turned on. If one has tripped off, turn it on again.

Before turning on the isolation switch, unplug all equipment in your laboratory, if you have not already done so.

Turn on the isolation switch.

If the fuse blows again or the circuit breaker trips, call in an electrician.

If not, plug the equipment under test into its own socket.

If the fuse blows or the circuit breaker trips again, there is a short-circuit in your equipment. Replace the fuse or reset the circuit breaker as before but do not plug in the offending equipment. Proceed with 6.

If the fuse does not blow when the equipment is plugged in and switched on, proceed with 5.

5. *Mains supply, power reaching socket but equipment not functioning*

If you have not already done so, open the plug and inspect the wiring. Rewire if faulty (see Section 3.5.3).

If the plug contains a fuse, check the fuse with a continuity tester. Replace if faulty.

If, when you switch on the equipment, the fuse blows again, proceed with 6.

Check any fuses in the equipment itself. Some of these may be installed in fuseholders mounted on the front or rear panels; others may only be accessible after the cover has been removed from the equipment. If faulty, replace the fuse with a new one of the same rating (see also Section 3.3.3).

Check the supply lead which carries the power to the equipment. Use a continuity tester to discover breaks in any of the wires in the lead. If faulty, replace the lead.

6. *Mains supply, equipment has a short-circuit*

The fault may be in the supply lead. With the equipment unplugged and turned off, and using the continuity meter, check the insulation between the live, neutral, and earth pins on the plug.

If a short-circuit is found, the lead should be replaced.

If no short-circuit is found, the fault is in the equipment itself. Call in a competent electrical or electronics repairman.

3.5.3 Wiring a plug

All power outlets in a science laboratory should be of the three-pin type. The pins may have a round or a rectangular cross-section (Fig. 3.24). Plugs of the latter kind are supplied with a 3-ampere or a 13-ampere fuse. Just inside the gap through which the cable enters the plug, is a strip of plastic held by two screws. This is the cord grip which clamps the cable.

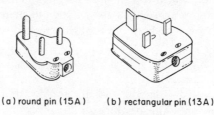

(a) round pin (15A)   (b) rectangular pin (13A)

Fig. 3.24 Three-pin plugs

The type of cable that is used with these plugs is the double-insulated type, i.e. it consists of three conductors, each covered in its own individual sleeve, and then covered collectively with an overall outer sheath. In older wiring the sleeves may be of rubber while braided cotton is used for the sheath. In modern cables, the sleeving and the sheath are both made of PVC. The conductors are identified by the colour of the sleeving. The most common colour codes are shown in Appendix 9.6.

The following wiring procedure may be used for both the round and the rectangular pin types.

Strip the outer sheath from the cable for a distance of 40 mm from one end (Fig. 3.25(a)). Open the plug to reveal the terminals. Clamp the unstripped part in the cord grip (Fig. 3.25(b)) ensuring that the sheath is securely held. Run the brown lead to the live terminal, marked L (or R in some round-pin plugs), the blue lead to the neutral terminal, mark N (or B), the green-yellow lead to the earth terminal. Cut each lead so that it just reaches the correct terminal (Fig. 3.25(c)). Strip 10 mm of sleeving from each wire. If the conductor consists of separate strands, twist these clockwise to keep them together (Fig. 3.25(d)).

Wind the wires clockwise around the terminal so that it follows the direction in which it will be tightened (Fig. 3.25(e)). Some terminals have a hole through which the wire is passed before screwing tight. Insert the correct fuse (3 A for lamps and equipment using less than 100 watts; 13 A for the rest) and screw down the plug cover.

Light-duty cable, rated at one ampere, has very thin conductors which may be damaged when tightened in the terminals. They are protected as follows. Cut each lead so that it reaches 10 mm beyond its terminal. Strip 10 mm of sleeving

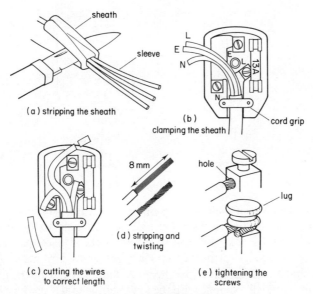

(a) stripping the sheath

(b) clamping the sheath

cord grip

8 mm

hole

lug

(d) stripping and twisting

(c) cutting the wires to correct length

(e) tightening the screws

Fig. 3.25 Wiring a plug

from the lead and fold back the conductor so that it lies flat against the sleeving. Insert the end of the lead, with the sleeving, into the hole of the terminal (Fig. 3.26). The screw is tightened against the sleeve, with the conductor being squeezed between the sleeve and the side of the hole. This eliminates the risk of the strands being cut when the screw is tightened.

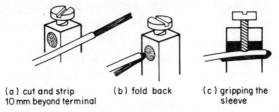

(a) cut and strip 10 mm beyond terminal

(b) fold back

(c) gripping the sleeve

Fig. 3.26 Using light-duty wire

Single-insulated two-core flexible cable is used for lamps and referred to as twin flex. As it is not usually thick enough to be held securely in the cord grip, it should be tied in a knot at a distance of 30 mm from the end (Fig. 3.27). Hold this knot in the cord grip but do not overtighten for fear of the conductor cutting through the insulation. The two leads are connected separately to either live or neutral terminal (it does not matter which). There is, of course, no connection to the earth terminal.

3.5.4 Soldering

The term soldering describes the process of joining metals together by means of a low melting metal or alloy known as solder. Brazing is similar to soldering but

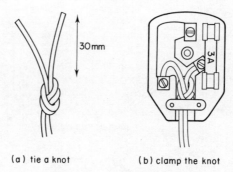

(a) tie a knot   (b) clamp the knot

Fig. 3.27 Using twin flex

uses harder solders with a higher melting point. As a rule, solders must have a melting point that is lower than that of the materials to be jointed but consideration must also be given to the nature of the articles themselves. For example, when soldering electronic components, excessive heat may not melt the components, but could permanently alter the characteristics of the devices.

Most of our work will be done with the low-melting solder used by radio and television repairers. It is available from electrical stores in various thicknesses and, as a rough guide, the thicker solders generally have a higher melting point than the thinner. Choose a thickness of 1.5 to 2 mm. It can be used for soldering brass if the surfaces are scrupulously clean (sanding may be necessary).

Electrical solders are supplied nowadays with a flux known as rosin, already present in the form of a core or even several cores (see Fig. 3.28). For this reason, if all your soldering is confined to electrical or electronic work, you may never have to purchase any flux at all. The solder is melted using a light-duty electrical soldering iron. In a single circuit there may be very many joints, e.g. in a 4-decade resistance box there may be 130 or more. Any one of these could cause a malfunction with resultant complaints from your pupils that 'the experiment does not work'. The overall reliability of such equipment depends mainly on the soldered joints and therefore these must be reliable in themselves.

The main nuisance is found with joints which look perfect but which, because of dirt between the conductors or tiny cracks in the solder, do not provide electrical continuity. These are known as dry joints. It is well to guard against them right from the start and to be aware of the conditions which produce them.

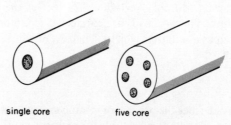

single core   five core

Fig. 3.28 Rosin-cored solder

Cleanliness is very important. There should not be any traces of grease or oxidation on the conductors. This would prevent the solder from adhering to the metal. Scrape the surfaces very lightly with an old razor blade and then tin the surfaces by applying a layer of solder. Most electronic components are ready-tinned by the manufacturer. This cuts down some of the work but, if they have been in storage for very long periods, cleaning may still be required.

After tinning, the conductors are brought together. One will be just a wire lead of the type attached to small resistors or capacitors; the other may take various forms:

1. a pin around which the lead may be wrapped;
2. a tag with a hole or eye through which it may be threaded; and
3. a hole in a copper strip bonded to a plastic board (see Section 3.4.5: note on strip boards).

A small hook is needed to hold the wire in place. It could just be a small right-angled bend around a pin or through the eye of a tag or through a hole in a strip board. Hold the soldering iron against the joint so that the lead and the pin or tag heat up simultaneously. You may find that a small amount of solder on the tip of the iron will help by making more intimate contact with the joint. When you are satisfied that the joint is hot enough, touch the tip with a length of solder (Fig. 3.29). The solder will melt and flow freely onto the joint. After a second remove the iron. The solder should have wetted both conductors, in this way providing both strength and electric contact to the joint.

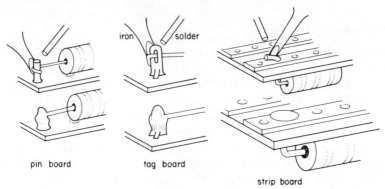

pin board   tag board

strip board

Fig. 3.29 Soldered joints

Two important points to remember are these: do not carry the solder to the joint on the tip of the soldering iron as the rosin will evaporate before the joint can be formed and, second, the conductors must be hot. Insufficient flux and heat will produce dry joints.

CHAPTER 4

Capital and labour

4.1 INTRODUCTION

The purpose of this chapter is to show how to equip a school science laboratory in the most effective way. Even if your funds are limited, you can still proceed in this endeavour if you use all the resources that are available to you. These resources are considerable and include the help which you can obtain from your pupils and their parents, from craftsmen and from local and foreign agencies. The chapter lays out a programme of self-help and self-sufficiency which, if you carry it out, will produce the results you are seeking.

4.2 ZERO BUDGET

We will start by assuming that you do not have any money to spend on materials

4.2.1 Scrap

One of the conditions for carrying through a programme of improvisation is that there must be some material with which the required apparatus is to be constructed. What is material? It is the stuff of which the objects around us are made. Some of these objects are useful, some are ornamental. One group is variously described as junk, rubbish, or scrap. It is usually discarded and generally regarded as so undesirable that people will pay to be rid of it. This scrap forms the cornerstone on which the zero budget strategy is based.

The material of which the scrap is made is of value to us if we can discover how it can be used. A little imagination helps. Look at the scrap and mentally run through the apparatus, whether for experiment or for demonstration, that you require. Match the scrap to each object in turn. In every case, think of the materials, the shape, the special properties demanded by the apparatus and compare it to that of the scrap. As soon as you do that you will be surprised at the range of possible applications. Consider, for example, a tin can. It can be described as a hollow, closed cylindrical container, made of thin metal sheet and covered with a paper label stuck on with adhesive. In looking for possible uses in a laboratory or classroom, we can enumerate in a couple of minutes, not less than ten uses which depend on its shape and six which rely on the materials. There are many more, but let us discuss only these in some detail.

1. Storage. Most obvious is the fact that it is a container and can be used as such for storing odds and ends. You can keep nails, screws, pencils, chalk, and other dry objects in them (Fig. 4.1(a)).
2. Beaker. It can be used for pouring liquids. During the Second World War, prisoners of war were kept busy making mugs out of tin cans and many people used these in their homes (Fig. 4.1(b)).
3. Calorimeters. The shape is right—a calorimeter is just a copper container. The fact that these are made of iron with a coating of tin does not affect the theory of calorimetry (Fig. 4.1(c), also Project 5.5.1).
4. Joule calorimeter. The plastic lid which is sometimes supplied with tin cans such as those containing breakfast oats, custard etc., is useful for holding electrodes, thermometers, and stirrers in such a way that there is no electrical contact between them (Fig. 4.1(d) also Project 5.5.2).
5. Leslies' cubes. These are only metal containers with different types of wall coatings. A simple experiment which could serve the same purpose as Leslies' cubes is to show that a tin can, containing hot water, cools faster if it is painted black than if painted white (Fig. 4.1(e)).
6. Thick lens. If both the top and the bottom of a tin can are cut out, a lens can be cemented into place at each end. This combination of lenses will behave like a thick lens (Fig. 4.1(f)).
7. Telescope. Tin cans come in different diameters and lengths. A telescope simply consists of two metal tubes, one of which can slide inside the other and each carrying a lens or set of lenses (Fig. 4.1(g)).
8. Instrument case. One of the main functions of an instrument case is to provide a protective, screened enclosure for an electrical circuit. The box-like shape is dictated partly by the chassis on which the equipment is built and also by the need for flat surfaces on which to mount the controls and terminals. Although rectangular biscuit tins may be used (Fig. 4.1(h)), there is really no reason why the chassis cannot be altered to fit into a cylindrical case (see also Project 8.1).
9. Styrofoam cutter. In Project 5.5.1 we have described how heated tin cans may be used to cut blocks of polystyrene foam (Fig. 4.1(i)).
10. Roller. Last, the cylindrical shape is also useful for rolling out plasticine or clay (Fig. 4.1(j)).

Let us now consider the materials of which the tin can is made.

1. If the tin can is opened out along its length, a flat sheet of metal results. This can be used for cutting out lettering stencils similar to those described in Project 6.3.2.
2. Conducting strips. Metre bridges require strips of conducting material to link the terminals to the slide wire (see Project 5.2.1).
3. The electrodes used in electrolysis experiments consist of small metallic plates which can be cut from a tin can.
4. Electrical cell. The tin can itself containing dilute acid may be used as the outer electrode of a battery (Fig. 4.1(k)). An inner electrode is made of a

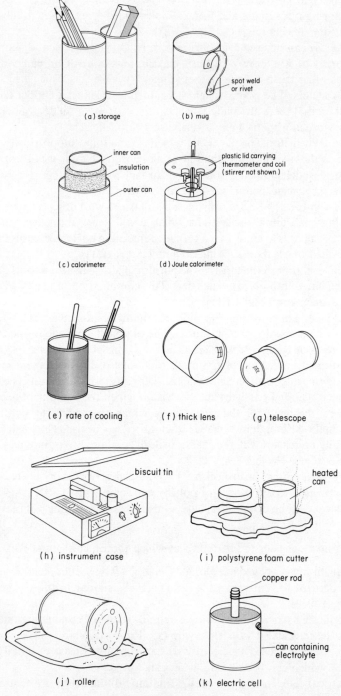

Fig. 4.1 Using tin cans

dissimilar metal such as a copper rod or copper wire wound into a coil to increase its submerged surface area.

5. Label. Tin cans often have very glossy, eye-catching labels which could be given to the arts master for use in collage work.

6. Glue. Heat the tin till the glue melts. Scrape off the glue with a knife and use it to stick labels onto hot bottles and jars.

Similar lists may be prepared for other items such as cardboard cartons, ballpoint pens, wastepaper, jam jars, etc. Try to get a feel for various materials such as paper, cardboard, wood, metals, glass, and plastics. Cut them up, bend and twist them, melt and burn them, grind them up. Even liquids can be subjected to a similar scrutiny especially those that are easily available such as cooking oil, petrol, kerosene, and even water. These could easily become substitutes for the classical materials which most textbooks require us to use. Why should the verification of Stoke's Law of free-fall through a viscous medium depend on the availability of steel ball-bearings and castor oil? Glass marbles and groundnut oil will do just as well. Discarded engine oil can be filtered through a large plastic funnel plugged up with a wad of steel wool (obtained from supermarkets). You can use this if you have reservations about using groundnut oil which, after all, is a foodstuff. Viscostatic automobile engine oil is relatively less temperature dependent than other oils so that more consistent results are possible.

Junk-hunting should be conducted as a campaign. Mobilize all the children in the school, work through the Parent Teachers Association and explain what you are trying to do. The parents have a vested interest in your success. They want to get the best education for their children and therefore they will give you their fullest support and cooperation.

Specify the material that you require. List 2 of Section 9.1 of the Appendix contains an inventory of the most useful scrap and where to find it. You will notice that rubbish dumps have not been included as a source of scrap. These are unhealthy, dangerous places and are best avoided.

Offices feature prominently as a source of material and it is certain that the headmaster will approve of the odd pin or paper clip from his office finding its way to your laboratory. The home is also a prime source. It may be a good idea for your pupils to inform you, in advance, of the articles which they can bring. This will avoid you ending up with a room full of orange squash bottles and powdered milk cans.

The car-breaker's yard is an abundant source of useful scrap. Consider the materials that go into making a car. The frame is made of metal, the engine consists of gears, pistons, and levers held together by innumerable nuts and bolts. Plastic, copper, and aluminium tubing carry various fluids around inside the car. Electrical wiring of all grades and colours abound: so do plugs, sockets, switches, fuses, and fuse holders.

One of the biggest problems when collecting scrap is the question of storage. It is a mistake to embark on an indiscriminate collection campaign. Decide on the particular project you have in mind and collect materials to that end. Keep these in cardboard boxes. In list 2 are indicated the items which you should collect as a matter of routine. These are characterized by:

1. those with a wide range of application, such as ballpoint pens, copper wire, polystyrene foam;
2. those which are fairly valuable such as fuse holders, switches;
3. those which are only occasionally obtainable such as copper tubing, plastic tubing.

Other items need only to be collected if and when needed. You may, as in the case of tin cans, specify only the particular size you require and whether it should have a replaceable metal or plastic lid. This applies also to cardboard boxes. The strongest ones are those used for expensive items like wines and spirits.

Articles which you intend to scrounge from the office could stay there till you need them. The exception is the spools on which typewriter ribbon is wound. These make reasonably good pulleys.

A jam jar with a screw-top lid can contain petrol into which you place bits of polystyrene. This will provide a continuous supply of polystyrene cement which can be used as an adhesive or as an waterproofing varnish.

4.2.2 Dual purpose equipment

Scrap can also be used in adapting existing laboratory equipment to serve a dual purpose. We have already mentioned that most wooden equipment is designed according to only four basic frames. Even dissimilar apparatus can be mounted on the same frame.

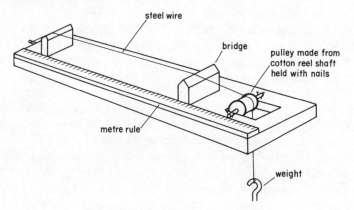

Fig. 4.2 Optical bench as sonometer

Fig. 4.2 shows an optical bench which can serve as a sonometer. We need to add a cotton reel as a pulley, a length of steel wire, screws, and bridges. A hole is made in the bench to make it easier to use the cotton reel as a pulley.

A stand such as is used for the optical screen of Project 5.1.3 may be adapted for a wide range of applications. Many different additions could be made to it

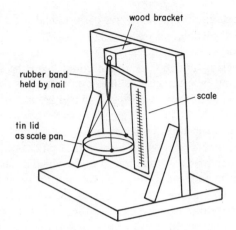

Fig. 4.3 Optical screen as Hooke's law apparatus

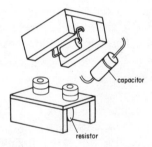

Fig. 4.4 Platforms for interchangeable components

and provided that they are demountable or, if they are mounted on the reverse side (Fig. 4.3), the screen can continue to be used for its original function.

Small wooden platforms (Fig. 4.4), are used for mounting two-terminal devices such as resistors. The components can be removed by desoldering and replaced with others. If they are fixed in place with nuts and washers, you will not even have to worry about the cost of solder. In a few minutes you can convert a set of mounted resistors into a set of capacitors.

4.3 LIMITED BUDGET

4.3.1 The right priorities

If you are fortunate to be allocated a sum of money to spend on your laboratory there is a temptation to grab the nearest catalogue of science and education equipment and spend it all on a massive overseas order. The fact that what you can order is only a tenth of what you really need may lend an air of futility to the occasion but even more frustrating is the knowledge that red tape in the form of import licences, exchange control procedures, etc. could prevent that order from reaching its destination until months have passed. The overseas firm, if it has a guarantee that it will get paid, may despatch the goods fairly soon after receiving the order and after a few months it will arrive at the seaport. Then follows correspondence, delays, and tussles which could keep the goods at the port warehouse for a long time before it is delivered to you.

Instead of following this line, we suggest that there is a feasible alternative: that you spend only a part of your money, locally or overseas, on essential materials and the rest on tools for constructing the equipment you require.

There are a number of factors which support the first option, not least of which is the fact that your primary function is to teach and that, by buying the equipment instead of building it yourself, you should be able to devote your efforts to teaching. This is true and it is not a factor which should be dismissed. However, things are seldom so clear-cut. All the possible repercussions of such direct spending, should be taken into consideration. To what extent can you justify spending on some items while many others may have to be neglected? You will probably face a long wait before the equipment arrives. After you have spent this grant you may not get another for some time.

These facts will lend force to the second proposition: that you embark on a programme of construction. This has the following advantages:

1. the tools and materials you require are obtainable locally;
2. the cost of making the equipment is a very small fraction of the cost of importing it;
3. you can give priority to immediate needs;
4. by careful budgeting you can keep some money in reserve for out-of-pocket purchases you may not be able to reclaim otherwise.

Ideally, you should make out an order for manufactured equipment only if it is impossible for you to construct it yourself, and only after you have purchased locally most of the tools you require with a sum set aside for materials. This is the procedure which, it is hoped, you will adopt and, with this in mind, we can now look at the details of your strategy.

4.3.2 Overseas purchases

There are many articles which we require and which are already imported into the country for reasons not directly related to this course. These are articles which are needed for day-to-day purposes. Tools, timber, sheet metal, electrical fittings are among the goods which fall in this category and may be purchased locally.

What we are concerned with are goods that are useful to us and which will not normally be available. Glass tubing and lenses, tuning forks, rubber stoppers, bunsen burners, thermometers fall in this category. There are also those items like brass woodscrews, or carbon resistors which are required by specialized industries but which are not imported in bulk. You may be able to buy these locally but the cost would be prohibitive especially if they are purchased away from the capital or seaports.

Stock List 5 of the appendix contains the articles which are required to be imported, but this should not prevent you from making your own selection. Give priority to the items which you require for simple basic experiments especially those with which you are yourself familiar.

Do not order the same article with a variety of differing specifications except when you require these for particular experiments, e.g. in Stock List 5, four kinds of thermometers are named. These are all the specifications you will ever require. Stirring thermometers are recommended because they are robust. The important range is − 10 to 110 °C as it covers almost all the experiments in your course. Very small quantities of the others are needed. The − 5 to 55 °C range are intended for the construction of an hygrometer (Project 7.2.1), but may be omitted if you decide to purchase the complete unit instead. One or two that reach up to 360 °C will be required for thermocouple experiments.

It will also be noticed that those thermometers which cover the range − 10 to 110 °C are always cheaper than those with other scales (all other specifications otherwise being the same). This is because it is the most popular and therefore the manufacturer produces more of this size than all the others put together.

The selection of test-tubes, glass and rubber tubes, and rubber stoppers, from the wide variety which is available, makes a good case study. If you glance over the prices of each you will find that certain types seem to be more economical than others. For example, test-tubes measuring 12 mm diameter are cheaper in terms of material than other types. You will also notice that the manufacturer offers the widest assortment of lengths with this diameter, such as 75, 100, and 125 mm. Obviously these sizes must be the most popular and your choice of test-tube would fall on the two which are cheaper still, i.e. 75 mm or 100 mm. The latter is generally more useful. Buying only one size simplifies the problem of storage and selecting accessories such as stoppers, test-tubes holders, brushes, racks, etc. The larger 150 mm by 25 mm tubes have a 70 ml capacity and, when fitted with a two-holed stopper, can be adapted for many of the applications for which small round-bottomed flasks are used.

Our choice of rubber stoppers has already been decided for us because we have ordered tubes and test-tubes of 12 and 24 mm diameter for which we require stoppers of sizes 11 and 23 respectively, each being supplied with the maximum number of holes available. Size 11 has one hole and size 23 has two. Size 27 stoppers have been included in our list as these are standard fitting for some aspirators, bell-jars and desiccators.

The holes in rubber stoppers have a diameter of 5 mm. This indicates that we will require tubing of at least this diameter. We have chosen 6 mm diameter tubing because of the tighter fit. Both standard wall and capillary tubing are chosen with this outside diameter. The latter is used in Project 6.2.6. The stoppers which we have chosen also allow us to enlarge our range of glass tubing to include the 12 mm and 25 mm sizes and this combination of tubes and stoppers will enable us to construct our own condenser (see Project 6.2.4).

You will note that five reels of 26G constantan wire are ordered. This gauge is recommended in the construction of the metre bridge (Project 5.2.1) and the styrofoam cutter (Project 8.4). It can, of course, also be used for copper–constantan thermocouples. Only one reel of the thicker 18G wire is required for making the primary standard resistances (Project 5.2.3).

The names and addresses of some suppliers are given. Most educational institutions tend to deal with these firms and you can write to them directly for catalogues and price lists which will be posted to you free of charge. Certain catalogues are particularly useful because they contain the complete layout and description of some experiments.

In spite of the extra cost, insist that the consignment be despatched to you by air parcel post which has the advantage that the goods will be delivered right to your local post office. It would already have been inspected and assessed for the customs duty which you pay when you collect the parcel. There is no need for shipping agents to step in and double the charges. In most countries no duty is payable on educational materials if it is addressed to the head of the educational institution. Inform the forwarding agency that the address should include this designation, e.g. Mr P. Ola, Headmaster or Dr M. Abdulkarim, Head of Department, etc. and that the parcel is clearly marked 'Contents: Educational Material'.

Very heavy or bulky pieces cannot be sent by parcel post. The maximum weight varies from country to country but usually the despatching firm will break up the order into smaller consignments to comply with the prevailing regulations. If any individual item exceeds the limits, you can specify that these alone should be sent by freight, again preferring air to surface.

Insist that all consignments be fully insured. An insured parcel can be traced and this discourages pilfering. If the articles are lost or damaged you can claim reimbursement from the post office or insuring agency.

Your headmaster should know how the order will be paid for. There may be a national centralized purchasing agent through whom you operate. It is the duty of this agent to ensure that the necessary foreign exchange is available to pay for the goods. Very often this agent simply issues a guarantee that the money will be paid. Some companies do not accept this and may insist that a banker's draft be received before they will despatch the goods.

Some countries appoint an overseas agency to look after its foreign purchases. Such a firm is usually just referred to as The Government Purchasing Agent. In the United Kingdom, the Crown Agents would attend to purchases on behalf of a foreign country especially if the payment has to be made from funds given as an aid to that country.

4.3.3 Sources of foreign currency

By reason of their foreign status, expatriates are allowed to remit their savings to their countries of domicile. Many are quite prepared to use their overseas accounts to pay for purchases which would be useful to the institutions for which they are working. Their only expectation is that they be remunerated as soon as the goods are received and they present the invoices. They could then return the money through the normal channels to their homes. This is quite legal, as far as we are aware, and in some countries it is encouraged. If you use this service you will probably find that it is the most efficient and economical available to you. The expatriate submits the order together with a cheque on his bank. The exporting firm usually sends off the consignment within days and with insured air parcel post the goods arrive about four to six weeks after the original order was posted. Any delay is due to the firm not having the goods in stock at the time of receipt of the order. In some countries you may have to apply for an import permit for the goods and to explain the source of the foreign currency. An expatriate may visit his home country at regular intervals. This is an excellent opportunity for him to shop around for any equipment or components which may be obtained at reduced prices. The articles in Stock List 4 may easily be brought back by him when he returns. He could be asked to pay duty on it at the port of entry but this does not happen very often.

You could apply for assistance in the form of goods from charitable organizations such as Oxfam, Caritas, World Council of Churches, Save the Children, Third World First, and many others. There is no harm in applying directly to these agencies. The worst they can do is to say 'No'. You would not have lost anything by asking. If you indicate the goods that you require and you do not ask for money, you may get what you want. With many there is the fear that the money will be misused. You may even find that your government insists that all financial aid should be channelled through some ministry or other. Gifts in the form of goods are let through without question although some overzealous customs officer may ask you to pay duty on it. Advise your benefactor that the duty is assessed on the insured value: so keep this as low as possible. Marking the parcel as an 'Unsolicited Gift' and 'Educational Material' with the Headmaster as the addressee, would also help.

Twinning is an aid-activity about which very few countries know as much as they should. This involves the establishment of close friendship ties between communities, between towns and even between countries. Very often this takes the form of visits by one group being sponsored or assisted by funds or offers of hospitality from the other. For your purposes, twinning between your school and, perhaps, a school in England, Germany, France, Ireland or the United States is required. It could mean that, when you launch a fund-raising campaign in your school, your twin would come to your assistance and raise some money on your behalf within its community. This is valuable foreign exchange and you could ask that the money be converted into needed equipment. The expatriates in your community could help to contact schools in their own countries and in this way bring about the twinning.

4.3.4 Local purchases

In the Third World, education is now a major growth industry. In most countries, the budget allocation for schools, colleges, and universities exceeds that of health and agriculture. Many business entrepreneurs are taking advantage of this situation by establishing firms for supplying educational and scientific equipment. With no knowledge of the goods they handle, they only act as middlemen whose profit on a transaction usually exceeds that of the main supplier.

Let me give you an actual example from personal experience. While working in Anambra State, Nigeria, I had decided to construct a caravan for touring around the country with my family. I required some 0.5 mm thick aluminium sheet and purchased some 4 foot by 8 foot pieces from a firm in Enugu, at a cost of 15 Naira (about £12 at the official rate of exchange). These sheets were available off-the-shelf, at the warehouse. A year later I had started work at Zaria, Kaduna State, in Northern Nigeria, about 850 kilometres away. There I discovered that a local businessman was selling the same 0.5 mm aluminium in smaller sheets of 3 foot by 6 foot, for 40 Naira. There is a railway line connecting Enugu to Zaria. I doubt if the transportation could have added more than one Naira to the cost of a sheet. There can be no justification, except greed, for making this exorbitant profit. I have bought carbon resistances, in Lagos, for ₦ 0.06 and discovered that in the rest of the country they were selling for ₦ 0.50 to ₦ 0.80 each.

My earnest advice to you is to avoid any middlemen. If you do not live near a main distributor, write to obtain the company's catalogues, price lists and conditions of sale. Ask for a proforma invoice for the equipment that you want to buy. You must give a brief description of the specifications of the articles in much the same way as it is given in Stock List 5, but be prepared to accept a substitute if an article with the correct specifications is not available. Strike a balance between immediate availability at a higher price and a long delay at a lower price. Bear in mind also that long delays could cost you money especially with the present high rate of inflation.

Be very suspicious of firms that quote a price without giving the specifications. On the other hand, if you had not given any details of the articles you asked for, who can blame them for thinking you are a fool and wanting to cheat you? A Kenyan teacher of my acquaintance asked two firms for a price quotation on ten beakers. One offered to supply them at a cost of 20 shillings and the other at 550 shillings. Neither the teacher nor the two companies gave any indication of size and material. My friend should have stated: 10 beakers, Pyrex, tall form with spout, 250 ml graduated. When he asked the firms for a description of what they were actually going to send him, the first thought he wanted disposable plastic tumblers and the other would have sent a set of cut-glass wine goblets. These just happened to be what they had in stock and so they felt that, because of the vagueness of the order, they could safely palm them off on him!

A more bizarre story concerns a technician who had received, from three firms, quotations for an anti-transpriner. I told him that I had never heard of such a device. He informed me ruefully that the school typist misread his order which had been for an auto-transformer. I wonder what he would have received from these firms.

4.3.5 Cash purchases

The purchases that we have described so far are fairly complicated and therefore we have discussed the procedure in some detail. You will now be pleased to know that the majority of the purchases which you have to make are no more complicated than the usual day-to-day shopping which you or your spouse have to do. This entails going to a shop or a stall at the market, choosing the items you require, perhaps asking the proprietor for advice, paying your money, and taking possession of the goods. As you are buying the goods on behalf of the school, you would in this case ask for a receipt on the basis of which you may reclaim your expenses and, if necessary, return defective articles.

In Stock List 1 of the Appendix (Chapter 9) we have indicated the tools and materials which you should order as a basis for your construction work. You will find that most of the projects depend of these. You will be surprised at how often you will have to replenish your stock.

Your shopping will be confined to hardware and electrical components shops and to timber and metal yards. Start off just by pricing the articles you want whether these are tools or materials. Whenever you meet a shopkeeper or dealer who is prepared to spend some time talking and advising you, make full use of every piece of information he can give you. He knows more about the quality of the goods than you do. Remember, listening to his advice does not place you under obligation to buy from his but I have found that a dealer that is prepared to discuss the relative quality of his products is more likely to be honest that one that adopts a take-it-or-leave-it attitude. Sooner or later you will come across one whose advice is sound and whose prices are reasonable. When that happens you should try to get most of your needs from him. When you become a regular customer he will be more prepared to allow you concessions such as giving you off-cuts and remnants at a much reduced price or of trying to obtain out-of-the-ordinary articles. The chances are that he makes regular trips to a big city where many of the things you want are available quite cheaply. This could save you special trips especially as he would know exactly where to get them.

4.4 MASS-PRODUCTION TECHNIQUES

Part II of this book deals with the construction of single pieces of apparatus. This is acceptable when there is an occasional need for increasing the range of available equipment. Sometimes more than just one piece of a particular item will be required as at the annual practical examination when large quantities of identical pieces of equipment are needed.

In this respect there are a few points which should be considered before producing these in bulk.

1. The experiments should be simple and straightforward.
2. The cost of producing the apparatus should be low so that you can provide a complete set for each student (perhaps after having split the class into two or three groups).

3. The equipment should be such that you could use all or most of it in your laboratory course.
4. Because of the need for secrecy, such apparatus must be produced well in advance of the examination so that the construction should not be associated with it.

4.4.1 Cheaper by the dozen

Mass-production is the process of manufacturing goods by methods which are specially adapted for the production of large quantities of identical standardized articles.

The step from constructing single pieces of diverse equipment to that of mass-production is not very great. A few organizational skills are required but as you are a teacher it is fair to assume that you would already have had some training in this respect.

Producing equipment in bulk is much less trouble and less time consuming and, as we shall prove, more economical than making the same number of items only as and when you need them, and there is a bonus. If you overproduce, you can always sell the surplus to other schools that do not have a construction programme. If you really get down to it, you can thereby quite conceivably finance your own programme and become quite independent of any government assistance.

4.4.2 The prototype

A prototype is a working model which is constructed for the purpose of assessing a particular design and should lead to a further design with an improvement in efficiency, reliability, and cost effectiveness.

A prototype enables the designer

1. to optimize the specifications and batch size,
2. to review the cost per item,
3. to review the complexity of construction carried out,
4. to assess the quality of the product.

We will discuss each of these objectives in turn both in broad outline and also with reference to a specific project. For this purpose we have chosen the optical bench (Project 5.1.1), which has a simple construction and is most likely to be the first article which you may wish to acquire in large numbers.

4.4.3 Specification and batch size

The material is supplied in standard sizes. On this the designs should be marked out, sometimes with templates, in such a way that the maximum number of articles can be derived from it. A template is a thin plate cut to the shape required, by which a surface of an article being made is marked out. A template can be made from paper, such as the patterns used in dress-making, from cardboard, or from metal sheet.

The above procedure for marking out should give an indication of the ideal batch size which, in this case, would be a multiple of the number of articles which can be made from the standard-sized material. The actual batch size will depend on your requirements and the proposed investment. If a sheet of plywood can be cut to produce six articles and your requirements run to 40, it would be reasonable for you to purchase seven sheets and thus produce a batch of 42 articles (a multiple of 6). On the other hand, you could produce batches of 6, as you can afford them, until you reach your target of 40 or 42.

The optical bench, as described in Project 5.1.1, consists of three constituents:

1. one base of 12 mm plywood, 2100 mm long and 130 mm wide;
2. five feet of 12 mm timber, 130 mm long and 20 mm wide;
3. two metre rules with a millimetre scale.

The first is to calculate the number of bases which can be cut from the standard sheet which measures 2438 mm by 1229 mm (8 foot by 4 foot). Clearly the cuts must be lengthwise along the sheet so that the longest dimension of the base (2100 mm) may be accommodated. The sheet should be reduced to a length of 2100 mm before the bases are cut (see Fig. 4.5). Allowance must be made for the

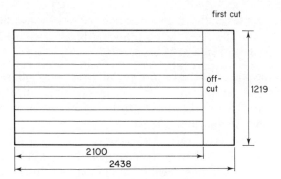

Fig. 4.5 Cutting the sheet

width of the saw-cut which is assumed to be 3 mm. If we are prepared to increase the base width to 133 mm, we could obtain nine bases with only eight cuts. Because of the limitations set by the width of the lamp box (Project 5.1.2), the width of the base cannot be reduced. The optimum batch size would appear to be nine articles.

4.4.4 Costing

The next step is to construct a complete prototype and draw up a list of the components which you used. Quantities, dimensions, and the cost of each must be shown and the total cost of the finished article should be estimated. Each item starting with the most expensive, is then scrutinized and a critical assessment is

Table 4.1 Costing the optical bench
Batch size: 9 articles (cheaper alternative components are shown in parentheses)

Part	Material	Require-ments per article	Size of standard material	Cost of standard material ($\aleph$)	Cost per batch ($\aleph$)
Base	Plywood, 12 mm	2100×133	2440×1220	20.00 (17.00)	20.00 (17.00)
Feet	Timber, 25×12	5 off 133 mm	3.7 m (12 ft)	2.00	1.98
Rules	1 metre length	2 off		1.30	23.40
Screws	1 inch by No. 8 (1 inch by No. 7)	10	144	3.00 (2.50)	1.88 (1.56)
	$\frac{3}{4}$ inch by No. 6 ($\frac{1}{2}$ inch by No. 4)	10	144	2.00 (1.50)	1.25 (0.94)
Adhesive	PVA	20 g	500 g (2 kg)	3.00 (6.00)	1.08 (0.54)
Varnish	Polyurethane (polystyrene cement)	100 g	450 g	11.00 (0.05)	22.00 (0.45)

Total: $\aleph$ 71.59
($\aleph$45.87)

made of the ways in which the cost may be reduced or by which the product can be improved without increases the cost. Such a breakdown of the cost of the optical bench has been made in Table 4.1.

1. We see that the polyurethane varnish constitutes almost a third of the cost of the bench. Polystyrene cement is not so hard-wearing, but when you put on three or four coats of this the cost of varnishing will not be more than $\aleph$ 0.05. This alone will save you $\aleph$ 23.50.
2. Changing from No. 8 to No. 7 screws could save another $\aleph$ 0.50.
3. A half-litre of adhesive will be quite enough for the project but if you kept the two-litre size as standard you will save another $\aleph$ 0.10 per article making $\aleph$ 1.00 on the lot.
4. The 12 mm plywood which you are using may also be purchased in bulk so you could get it for $\aleph$ 17.00 per sheet.

Proceeding in this manner, it is quite conceivable that you can reduce the overall cost from what it was to less than $\aleph$ 50.00, i.e. $\aleph$ 5.00 per item.

4.4.5 Construction

Constructing the prototype also helps to determine the most efficient way in which each part could be made and shaped, the structural relationship between one part and another, the problem of assembling the parts, and the sequence in which protective measures such as painting, greasing, and oiling, and various tests and quality controls should be incorporated in the production. In general,

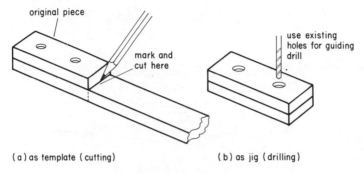

(a) as template (cutting)   (b) as jig (drilling)

Fig. 4.6 Using original piece

the following suggestions would be useful.

1. All parts serving the same function should be made identical within convenient tolerances.
2. Identical parts are more easily produced by simple repetitive work. The use of templates and jigs is recommended.
3. If material has to be cut up into small parts on which further individual work needs to be done, you may find it easier to reverse the order by doing the work on the parts before separating them from the bulk of the material (see Fig. 4.8).
4. When the material is thin, several pieces may be clamped together and machined simultaneously (Fig. 4.7). This is particularly useful when drilling holes in sheets of metal or hardboard. Do not pile these pieces to a height of more than 30 mm especially if the diameter of the bits is less than 2 mm, because the bit could be deflected to an angle.
5. Filing, planing, and sawing may all be done with a number of sheets clamped together. In fact sawing metal sheets is made easier by clamping them together.

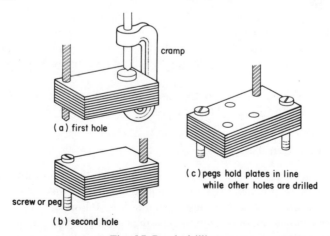

(a) first hole

(b) second hole

(c) pegs hold plates in line while other holes are drilled

Fig. 4.7 Batch drilling

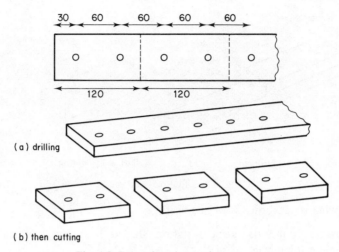

(a) drilling

(b) then cutting

Fig. 4.8 Reversing the work sequence

Ideally all the articles in the batch should undergo the same treatment simultaneously. If this is not feasible, then whatever work that is required should be performed on each, one after the other, in a repetitive fashion.

The entire batch should have completed one stage before proceeding to the next. No part or article should be allowed to lag behind the others.

Applying these suggestions to the optical bench, we note that each bench requires five feet, each foot requires two clearance holes for the screws, making a total of 90 holes in 45 pieces of timber. Now let us satisfy the criterion that these 45 pieces should be identical and interchangeable. If they are not, then each pair of holes in the base will have to be matched to the particular foot that we want fitted. It also means that the foot must be fitted immediately or it will get mixed up with the others and time will be lost retrieving it.

The task of making these components is simplified by producing them in batches of five each. For each batch a strip of timber 600 mm long of the correct cross-section (20 mm by 12 mm), is drilled with clearance holes at intervals of 60 mm, starting 30 mm from one end (Fig. 4.8). Each strip is then cut into five pieces.

For drilling the starter holes in the base, you could use a jig made of metal or plywood, as shown in Fig. 4.9(a) and (b).

4.4.6 Quality control

One of the reasons for taking such pains to ensure that the articles are identical in size and shape is that there is then a greater likelihood that they will also be identical in accuracy, reliability, and other qualities. It is most exasperating for a science master to have a pupil complain, at the height of a practical examination, that he has been unfairly assigned a piece of equipment which is not as accurate as

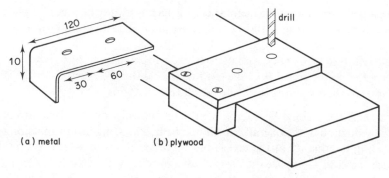

(a) metal (b) plywood

Fig. 4.9 Purpose-built jigs

those of his classmates. Quality control tests are therefore just as important as the actual construction.

These tests may be performed at any stage in the manufacture of the article, as it is easier to correct a possible fault before the assembly is complete. If you do not, you may end up by botching the job. A botched job is one in which errors, made during the construction, have had to be corrected.

The final stage has now been reached. This is to subject the prototype to tests to ascertain that it will serve the purpose for which it has been designed. There are three points on which the bench must be checked.

1. If placed on a level surface it should not wobble (Fig. 4.10(a)). If any of the feet appear to be higher than the rest, rub it down with sandpaper. This test should be done before applying the varnish.

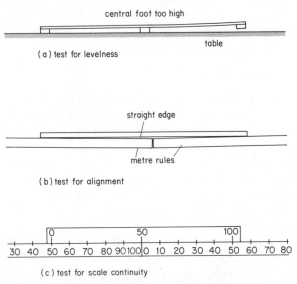

(a) test for levelness

(b) test for alignment

(c) test for scale continuity

Fig. 4.10 Testing the optical bench

2. Test the alignment of the metre sticks by placing a straight edge alongside the two bench rules (Fig. 4.10(b)). If they are at an angle to each other, this fault should be corrected.
3. Place a third metre stick with its zero at the 50 cm mark of one of those on the bench. The 100 cm mark of the test rule should then be exactly over the 50 cm mark of the second rule on the bench (Fig. 4.10(c)).

The tests 2 and 3 could be done while the second rule is being fixed into place.

The reduction of the overall cost should be balanced against the possibility of degrading the quality of the article but there are limits to which you need to reduce the cost. Compare the cost of your product with what is commercially available. Yours could cost 80% less. A strong case therefore exists for improving the quality and allowing the cost to rise if you can afford it. A higher quality could take into consideration such points as robustness, reliability, ease of maintenance. These could save the time and money that would have been needed for repairs.

4.5 DIVISION OF LABOUR

It is not possible for you to carry by yourself the full burden of a construction programme. You must have some form of assistance, which will enable you to allocate particular aspects of the tasks to others. Once again we look to industrial practice to give us a hint on how this is to be done.

The labour force of a factory is divided into four groups: managerial, skilled, semi-skilled, and unskilled. For our purposes, you, the teacher-cum-constructor, will have to fulfil two of these tasks: managerial and semi-skilled. You will therefore need some skilled persons, to help you cope with these jobs which require specialized knowledge or tools, and some unskilled persons, to handle the simpler, repetitive, and time-consuming work.

4.5.1 Artisans and craftsmen

Sooner or later you will have to call on the assistance of a carpenter, welder, or electrician to handle essential tasks which, you feel, they will handle with greater competence than you. Of course, the cost of their services will have to be added to that of the equipment you are making.

Be very clear and precise about what you require. I know a man who asked a carpenter to make him a table and gave a drawing similar to that in (Fig. 4.11(a)). This was quite an artistic picture of a table shown in perspective. The carpenter produced a table exactly like that in the picture—with one leg about one-third of the length of the other three.

Soon after you start dealings with a carpenter you will discover that even if he had never passed a City and Guilds examination or had any similar formal training, he will understand technical drawing. In fact this may be the only type of drawing he will understand. If my friend had presented the carpenter with a

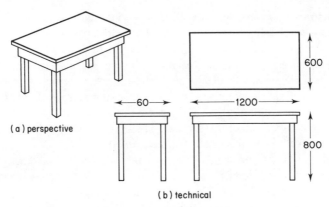

(a) perspective

(b) technical

Fig. 4.11 Drawing a table

sketch such as (Fig. 4.11(b)) he would undoubtedly have obtained what he wanted.

Give him all the specifications regarding the dimensions, materials, and finish. If you are unsure about any details, ask for his advice, but be certain that he understands your requirements. Before you allow him to proceed with the job, ask for a quotation. From your knowledge of the materials and of the general expenses and overheads of the carpenter, you may be in a position to decide if the price is reasonable. Beware if the price is too low because it could indicate that he has misunderstood something. If you think his price is too high, you are free to get a quotation from someone else.

The cost of making an article depends on the materials, fixing, and labour. The labour charges are quite complicated and depend very much on the overheads of the craftsman. He has to make a living for himself and his family. He has to have a place to work, tools, materials, etc. Take a friend along as a witness when you finally submit the job to the carpenter. In his presence, state clearly your requirements including details and stipulate that the money will be paid when the work is completed. The carpenter may ask for an advance. This should never be more than half the final cost and should only be necessary if it is clear that he does not stock the materials needed. Insist on a receipt.

When the article is completed, again take your witness along and, in his presence, test it, make any comments on the quality of the workmanship, and point out any flaws. If you are satisfied, pay the full amount owing to him and get a receipt.

Welding, like carpentry, is also a skilled occupation. There is usually at least one welder operating nearby, perhaps with a car-repair workshop. Welders keep a stock of sheet metal, such as galvanized iron, of various gauges. If you require metals such as aluminium, copper, or brass in gauges which they do not stock, they may obtain them for you or they would inform you where they may be obtained. Furthermore they would have equipment such as tin shears, a guillotine or perhaps even a bending machine. Some welders are engaged in making heavy-duty structures such as climbing frames, slides, and swings for children's playgrounds. Your school may very likely have close ties with such a person. If you make friends with him he would introduce you to dealers who may give you special concessions on materials because of your association with him. The success of such a friendship will depend on the honesty and sincerity with which it is approached. Explain exactly what you are doing as regards equipping the laboratory and get him involved in the planning of any projects. He should get reasonable recompense for any services which he renders, and all transaction should be above board, receipted, and accounted for.

In general, a craftsman, whether a carpenter or a metal worker, is good at duplicating factory-made articles. Ask him to construct the copy in such a way that it can be taken apart again. Ensure that he uses only screws or nuts and bolts. You could then have a prototype which you can dismantle in order to examine each part and ascertain how it has been made.

The prototype may require materials or techniques with which you are not familiar. If this is so, he may be able to suggest alternative ways of doing it. It may also indicate that you will require his services in a mass-production run. Either you turn the whole project over to him and let him turn out the number you require or you could get him to construct only that part of the article which calls in his special skills. You could also cut out all the parts and the commission him to assemble it. This would be the system you could adopt for equipment which requires welding. Project 6.1.3 describes how the services of a welder may be invoked in the mass-production of metal tripod stands.

4.5.2 Pupil power

In every school curriculum the pupils are required to undergo some physical activity, in which they perform tasks and expend energy to develop their coordinating skills and to learn to work within a team. All the physical, social, and creative needs of the child can be met within a construction course or participating in the production line. Your pupils provide a labour force which is always available to you, if you can use it effectively.

In Section 4.4, the need for simple repetitive techniques in a mass-production run was stressed. If such is the case, you can use your pupils to construct and assemble the articles. Almost any job, even if it appears to be complicated, becomes quite simple if it is repeatedly done. Someone who has never done any previous soldering can cope with a task that involves nothing more than soldering two wire leads to the ends of a carbon resistor.

Pride in one's manual accomplishments, is a reward in itself and should be promoted as an incentive. By participating in a course such as this, the pupils develop their manual skills and obtain a familiarity with laboratory equipment which transcends that which is provided by an experimental course alone. The acquired familiarity with tools and machines, and the feel for materials will stand him or her in good stead in later years. They would already have found fulfilment in a scientific pursuit before they have reached university level. The prospects are exciting, don't you agree?

Part II:

Projects

CHAPTER 5

Physics

INTRODUCTION

The projects which are discussed in this chapter mainly consist of wooden structures and may therefore be tackled immediately after you have familiarized yourself with the techniques outlined in Chapter 1. They are discussed under the following headings: frame, tools, description, requirements, and procedure, accompanied by diagrams in every case.

Frame

The four basic frames are the structures on which most of the designs are founded. In a few cases, where such a frame cannot be identified, none is mentioned, but a full description of the construction is then given.

Tools

It is assumed that all the tools of kit A have been purchased. In addition, many of the projects may require the use of a G-cramp or a soldering iron. Very few projects in this chapter require any other tools but the possession of an electric drill and a machinist's vice would certainly simplify your work. The multimeter would be quite useful for testing electrical connections, battery voltages, resistances values, etc. In none of the projects is it assumed that you have these low-priority tools which, as we have already explained, are only purchased when you can afford them.

Description

This is a concise outline of the specifications of the finished article and usually refers to the first insert of the diagram. In some cases an appropriate experiment involving the apparatus is described.

Requirements

This contains an itemization of the individual pieces required for the construction. In every case these are tabulated without any column headings e.g.

base	plywood, 12 mm	1–08	500 × 20	1
feet	timber, 25 × 12	1–05	120 mm	4
rod	glass, 6 mm diam.	5–23–02	150 mm	1
	socket	3–24		

The unseen headings are:

| Part | Specification | Stock No. | Dimension | Quantity |

The part is named according to the frame and will be identified from the description given in Chapter 1. All dimensions are given in millimetres and, whenever the units are not indicated, these are assumed to be millimetres. A translation into inches is given whenever you may find difficulty in getting the exact metric size. On the whole, it is assumed that all the materials in the basic stock list (list 1 of the Appendix) are available for the project. Sometimes additional work such as sawing and planing of stock timbers may be necessary.

The specification will usually be the same as that given in the stock list in which the item appears.

The word 'timber' is used to describe sawn wood, preferably one of those mentioned in Table 1.2, planed to the desired cross-section. The specified cross-section is approximate and you may use material varying by as much as 20% less to 50% more in most cases, in which case some of the dimensions of the other pieces may have to be adjusted in compensation.

The first digit of the stock number refers to the stock list appearing in the Appendix, e.g. stock number 3–23 is taken from stock list 3. Generally, the lower the list number, the more accessible the item should be. The list number is therefore an indication of the amount of advance planning the project requires. Thus:

List 1	Basic Stock	Immediate availability
List 2	Scrap or scrounged materials	Up to 1 month
List 3	Local purchases	Up to 2 months
List 4	Personal overseas purchases	Up to 6 months
List 5	Overseas orders	Up to 2 years

The reference number will help you to draw up orders for the projects which you are planning. A few items, especially those appearing in stock lists 4 and 5 may have more than one reference number, indicating that alternate sources exist.

Fixings are nails, woodscrews, and vinyl adhesive. No mention of these are made in the requirements list because it is assumed that:

1. you have at hand all the fixings in the basic stock list 1;
2. you will choose the most suitable fixing for the particular project, preferring woodscrews to nails and using adhesive for all joints, unless specifically instructed not to do so.

In those cases in which fixings not in the basic stock list are used, they will be
mentioned in the requirements list and their stock number given. Whenever one
type of fixing is preferred to another, this fact will be pointed out in the
procedure.

Procedure

The details for constructing the basic frames have been given in Chapter 1
(Sections 1.6.1 to 1.6.4). It is assumed that you are familiar with the techniques of
marking, cutting, fixing, etc. that are involved in each. Any work which is specific
to the project is then described with a degree of detail which depends on the
complexity. Occasionally a tool, not featuring in any of our kits, may be
mentioned. This only happens if it is felt that many woodworkers would,
perhaps, possess it already. The use of this tool for the specific job would be
described but we would also show how the same task may be undertaken using
only the prescribed kits.

Diagrams and inserts

A set of diagrams appears with each project. This includes a view in perspective
of the finished article and various elevations in the form of technical drawings.
Further details of certain aspects of the apparatus are then presented as subsidiary
Inserts labelled (a), (b), etc. These will be referred to in the text as Ins.(a), Ins.(b),
etc. The reference number for the diagrams and accompanying inserts cor-
responds to that of the project, i.e. Fig. 5.1.3 and its inserts refer to Project 5.1.3.

5.1   OPTICS

5.1.1   Optical bench

Basic frame: bench
Tools   : kit A

Description

The bench is 2100 mm long, 125 mm wide and about 25 mm high. It is fitted with
a two-metre rule (two one metre rules end-to-end).

Requirements

base	plywood, 12 mm	1–13	2100 × 130	1
feet	timber 25 × 12	1–03	130 mm	5
metre rule	single scale	5–11–01		2
misc.	glue, screws			

Procedure

Assemble the bench as described in Section 1.6.1. The two metre rule may be
obtained by cutting a double-scale metre rule down its length into two pieces.

118

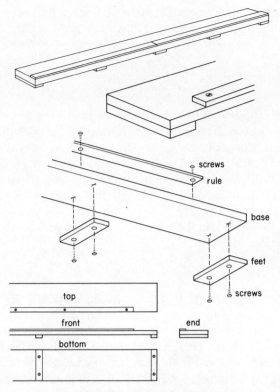

Fig. 5.1.1 Optical bench

This should be done very carefully so that the rules are equally wide. If necessary, the wider piece could be planed or sanded until the widths are the same. Varnish the cut edge of the rule as soon as possible, otherwise the uneven drying of the wood could produce warping. It is also advised that the optical bench itself should be varnished for the same reason as warping can produce very frustrating problems when trying to keep the optical components on the bench properly aligned.

The large number of feet attached to the undersurface will also reduce warping.

The tests for the correct positioning of the metre sticks are described in detail in Section 4.4.6.

5.1.2 Lamp box

Basic frame: box
Tools   : kit A

Description

The lamp is enclosed in a box measuring 250 mm high on 100 mm by 100 mm base. Light emerges from the box through a hole of 25 mm diameter. Ventilation of the box may be provided through small holes which are drilled into the walls of the box.

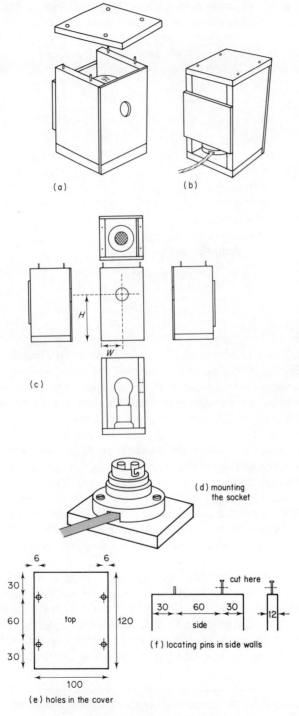

(a) (b)

(c)

H

W

(d) mounting
the socket

6 6

30

60   top   120

30

100

(e) holes in the cover

cut here

30 60 30

side

12

(f) locating pins in side walls

Fig. 5.1.2 The lamp box

The construction of the box varies from that described in Section 1.6.3 in that the top and bottom are made of plywood or, preferably, timber, 12 mm thick. The top is not fixed permanently but is used as a cover which can be removed to allow the lamp to be changed when necessary.

Ventilation is also provided by leaving a space above and below the rear panel.

Requirements

base	timber, 100×12	1–01	120	1
cover	timber, 100×12	1–01	100	1
	or plywood, 12 mm	1–13	100×100	
panel, front	hardboard	1–18	250×100	1
panel, rear	hardboard	1–18	150×100	1
side	timber, 97×12	1–01	238	2
lamp socket	surface-mounted	3–49		
wire	cable, twin flexible			
	5 A	3–42		1.5 m

Procedure

Attach the flex to the lamp socket. Mount the socket in the centre of the base of the lamp box. You may have to make a gap in the base of the lamp socket itself to avoid trapping the flex (Ins. (d)). Assemble the lamp box, positioning the shortened rear panel so that a gap of 25 mm remains above and below it. As the top of the box is not permanently fixed, the box has to be strengthened structurally by using timber (and not plywood) throughout the construction. Screws, driven into timber, hold better than when driven into plywood.

Drill four holes of 2 mm diameter on the cover in the positions indicated in Ins. (e). With the cover in position, push a bradawl through each hole in turn to mark its position in the sides of the box. Remove the cover and drive one-inch nails into the marks leaving about 12 mm of the top of the nail exposed. Using a hacksaw or, if you have it, a pair of pincers, cut off the heads as shown in Ins. (f). The nails then become pins or pegs for keeping the cover in position. It is also possible to use hardboard nails or panel pins and avoid the necessity of cutting off the heads.

The type of socket used will, when the 40 W lamp is in place and when mounted on the 12 mm base, determine the height, H, from the lamp filament to the undersurface of the base. This height, H, will be regarded as standard for the accessories to the optical bench and will determine the height above the bench at which the optical components such as the lenses, gratings, etc. will be located. It is important for standardization that you use the same lampholders for all your lamp boxes.

For similar reasons the distance, W, is also critical, should be measured and used as a standard for the horizontal alignment of the bench components.

5.1.3 Optical screen

Basic frame : stand
Tools   : kit A

Description

A stand 250 × 100 × 75 with a hoarding covered with plain white papter. The following variations may be incorporated:

1. no aperture.
2. single aperture, 8 mm diameter with cross-wires.
3. single aperture, 30 mm diameter with lens.
4. multiple aperture for corona experiment.
5. single aperture 20 mm diameter with straight-edge diffractor.

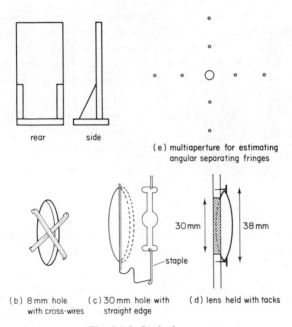

rear   side

(e) multiaperture for estimating angular separating fringes

30 mm   38 mm

staple

(b) 8 mm hole with cross-wires   (c) 30 mm hole with straight edge   (d) lens held with tacks

Fig. 5.1.3 Optical screen

Requirements

base	timber, 75 × 12	1–02	100	1
hoarding	plywood, 6 mm	1–14	100 × 250	1
brackets	timber, 40 × 20	1–75	75	2
fixings				
misc.	paper, staples, mosquito netting			

Procedure

Paste a sheet of white duplicating paper on the front face of the hoarding. Varnish the surface of the paper with clean polystyrene cement (see Section 1.5.4) to make it resistant to dirt. These screens may be used with various modifications.

In Ins. (b) the cross-wires can be made quite easily by injecting two staples at right angles to each other across the aperture. An office stapler is used for this purpose. The points of the staples protruding through the hoarding, should be turned to make it hold permanently.

A single staple placed vertically across the hole makes a good narrow object for studying diffraction fringes.

The large hole of 30 mm diameter in Ins. (c) is cut with a fretsaw and may be used for two purposes: either for studying straight-edge diffraction by stapling a razor blade partially across the aperture, or for holding a lens. The lens may be held in place with three or more shoe tacks.

The multihole screen is used in diffraction experiments for estimating, in a very simple manner, the angular separation between fringes. The holes are arranged at 10 mm intervals along a vertical and a horizontal line (see Ins. (e)). The central hole is much larger than the others because it provides the main source of light for the diffraction pattern. The use of this screen in studying diffraction patterns is discussed briefly in Section 9.2.

5.1.4 Lens holder

Basic frame: stand
Tools   : kit A

Description

The dimensions of the lens holder are designed for use with lenses of 38 mm (1.5 inch) diameter. It is recommended that only this diameter lens should be ordered.

Requirements

base	timber, 75×12	1–02	118	1
hoarding	plywood, 6 mm	1–14	$(H + 3) \times 118$	2
bracket	timber, 40×20	1–04	50	1
fixings				

Procedure

The hoarding may be made of two pieces of 6 mm plywood glued together. Before gluing the pieces are matched and the vees are cut. Then, the inside of each vee is chamfered on one side only (Fig. 5.1.4 (d)) so that when the pieces are

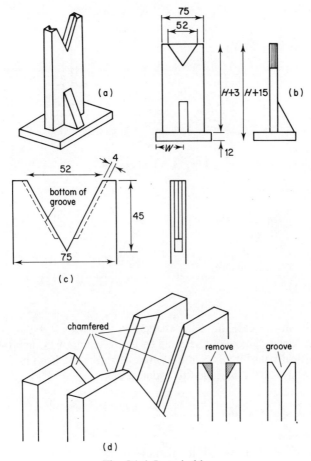

Fig. 5.1.4 Lens holder

finally assembled, a groove is formed by the two chamfers. The pieces must be glued together and cramped tightly till the glue is set. Screws passing through the hoarding into the bracket will help to hold the two pieces together. This method will only succeed if matching is perfect and the adhesive is reliable.

The groove should be 4 mm deep. If the dimensions are strictly adhered to, a lens of 38 mm diameter should sit in the vee with its centre at a height, H, above the level of the bench.

5.1.5 Optical pin

Basic frame: stand
Tools   : kit A

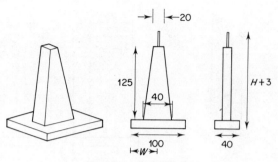

Fig. 5.1.5 Optical pin

Requirements

base	timber, 40 × 20	1–04	100	1
hoarding fixings	timber, 40 × 20	1–04	120	1
misc.	nail, 40 mm	1–33		1

Procedure

The brackets, in this case, have the shape of a truncated (top cut off) isosceles triangle. It is firmly glued and screwed to the base and a $1\frac{1}{2}$ inch (40 mm) nail is driven vertically into it to a depth of about 10 mm. The head of the nail is cut off and the shaft of the nail filed to a point.

5.1.6 Grease spot photometer

Basic frame: stand
Tools   : kit A, hole-saw (if available)

Description

A photometer allows the user to compare the luminosity of two light sources usually by equalizing the illumination produced by the sources on two separate surfaces. An attempt is usually made to bring the surfaces close to each other to make comparison easier.

    The grease spot photometer is such a comparison-type instrument and works on the principle that, while paper is normally opaque, grease or oil will make it translucent. Consider a piece of paper with a centrally placed spot of grease as in Ins. (a). If the paper is illuminated only from one side, then on the illuminated or bright side, the spot which transmits light, appears dark in a background of lighter paper which reflects the light. On the dark side, however, the spot appears brighter, due to the transmitted light.

    If the paper is illuminated by two sources shining on opposite surfaces, the grease spot may appear to have almost the same brightness as the paper. When

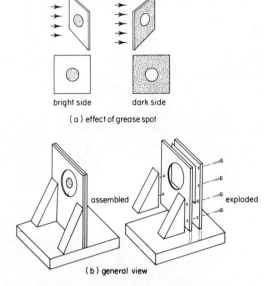

bright side   dark side

(a) effect of grease spot

assembled   exploded

(b) general view

Fig. 5.1.6 Grease spot photometer

the distances between the lamps and the photometer are adjusted, a stage may be reached when the grease spot disappears because it is then exactly as bright as the surrounding paper. The illumination is therefore the same on either side.

Requirements

base	timber, 100×12	1–01	100	1
hoarding	plywood, 3 mm	1–15	200×100	2
	or hardboard	1–18	200×100	
bracket	timber, 40×20	1–04	75	2

Procedure

Clamp the two plywood pieces together with the edges lined up exactly. Using a fretsaw cut a hole of 25 to 50 mm diameter (the bigger the better) with its centre at a distance $H - 12$ mm from the lower edge. Insert a piece of paper about 60 to 70 mm square between the boards so that the hole is completely closed. Apply adhesive between the boards and the corners of the paper and clamp together. When these are well bonded remove the clamps and holding the boards horizontally, place a small blob of clear grease (petroleum jelly) or clear non-volatile oil (bicycle oil) at the centre of the paper. The easiest method is to dip your forefinger lightly in the grease and then to transfer some to your thumb by rubbing it against your forefinger. Hold the centre of the paper between your thumb and forefinger and gently work the grease into the paper. A spot between 10 and 20 mm diameter should be sufficient.

The completed hoarding can then be fastened to the base and brackets in the usual way.

5.2   ELECTRICITY

5.2.1   Metre bridge

Basic frame: bench
Tools   : kit A, hacksaw

Description

The bridge is fixed to a frame 1050 mm long and 100 mm wide. A metre length of 26G constantan wire is stretched along a metre stick. Connections to the terminal are made through strips of aluminium or copper. The terminals are brass woodscrews to which connection may be made with crocodile clips.

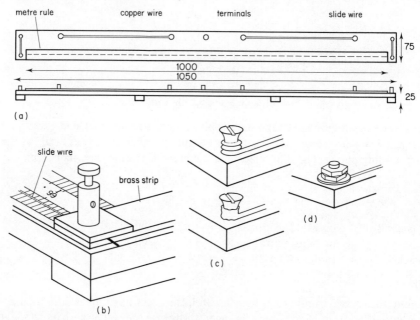

Fig. 5.2.1   The metre bridge

Requirements

base	plywood, 12 mm	1–13	1050 × 75	1
	or blockboard, 12 mm	1–10	1050 × 75	
feet	timber, 25 × 12	1–03	75	3
metre rule	single scale	5–11–01		1
wire	constantan, 26G	5–10–05		1.2 m
conductors	see text			
terminals	insulated type	5–16–11		11
	or brass type	5–16–10		11
	or woodscrews brass	4–28		11
	with crocodile clips	4–45 or 5–10–02		11

Procedure

The metre bridge which usually appears in catalogues of science educational equipment has brass strips and brass posts which provide the electrical interconnections and terminals. These are shown in Ins.(a). If brass or copper strips of almost 10 mm by 3 mm cross-section and terminals such as stock numbers 4–22 and 4–23 are available then this type of bridge can be constructed quite easily. However, this is not always the case and substitutes may have to be sought.

An alternative form of bridge may be made by using copper wire and brass woodscrews as in Ins. (c). The loose components such as resistances, battery, etc., are connected to the screws by means of crocodile clips. In this case the heads of each screw protrudes about 10 mm above the surface. The copper wire, usually of 1.5 mm² or 2.5 mm² section, is wrapped tightly around the screw and impregnated with solder. Steel screws may also be used in this way but it is more difficult to get the solder to cling effectively. The screws have to scrupulously clean and a much higher temperature is required. Brass is, of course, the preferred metal because of its low contact resistance, but steel screws tinned all over with a layer of solder are just as good. It is slightly more complicated to provide terminals for the constantan wire because this can not be soldered. A nut-and-screw junction must be used and for this we choose machine screws of 4 to 6 mm diameter. Drill a clearance hole through the base and insert the screw through it from the bottom up. The constantan and the copper wires are then secured with nuts and washers as shown in Ins. (d).

A junction such as this which brings together a variety of metals will undergo rapid corrosion and deterioration because of electrolytic action. It is advisable to seal it off from the atmosphere by applying a small amount of petroleum jelly to the components before assembly.

Try to position the screws in such a way that contact between the constantan wire and the washers takes place close to the ends of the metre rule. This will reduce the end-error. A locking nut will prevent the joint from loosening but, if it does, it can be undone and retightened. Do not use this joint as a screw-down terminal for free components as repeated undoing and tightening of the nuts will alter the length and tension in the slide-wire and so affect the accuracy and consistency of the measurements.

A jockey (sliding contact) may be made from the earth-pin of a discarded 13-ampere plug (see Section 3.5.3).

5.2.2 Potentiometer

Basic frame: bench
Tools   : kit A

Description

A bench measuring 1100 mm long, 50 mm wide and about 25 mm high, fitted with a metre rule and a one-metre length of 26G constantan wire.

Requirements

base	plywood, 12 mm	1–13	1050 × 50	1
	or blockboard, 12 mm	1–10	1050 × 50	
feet	timber, 25 × 12	1–03	50	3
metre rule	single scale	5–11–01		1
wire	constantan, 26G	5–10–05		1.2 m
conductors	see text			
terminals	as for Project 5.2.1			

Procedure

Assemble the bench and mount the scale, wire and terminals in the manner described for the metre bridge.

It is well to point out that the metre bridge (Project 5.2.1) already contains the elements of a straight wire potentiometer—all you have to do is to ignore the interconnecting strips. The metre bridge is therefore a dual purpose instrument and should be used as such.

Fig. 5.2.2 Potentiometer

5.2.3 Standard resistances

Tools: kit A, sharp knife for whittling

Description

Standard resistances are ones for which the values are known with good accuracy and which can therefore be used for determining, by comparison, the values of unknown or inaccurate resistances. Those obtained from educational suppliers usually have an uncertainty of 0.1% which is much less than will normally be required in a school laboratory. For this project we will discuss the production of standards of 1% uncertainty which can be obtained just by careful linear measurement and without the need for expensive calibration equipment.

Modern techniques for producing wire allow the tolerances, i.e. permitted inaccuracies, in composition and diameter to be maintained at very low levels. Constantan wire of 26G will have a resistance of 2.91 ohms per metre and this value can usually be maintained within 2% uncertainty. Obviously thicker wire will be more accurate than thinner and, as the length of wire required will be longer, the overall accuracy increases. Only fix the length with an error less than 0.2% in order to produce a resistance with the accuracy set only by the tolerance of the stated specifications of the wire.

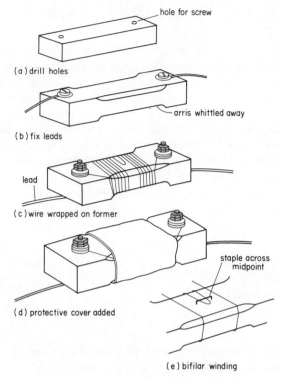

(a) drill holes

hole for screw

(b) fix leads

arris whittled away

(c) wire wrapped on former

lead

(d) protective cover added

staple across midpoint

(e) bifilar winding

Fig. 5.2.3 Standard resistances

Purchase a 250 g roll of 18G constantan wire from which three 1-ohm and three 2-ohm primary standards may be made by using exactly 2445 mm and 4890 mm of the wire respectively (allowing an additional 20 or 30 mm for wrapping around the terminals).

These primary standards may then be used for the accurate measurement and adjustment of 1, 2, 5, 10, and 20 ohm resistances made from 26G wire. About twelve of each of these sizes (a total of 60 secondary standards) can therefore be made from one 250g roll of the thinner wire. The measurements are made by metre bridge or potentiometric methods. In fact if only ten of each of the secondary standards are made, there would still remain enough wire for over 30 metre bridges.

Requirements

bobbin	timber, 25 × 12	1–03	70	1
wire	constantan, 26G or	5–10–05		as needed
	constantan, 18G	5–10–06		as needed
terminals	nuts and bolts or	3–27		2
	woodscrews, brass	4–28		2
	with crocodile clips	4–45 and 5–10–02		2

Procedure

The wooden former or bobbin is fitted with two small machine screws to which the ends of the wire leads will be tied. Whittle away the edges or arrisses of the former as shown in Ins. (b). This will make it easier to wrap the resistance wire and will prevent damage to the enamel coating.

The constantan wire should be wrapped around the bobbin with a bifilar winding. This reduces the inductance of the resistance and makes it suitable for use with alternating current as well as direct current. Before winding, find the exact midpoint of the wire. Make a U-loop at this point and staple it halfway along the length of the former. Then wrap each half of the wire starting from the middle and, keeping each turn tight and closely packed, work your way carefully to the end of the wire before wrapping it around the screw and securing it with the nuts and washers. Protect the winding with a layer of insulation such as PVC tape or sellotape.

5.2.4   Resistance boxes

Basic frame: box
Tools   : kits A and D

Description

The resistance box contains cheap carbon resistors of 2% tolerance. This accuracy is usually adequate for most secondary school experiments. Variation of the total resistance is made by moving a crocodile clip from one brass-screw terminal to another.

Requirements

ends	timber, 75 × 12	1–02	50	2
sides	timber, 50 × 12	1–02	100*	2
top	hardboard	1–18	100* × 100	1
bottom	hardboard	1–18	100* × 100	1
fixings				
terminals	woodscrews brass	4–28		10 per decade
	with crocodile clips	4–45 and		
		5–10–02		1 per decade

* For a decade box allow a further 80 mm for each additional decade. A maximum of four decades is common.

Procedure

Assemble the box with glue and screws or glue and $\frac{3}{4}$-inch nails but leave the top free. This should not be glued and should only be fixed with No. 6 screws which may be removed to provide access for repairs.

The terminals are $\frac{3}{4}$-inch by No. 6 brass screws driven through the top so that about 6 mm projects below and above the plywood.

 131

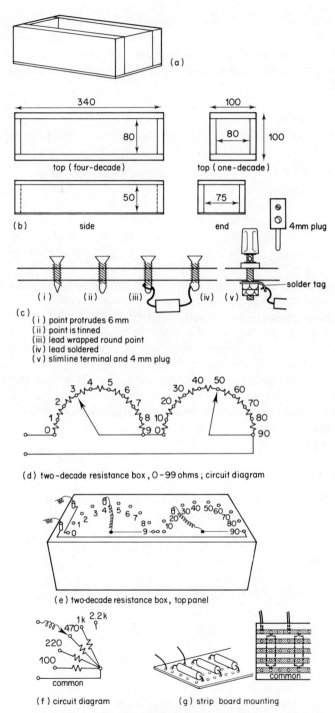

(a)

top (four-decade)   top (one-decade)

(b)   side   end   4mm plug

solder tag

(i) (ii) (iii) (iv) (v)

(c)
(i) point protrudes 6 mm
(ii) point is tinned
(iii) lead wrapped round point
(iv) lead soldered
(v) slimline terminal and 4 mm plug

(d) two-decade resistance box, 0-99 ohms; circuit diagram

(e) two-decade resistance box, top panel

common

(f) circuit diagram   (g) strip board mounting

Fig. 5.2.4 Resistance boxes

Tin the points of the screws thoroughly before soldering the resistors or capacitors to them (Ins. (c)). In place of screw-and-crocodile-clips connectors, you could use a combination of slimline terminals and 4 mm 'banana' plugs which are quite economical and can be used for many other applications (see Fig. 3.17).

(a) Decade resistance box

Components

For a four-decade box, 0 to 9999 ohm used with a 2 volt supply

resistors	carbon, 2 W or wire-wound, 2 W	5–17–07 or 5–17–08	1 ohm	9
resistors	carbon, 0.5 W	5–17–05	10 ohm	9
resistors	carbon, 0.5 W	5–17–05	100 ohm	9
resistors	carbon, 0.5 W	5–17–05	1000 ohm	9

Note on components   As it is important that the resistances should be nearly identical, they should be from the same batch (see Section 3.4.3).

Before mass-production of these boxes is undertaken, decide on the resistances you will require and then place a single order for the entire consignment, preferably in packs of hundred which may be obtained from companies like Electrovalue Ltd or Radio Resistor Company. If you obtain these through someone travelling overseas you could spend a small fraction of the local cost. For decade boxes the resistances, in general, may have a rating of 0.5 W. This is based on the assumption that the working voltage supply will be about 1.5 V.

Low value resistances could be specially wound using 26G constantan wire with double cotton covering (see Project 5.2.4).

Procedure

A decade consists of nine resistors connected in series and soldered directly on the ends of the brass screw terminals. Each decade is connected directly in series with the next.

A floating lead, ending in a crocodile clip, is connected to the last resistor of every decade (Ins. (d)). Variation of the total resistance is made by moving the crocodile clip to the appropriate screw. The crocodile clip-and-screw connectors may be replaced by 4 mm plug-and-socket connectors, as shown in Ins.(e).

(b)   Resistance substitution boxes (100 mm long)

Components

resistors	carbon, 0.5 W	5–17–05
One each of	100, 220, 470, 1000, 2200, 4700	
	10 k, 22 k, 47 k, 100 k, 220 k, 470 k	
	1 M, 2.2 M, 4.7 M, 10 M (total of 16)	

Note on components The resistors need not be from the same batch although this may be an advantage if you are considering making a large number of identical units. These lend themselves easily to mass-production and, very conceivably, you could get each pupil in your class to make one.

As the lowest value resistor is 100 ohms, the boxes may be used for supplied potentials up to 6 V if all the resistors are of 0.5 W rating. By increasing the ratings, higher potentials may be tolerated.

Procedure

Because of the need for a common point (Ins. (f)), the resistors cannot all be soldered directly onto the screws. Instead they are mounted on a strip board as shown in (Ins.(g)). A single lead is then taken from the common strip to the common terminal. Further leads are connected between the other end of each resistor and the corresponding screw on the top of the box.

5.2.5 Capacitance boxes

Basic frame: box
Tools   : kits A and D

(a) Decade capacitance box

Description

We shall confine ourselves to one-decade boxes as it is seldom that more then one decade is required. Usually 0–to–10 microfarads (μF) is the most common but some 0–to–1 μF boxes should be available. Polystyrene or polyester capacitors of 100 V rating are used. They usually have a tolerance of only 5% which is sufficient for our purposes although 10% is quite acceptable if they are definitely from the same batch.

Components

For 0–to–1 μF box:
capacitors polyester, 100 V   5–17–02   1 μF   10

For 0–to–1 μF box: 5–17–02   0.1 μF   10
capacitors polyester, 100 V

Procedure

To add together the values of capacitances they have to be connected in parallel. This presents a problem when using our 'screw and croc-clip' connectors because a crocodile clip has to be provided for each of the ten capacitors. A less

134

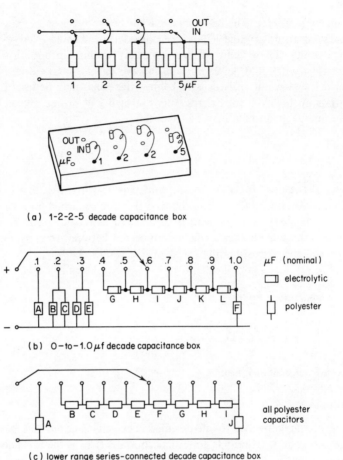

(a) 1-2-2-5 decade capacitance box

(b) 0-to-1.0 µf decade capacitance box

(c) lower range series-connected decade capacitance box

Fig. 5.2.5 Capacitance boxes

cumbersome method is to use the 1–2–2–5 arrangement which is usually employed when weighing with chemical balances. This is shown in Ins. (a) and only four connectors are needed. Each selector clip (or plug, if these are used) is provided with two terminals marked IN and OUT. The former indicates that the setting has been included in the total value appearing at the output terminals. The OUT terminals are included for neatness and to reduce the wear inflicted on the leads if they are allowed to dangle about when not in use.

The network in Ins. (b) is more elegant. Only one floating lead is required and the face-panel resembles that of the decade resistance box. Six polyester (5% tolerance, 100 V d.c. working) and six electrolytic capacitors (20% tolerance, 10 V d.c. working) are required. The electrolytic capacitors may be from the E6 or the E3 series. The former are marginally more accurate. The overall inaccuracy is about 10%. As a polyester capacitor (F in the requirements list) is always connected in series with the electrolytics, the unit, as a whole, may be used at 100 V. It should be noted that electrolytic capacitors are polarized, with a

Table 5.2.5 Series-connected capacitance boxes

| Capacitor | 0–to–1μF | | 0–to–0.1 | 0–to–0.01 |
	E6 series	E3 series	μF	μF
A	0.1	0.1	0.01	0.001
B	0.1	0.1	0.056	0.0056
C	0.1	0.1	0.12	0.012
D	0.15	0.15	0.18	0.018
E	0.15	0.15	0.33	0.033
F	1	1	0.47	0.047
G	2.5*	2.2* or 2.5*	0.56	0.056
H	3.2*	2.2* or 2.5*	0.68	0.068
I	3.2*	4.7* or 5*	1.0	0.1
J	5*	4.7* or 5*	0.1	0.01
K	10*	10*	—	—
L	10*	10*	—	—

*electrolytics

stripe indicating the negative end. The output terminals of the box must therefore be clearly marked as positive or negative. Because of the cost of large polyster capacitors, this system is recommended for 0–to–1 μF boxes. For lower ranges, 0–to–0.1 or 0–to–0.01 μF, all the capacitors may, and should be, polyester types. The accuracy will be improved considerably and, with a slightly revised network (Ins. (c)) fewer capacitors are required. Table 5.2.5 gives a list of the components required for these series-connected decade boxes. The mounting of these components was discussed in Section 3.4.5 and is shown in Fig. 3.23.

(b) Capacitance substitution box

Components
capacitors polyester, 100 V or   5–17–02
          polystyrene, 100 V   5–17–02
One each of   100, 220, 470, 1000, 2200, 4700 picofarads
            0.01, 0.022, 0.047, 0.1, 0.22, 0.47, microfarads

Procedure

As only one capacitor is substituted at a time, the connections are similar to those of the resistance substitution box.

     Resistors, being quite small (10 mm by 3 mm diameter) can be soldered directly to the terminal screws. The average capacitor is much larger (about 15 mm long and 5 mm diameter). If they are crowded together, the reliability of the soldered joints is affected and servicing which involves the replacement of components becomes a bother. A solution to this would be to mount the capacitors together on a terminal board or group panel, (stock number 5–16–04) but if this is not available a substitute can be made from 3 mm plywood and solid copper wire (see Section 3.4.5). After the components are mounted in position, connection between the board is fixed to the inside of the box by screws driven through it into the bottom. The procedure for making and using the board is shown in Ins. (a).

In a 'conveyor-belt' run, one pupil could concentrate on making the boards while another could complete the connections to the top panel.

5.2.6 Multiple socket board

Description

This is an essential item in any laboratory or workshop because it allows a variety of devices to be operated from a single mains socket. It consists of up to four three-pin sockets mounted on a wooden board. Power is brought to the board by means of a three-core double-insulated cable connected to the board at one end

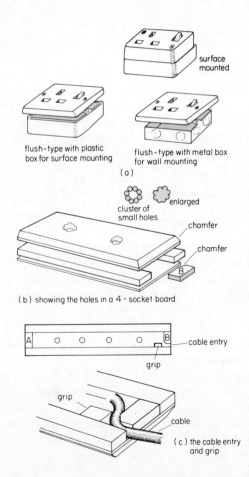

surface mounted

flush-type with plastic box for surface mounting

flush-type with metal box for wall mounting

(a)

cluster of small holes

enlarged

chamfer

chamfer

B

(b) showing the holes in a 4 - socket board

A   B cable entry

grip

grip

cable

(c) the cable entry and grip

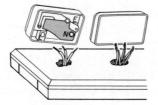

(d) remove sockets and press wires through holes

Fig. 5.2.6 Multiple socket board

and terminating in a three-pin plug. It is essential that a good earth connection should exist between the mains socket and the multiple outlets.

The sockets which are ideal for this application are the 13-amp surface mounted type, which have pins with rectangular cross-section. Purchase a good quality make and avoid cheaper brands. The undersurface of the socket reveals three hollow brass terminals into each of which the wire ends may be inserted and gripped by a screw. These terminals can accommodate two or three 15-ampere wires so that the sockets may be connected in parallel. Ins.(a) shows various sockets including a flush, low-profile type fitted to a plastic box-shaped base. This serves the same purpose as the surface-mounted type. The flush-type may, as a last resort, be used with a metal box if a plastic box-shaped base is not available.

Requirements

base	plywood, 12 mm	1–13	500 × 100	1
sides	timber, 25 × 12	1–03	500	2
end A	timber, 25 × 12	1–03	50	1
end B	timber, 25 × 12	1–03	44	1
bottom	hardboard	1–18	500 × 100	1
sockets	3-pin, 13 A, surface mounted, with switch.	3–52		4
plug	3-pin, 13 A, (rectangular pins)	3–50		1
cable	3-core flexible 15 A	1–42	5 metres	
cable	twin-and-earth 1.5 mm^2 solid core	1–40	1 metre, cut into 200 mm lengths	

Procedure

Make four holes at distances of 100 mm along the centre line of the base, each hole measuring about 25 mm across. They may be made by drilling a cluster of 6 mm diameter holes and breaking away the surplus wood (Ins.(b)). Chamfer the top edges of the base and also chamfer one of the corners of end B as shown in Ins.(b). Fix the ends and sides to the base with 25 mm nails driven through the plywood into the timber. A gap of 5 mm is left at the end B. This provides a cable entry (Ins.(c)). Fit the flexible cable into this gap. Movement of the cable may be restricted by nailing a strip of wood across the entry as shown. This puts a kink into the cable and will grip it firmly whenever the cable is pulled on. Temporarily fix the sockets into position over the holes, ensuring that the sockets are neatly arranged and that no part of the sockets will obstruct the passage of the wires through the holes.

Solid core wire may be used for the interconnections between one socket and the next. The correct colour coding must be observed depending on local practice (Section 9.6). Strip the outer sheath from the cable so that each wire is covered only in its own individual sleeve. For the interconnections between the sockets, cut three lengths, 200 mm long, of each colour. Strip off the sleeving to a distance of 15 mm from each end. The earth wire may already be bare but this is not a problem, provided that there is no likelihood of it coming into contact with the current-carrying wires. Remove the sockets. Pass the wires through the holes in the base before inserting the ends into the terminals. If more than one wire is to be inserted into a terminal, twist the ends together before doing so (Ins.(d)).

Finally connect the three wires from the flexible cable to the last socket. The sockets may now be screwed down permanently. Press the cable in the gap provided for it. Using $\frac{3}{4}$-inch by No. 6 screws (stock number 1–24) fix the hardboard cover in position.

5.2.7 Making permanent magnets

Sewing and knitting needles, hardened bolts and rods made of steel are ideal for turning into permanent magnets. This may be done by one or a combination of three methods.

1. Stroke the steel rod with the end of a magnet. Hold the magnet obliquely against the rod and stroke several times from one end to another—always in the same direction (Ins.(a)).
2. Hold the rod along the direction of the earth's field at your location. If you happen to have a dip-circle (i.e. a magnetic compass which is held in such a way that the needle can only rotate in a vertical plane) you should determine, I, the angle of inclination of the magnetic lines of force. If not, it is possible to obtain an approximate value of I from the relationship

$$\tan I = 2 \tan \lambda$$

where λ is your angle of latitude.

Having obtained I, you should now be able to hold the rod in one hand in a north–south direction and at an angle, I, to the horizontal. Holding a hammer in the other hand, hit the end of the rod repeatedly (Ins.(b)). Occasionally hold the rod near a compass needle to find out if it has become magnetized.
3. The most efficient method requires the use of a solenoid. This is wound with 1-ampere flexible insulated wire on a tube which is just large enough to hold the

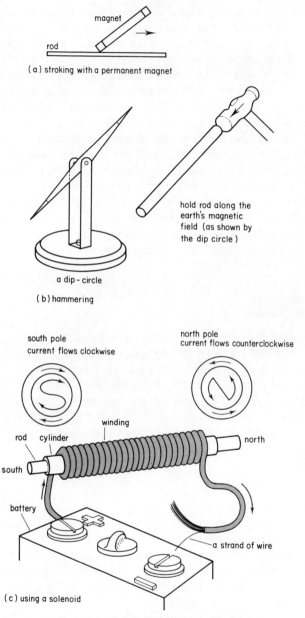

(a) stroking with a permanent magnet

hold rod along the
earth's magnetic
field (as shown by
the dip circle)

a dip - circle

(b) hammering

south pole
current flows clockwise

north pole
current flows counterclockwise

winding

rod   cylinder

north

south

battery

a strand of wire

(c) using a solenoid

Fig. 5.2.7 Making permanent magnets

rod. If knitting needles are being magnetized, the solenoid may be wound on the outer tubes of ballpoint pens. Only one layer of turns is necessary and, as the solenoid may be required more than once, it is worth wrapping adhesive tape around the ends of the solenoid to keep the winding in place permanently.

140

Place the rod to be magnetized in the solenoid. Attach one of the solenoid leads to a terminal of an accumulator. The insulation is stripped from the other lead to a distance of about 80 mm from the end. Separate one strand from the others and touch this on the opposite terminal (Ins.(c)). The sudden surge of current will fuse this strand almost immediately but not before it had produced a large magnetic field in the solenoid. Sufficient remanent induction would remain in the rod to produce a permanent magnet but it could be increased by touching further strands to the terminal.

If you do not wish to draw such heavy currents from your battery, you could pass a lower current continuously through the solenoid. Control the level of the current with a rheostat. While the rod is in the magnetic field of the solenoid, hammer one end to induce permanent magnetization.

The poles of the magnet, are identified as follows. With the solenoid pointing towards you, a south pole is produced if the current is flowing in a clockwise direction; a north pole is produced if the flow is counterclockwise. Other mnemonics are shown in the diagram.

5.3   MECHANICS

5.3.1   Pulleys

When pulleys are available at a hardware store, they are often inexpensive. The following suggestions are therefore adopted only when no immediate supply is at hand. A pulley is usually a wheel with a groove around its edge, along which a string can pass. It is used to alter the direction of movement of the string and, in experimental applications, it is assumed that the wheel bearings have low friction so that the tension along the string is unaltered when passing over the pulley. This last requirement is more important than that the pulley should be wheel-shaped.

(a)   *The smooth edge*

This is the simplest and consists of a metal plate with a smoothly rounded edge.

Using a file, followed with fine emery paper, give a rounded contour to the edge of the plate. Apply some metal polish to a cloth and, using the action shown in Ins.(a), rub the edge until it is perfectly smooth. Brass is the preferred metal for this application because of the ease with which it can be polished. Friction is reduced further by applying a layer of oil or petroleum jelly to the metal and by using nylon thread instead of string.

Drill countersunk holes in the plate by which it can be screwed to a wooden board.

(b)   *The smooth pin*

This is a variation of the smooth edge and has the advantage that, as it is constructed from a brass machine bolt, it is self-mounting, i.e. it holds itself in

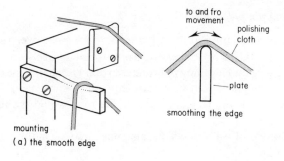

(a) the smooth edge

smoothing the edge

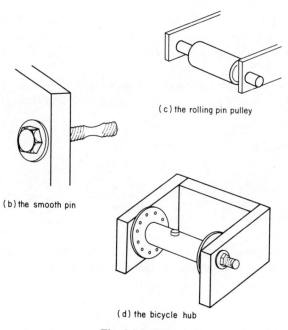

(b) the smooth pin

(c) the rolling pin pulley

(d) the bicycle hub

Fig. 5.3.1 Pulleys

position. Bolts of any size may be used. We will assume that 8 or 9 mm bolts are used. -

Drill a 9 mm hole in a board where the pulley is to be placed. Using two washers, one on each side, insert the bolt through the hole so that the threaded portion protrudes from the working surface of the board. Tighten it with a nut or even with two nuts, using the second for locking the first.

Take a round file and cut away the threads to form a slight constriction about 6 to 10 mm from the top of the bolt. Soak a 0.5 m length of string in metal polish, wrap it once around the constriction and then, with the to-and-fro action mentioned above give it a smooth pulley surface.

(c)   *The rolling pin pulley*

A short length of metal tubing of 6 to 10 mm bore is slipped over a smooth 4-inch (100 mm) round nail (Ins.(c)). The tube is able to rotate freely around the nail in much the same way that a rolling pin rotates around its shaft. The space between the tube and the nail is packed with petroleum jelly. This type of pulley usually improves with age as any roughness inside the tube would gradually be worn away.

There is a variety of ways in which this pulley may be mounted. Only one of these is shown.

(d)   *The bicycle hub*

The best makeshift pulley is the bicycle hub, although it is rather bulky. It is recommended whenever strength and very low friction are essential. I once used these very effectively to operate a set of quite heavy stage curtains for a theatre in Ghana.

Obviously, no constructional skill is required and, as the axle has threaded ends, this pulley is easily mounted in a box-like enclosure (Ins.(d)).

5.3.2   Pulley board

Frame: stand
Tools : kits A and C

Description

The pulley board is free-standing, measuring 1000 mm high and 600 mm wide. It has four grooved, solid pulleys made from machine bolts.

Requirements

hoarding	plywood, 12 mm	1–13	1000 × 600	1
base	plywood, 12 mm	1–13	600 × 400	1
brackets	timber, 100 × 12	1–01	600	2
feet	timber, 25 × 12	1–03	100	4
pulleys	machine bolts and nuts	3–65		4
	9 mm diam., 75 mm			
	long with washers			

Procedure

Fix the feet under the base, one being placed diagonally across each corner (Ins. (a)). Complete the assembly of the stand as described in Section 1.6.4. Drill four holes of 9 mm diameter in the hoarding in the positions indicated. Insert the

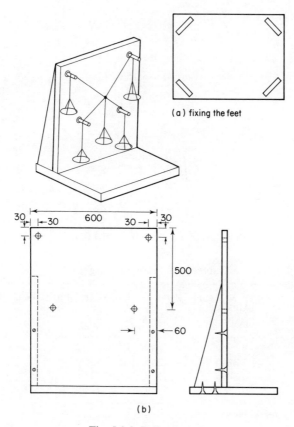

(a) fixing the feet

(b)

Fig. 5.3.2 Pulley board

bolts and washers in the holes and, using the techniques described in the last project, convert them to smooth pin pulleys.

5.3.3 Hanging weights

Tools: kits A and C

Description

The weights are made from lengths of reinforcing rod weighing exactly 100 g. These are bent into the form of closed rings. The weight holder is also made from iron weighing 100 g and is bent into the form of a hook on which the circular weights may be suspended.

Requirements

See text.

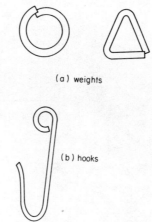

(a) weights

(b) hooks

Fig. 5.3.3   Hanging weights

Table 5.3.3   Hanging weights

Diameter of rod (mm)	Mass per metre (g)	Length (in mm) to be cut for			
		100 g	200 g	500 g	1 kg
6	220	450*			
9	500	200	400*		
12	890	113	225	565*	
16	1580		127	315	630*

*recommended length for hooks

Procedure

Table 5.3.3 gives the lengths of iron rod which correspond to the standard weights you may require. These values should be correct within 5% unless the rod has an appreciably non-linear cross-section. For improved accuracy you could start with a slightly longer length, weigh it on a balance and then adjust the length until the correct weight is obtained.

The rod is bent into a circle or triangle (Ins. (a)). Choose rods which are less than 200 mm long, so that a ring can be formed with a single loop. If a vice is available, the process of bending the rod will be made easier.

The hooks on which the weights would be hung are also made from iron rod. Lengths exceeding 500 mm are cut. A fairly tight 'eye' is made at one end and a U-bend is formed about a third of the distance from the other end (Ins. (b)).

5.3.4   Centrifugal force apparatus

Requirements: ball-pen tube, string, two small weights
such as a pair of heavy washers

Description and procedure

The apparatus is very simple. Pass the string about 1.5 m long, through the tube and tie a washer to each end.

In use the tube is held vertically in the hand while the upper washer is twirled overhead. As the angular velocity increases, the centrifugal force acting on the washer is transmitted through the string. The rotating part of the string increases and so the lower washer is pulled up. A knot, tied in the string about 100 mm from the lower end, is used to indicate that the rotating length, r, has now reached a predetermined length. By controlling the rate of rotation of the string, the knot can be held fairly steady at this position while the period of rotation, T, is measured with a stop-watch. The acceleration due to gravity, g, may therefore be calculated from the formula

$$g = 4\pi^2 mr / MT^2$$

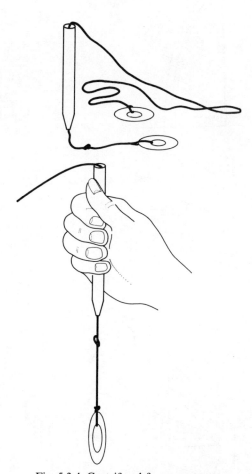

Fig. 5.3.4 Centrifugal force apparatus

146

where m and M are the masses of the upper and lower washer respectively, with M being about twice as heavy as m.

For best results, the string should be made of nylon or a similar plastic material that will offer only slight frictional resistance at the point of contact with the tube. The weight of the string should also be small compared to that of the washers. The string should be light but strong. If the string broke, the washer could go flying amongst your pupils. Smearing petroleum jelly on the string could reduce the friction and prolong the life of the string. To be on the safe side, inspect the string closely before starting the experiment.

5.3.5 Friction board

Frame: platform
Tools : kit A

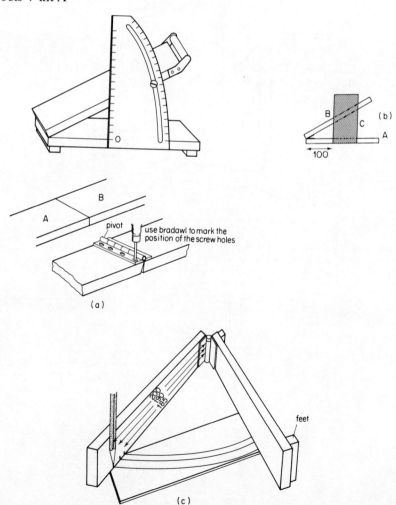

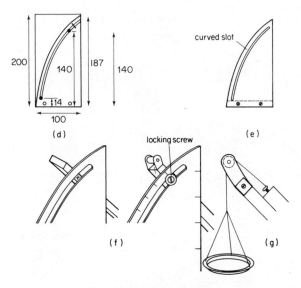

Fig. 5.3.5 Friction board

Requirements

base A	plywood, 12 mm	1–13	300 × 100	2
platform B	plywood, 12 mm	1–13	300 × 100	2
protractor	C plywood, 6 mm	1–14	200 × 100	1
hinge	piano hinge	3–24	100 mm long	1
feet	timber 25 × 12	1–03	100 mm	2

Procedure

Place the pieces A and B end-to-end and line up the hinge, pivot upwards, along the join (Ins. (a)). Use a bradawl or a sharp nail to mark the position of the screwholes. After drilling the starter holes, fix the hinge in position as shown.

The piece C is then screwed into position onto A as in Ins. (b). Make three notches along the inside edge of B at distances of 200, 190 and 185 mm from the pivot end. Place the point of a pencil in each of these notches, in turn, and using B as the arm of a compass, describe three arcs on the inner face of C as shown in Ins. (c). When C is now unscrewed it will be marked as in Ins. (d), with the largest arc ending at a distance of approximately 187 mm from the lower end. Using the fretsaw cut along this arc. Drill a starter hole between the smaller arcs at a distance of 140 and 14 mm from the lower end. Insert the blade of the fretsaw through either of these holes and carefully cut along both of the smaller arcs in turn. C will now have a shape shown in Ins. (e). Smooth the cut edges with emery paper.

Fix C back in position against A and pass in the bradawl through the curved slot, mark the edge of B. Fit a washer on a roundhead screw and drive the screw

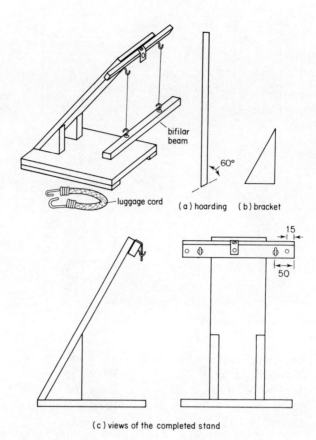

bifilar beam

luggage cord

(a) hoarding   (b) bracket

60°

15

50

(c) views of the completed stand

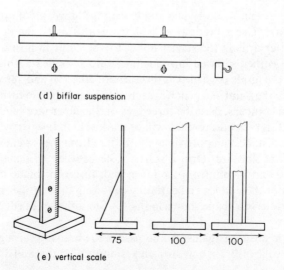

(d) bifilar suspension

75   100   100

(e) vertical scale

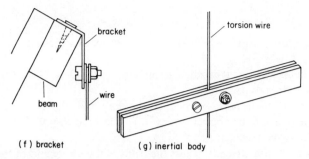

bracket

torsion wire

wire

beam

(f) bracket

(g) inertial body

Fig. 5.3.6 Suspension stand

through the slot B (Ins.(f)). Attach a rolling pin pulley (Project 5.3.1) to B. Attach the feet to A.

The protractor may be graduated in degrees along the curved edge or in millimetres along the vertical edge.

Accessories for the friction apparatus

Weight pan   This is made from the lid of a tin can. Drill three equally spaced holes along the edge of the lid. Tie a 150 mm length of string to each hole and knot the free ends together (Ins.(g)).

Sliding mass   This is a block of wood (plywood or solid timber) measuring 100 by 40 by 20. String can be tied to a small screw driven into one end of the block. In use, the string passes over the pulley and leads to the three strings attached to the pan. The locking screw is used to fix B at any angle A. The feet may be attached to A. The protractor may be graduated in degrees along the curved edge or in millimetres along the vertical edge.

5.3.6   Suspension board and accessories

Frame: stand
Tools : kit A

Description

The stand, which is 450 mm high and 300 mm wide, has a narrow hoarding which slopes forward at an angle of 60°. A beam placed across the top of the hoarding, holds two or three screw hooks (cup hooks) from which various objects may be suspended.

Requirements

hoarding	plywood, 12 mm	1–13	500 × 200	1
base	plywood, 12 mm	1–13	300 × 300	1
bracket	timber, 100 × 12	1–01	175	2
beam	timber, 25 × 12	1–03	300	1
hooks	screwhooks	3–38		2

Procedure

One end of the hoarding is cut at an angle of 60° to the face (Ins. (a)). This becomes the lower end.

The bracket is also cut at an angle of 60° (Ins. (b)). (Do this very precisely. It is not as easy as it sounds.)

Fix the hoarding, at its lower end, to the diagonal edge of the brackets and mount it on the base as shown in Ins. (c). The hoarding will therefore slope forward across the base.

Fix the beam symmetrically across the front of the upper end of the hoarding. Drill a 6 mm hole at a distance of 15 mm from each end of the beam. Also fix a screw hook at a distance of 50 mm from each end, and one in the middle. In the diagrams a metal bracket with a hole is shown at the midpoint of the beam. The holes and hooks may be used, with the appropriate accessories, to perform a number of experiments. Some of these accessories are described below.

Accessories for suspension beam

(a) *Bifilar suspension beam*

Requirements

beam	timber, 40 × 20	1–04	300	1
hooks	screwhooks	3–38		3
	or nails, 25 mm	1–32		3

Procedure

Insert a screw hook into the face of the beam at a distance of 50 mm from each end (Ins.(d)). The bifilar beam is suspended with string from the corresponding hooks on the stand.

(b) *Hook's law apparatus*

Description

A spiral spring is hung from the central screw hook. A scale pan such as is described in Project 5.3.5 is attached to the lower end of the spring. A short elastic cord with hooks (stock number 3–66), such as those used for strapping parcels to bicycle carriers, could be used instead of a spiral spring.

Measurements of the extension of the spring or cord is made with an ordinary 300 mm school ruler mounted vertically on a small stand.

Requirements   *(for vertical stand)*

base	timber, 75 × 12	1–02	100	1
bracket	timber, 40 × 20	1–04	70	1
scale	wooden ruler 300 mm	3–86		1

Procedure

Fix the ruler to the stand as shown in Ins.(e).

(c)   *Torsion pendulum*

Requirements   (for bracket)

bracket	steel strip, 12 × 3	3–30	50	1
fixing	nut and bolt,	3–27	15	1 set
	4–6 mm diam.			2
	washers for above			

Procedure

Drill a 6 mm hole about 10 mm from each end of the strip. Bend the strip at 20 mm from one end, to form an angle of 120°. Kit the strip, using 1-inch by No. 8 woodscrews, to the narrow edge of the beam. The longer arm of the bracket will point vertically down. Fit the screws, washers, and nuts to the lower arm (Ins.(f)).

Requirements   (for oscillating inertial body)

body	steel strip, 12 × 3	3–30	200	2
fixing	nuts and screws	3–27		2 sets
	4–6 mm diameter			
	washers for above			

Procedure

Clamp the two strips together and drill 6 mm diameter holes through both, simultaneously. The holes should be about 6 mm on each side of the midpoint.

Pass the screws through the holes and bolt the strips together.

The torsion wire is inserted at the midpoint between the two strips and clamped by means of the screws (Ins. (g)). The other end of the wire is held by the screws attached to the bracket.

It may be necessary to place a heavy weight, such as a tin can filled with sand, on the base of the stand to keep it steady while this experiment is performed.

5.3.7   Demonstration vernier scale

Basic frame: stand
Tools: kit A

Description

This is intended for demonstration but it is good practice to have a number of these on hand, each with a different type of vernier scale.

152

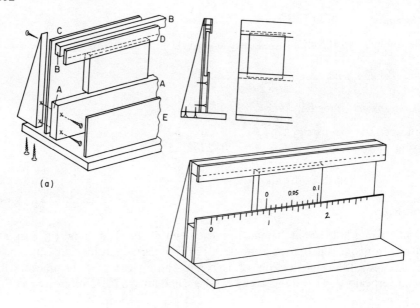

(a)

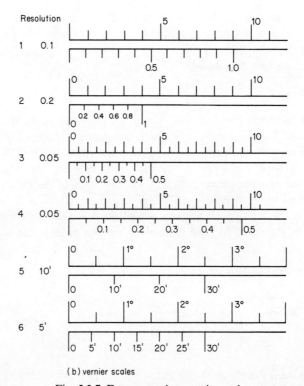

(b) vernier scales

Fig. 5.3.7 Demonstration vernier scale

Requirements

base	plywood, 12 mm	1–13	600 × 100	1
hoarding A	plywood, 12 mm	1–13	600 × 80	1
hoarding B	plywood, 12 mm	1–13	600 × 20	2
hoarding C	plywood, 3 mm	1–15	600 × 200	1
hoarding D	plywood, 3 mm	1–15	600 × 30	1
hoarding E	plywood, 3 mm	1–15	600 × 90	1
brackets	timber, 40 × 20	1–04	200	3
feet	timber, 25 × 12	1–03	100	3
slide	plywood, 12 mm*	1–13	150 × 95	2

* sanded to reduce the thickness to 10 or 11 mm.

Procedure

Start by fixing the two extreme brackets to the base using one-inch screws. Three sections of the hoarding, namely A, B, and C, can then be fixed in position on the brackets (Ins.(a)). Check that the sliding scale is able to move quite freely in the space between B and C. Pin D and E to B and C respectively. Apply a coat of white paint to the outer surfaces of D, E, and the slide.

It is advisable to make two sliding scales for the same equipment. These could be permanently installed and made accessible to the pupils for their use and self-instruction.

To increase the versatility of the equipment various other interchangeable slides could also be made. A few of these are shown in Ins. (b).

5.4 PROPERTIES OF MATTER

5.4.1 Hare's apparatus

Basic frame: stand
Tools: kit A

Description

Hare's apparatus is used to compare the densities of miscible liquids. The liquids are drawn up into the two tubes by sucking air out of the system and then sealing off as shown in Ins.(a). the reduced pressure holds each liquid in the tubes to a height which is inversely proportional to its density.

Requirements

base	plywood, 12 mm or	1–13	100 × 100	1
	blockboard, 12 mm	1–10	100 × 100	
hoarding	plywood, 6 mm	1–14	300 × 100	1

brackets	timber, 40 × 20	1–04	100	2
clamps	timber, 14 × 12*	1–03	100	2
	timber, 8 × 12*	1–03	100	2
	or terry clips	5–10–03		
tubes	glass†, 6 mm o.d.	5–23–07		2 of 250 mm
T-tube fixings	glass†	5–23–03		1

* Stock 25 × 12 timber should be cut lengthwise to produce these pieces.
† May be made from polystyrene (see Section 2.5.2).

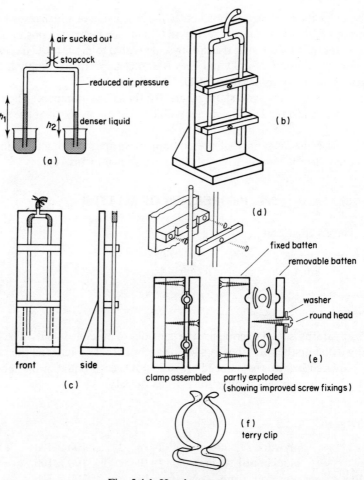

Fig. 5.4.1 Hare's apparatus

Procedure

Construct the stand as in Ins.(b). the clamps are intended to hold the tubes in place, without much stress on the glass. They should be quite square and identical in every respect. Even then, it is advisable to place pieces of rubber, plastic, or cloth between the glass and the wood to take any remaining irregularities.

The removable batten is clamped to the fixed batten by means of a screw. The clearance holes through it should be large enough for the screws to fit quite loosely. When the screw is tightened, the batten should be free to flex slightly.

If you happen to have them, you may use terry clips (stock number 4–46 or 5–10–03) to hold the tubes in position. These are easier to fix and possibly cheaper.

The tubes may, of course, be made from the transparent polystyrene outer-sleeve of ballpoint pens, as described in Section 2.5.2.

5.4.2 Manometer

Basic frame: stand

Requirements

See text.

Procedure

The same stand, constructed for the Hare's apparatus (Project 5.4.1), may be used for this project. In fact some manufacturers also mount the manometer on the reverse side of the hoarding as it saves materials and expense.

The U-tube can be made of glass, as described in Section 2.4.6. However, transparent flexible tubing such as clear PVC or polyethylene, obtainable from

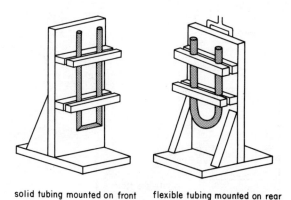

solid tubing mounted on front   flexible tubing mounted on rear
of stand   of Hare's Apparatus

Fig. 5.4.2 Manometer

motor car spares dealers, may also be used if it is mounted in such a way that the tube is fairly firmly held in position. In all cases, the U-tube may be fastened by the same method described for Hare's apparatus.

5.5   HEAT

5.5.1   Calorimeters

Tools: kits A and C

Requirements

See text.

Procedure

Calorimeters are easily improvised from tin cans. In general, a 140 g (5 oz) tomato paste can will fit into a 280 g (10 oz) or 420 g (15 oz) can.

Insulation is obtained from polystyrene or styrofoam (see Section 2.5.2). Place sheets of styrofoam on top of each other to form a pile 75 mm high (the height of a 10 oz can). Heat the open end of the can by holding it over a gas flame. Holding the can in a cloth to protect your hands, press the hot open end firmly down on the pile of sheets to obtain a solid cylinder of foam which fits in the can.

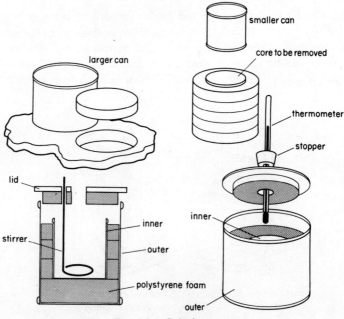

Fig. 5.5.1 Calorimeters

Sometimes it may be economical to cut a number of 75 mm diameter discs from a single sheet especially if this is an irregular piece. Make a pile of these discs about 75 mm high and, using a 5 oz can, cut out a concentric inner cylindrical core of 50 mm diameter. You will then be left with a hollow cylindrical sleeve of styrofoam, about 75 mm high and with an external and internal diameters of 75 mm and 50 mm respectively. Place a disc of styrofoam about 6 mm thick, 75 mm diameter, at the bottom of a 10 oz can and insert the hollow cylinder.

The heat generated when the core is cut may weld the layers together but if it does not, apply a vinyl adhesive like Uhu. Adhesives like Bostik are benzene-based and will dissolve the plastic. Place the smaller can inside the foam insulator.

A lid for the calorimeter is made from a disc of hardboard of 80 mm diameter. Glue a spare styrofoam disc concentrically to it. Drill a 12 mm hole in the exact centre of the lid. A No 11 stopper carrying the thermometer is inserted in this hole. Another hole, 2 to 4 mm diameter is drilled 20 mm from the centre. This can be used for inserting a stirrer made from wire about 1 or 2 mm thick. It consists of a circular loop, 40 mm in diameter, with a handle arranged at right angles to the plane of the loop. The handle protrudes through the hole and is moved vertically up and down to agitate the contents of the inner calorimeter.

5.5.2 Joule calorimeter

Tools: kits A and D

Requirements

lid	hardboard	1–18	80 mm diam.	1
leads	copper wire, 2.5 mm^{2}*	1–41	100 mm	2
heater	constantan, 26G	5–10–05	400	1
stopper	rubber, No 11	5–29–01		1
stirrer	copper wire, 2.5 mm^{2}*	1–41	400	1

* From PVC covered, twin-and-earth, solid-core cable.

Procedure

The Joule calorimeter is an extension of Project 5.5.1 and requires only a heating coil to complete it.

Cut two pieces of thick copper wire about 25 mm long. The copper wire is obtained from 2.5 mm^{2} solid-core mains cable. Use a sharp one-inch nail to make two holes in the lid 10 mm from the centre on opposite sides of the central hole for the thermometer. Remove the insulator and insert the lengths of wire into the holes, leaving about 10 mm protruding above the lid. These may be held in position with blobs of solder above and below the hole. It is important that they should fit tightly so do not make these holes larger than necessary. Replace the

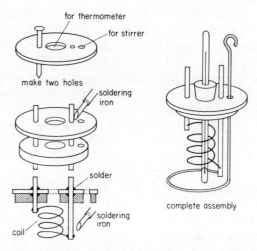

Fig. 5.5.2 Joule calorimeter

insulator. Cut a 400 mm length of 26G constantan wire and wind it into a loose coil of $5\frac{1}{2}$ turns of 25 mm diameter with about 5 mm separation between the turns. Wrap the ends of the coil around the lower ends of the copper wire and fix it with solder to make a good electrical joint.

With the stirrer in position the lid is now ready for use to complete the Joule calorimeter.

If properly assembled the coil should not come into contact with the stirrer when this is moved vertically. The inner calorimeter will confine the horizontal movement of the stirrer and prevent it from touching the coil.

5.5.3   Bimetallic strip

Tools: kit A, hacksaw

Requirements

See text.

Procedure

Any two metals may be used especially if their expansion coefficients differ widely. Take two strips identical in length and width though not necessarily in thickness and fix them firmly to each other.

As bimetallic strips are usually subjected to quite rough handling, very often being stored away in a drawer with other odd-shaped pieces of metal, it is advisable to use metal strips about 1 mm thick. Thinner pieces may be doubled or tripled for strength. Table 5.5.3 gives these coefficients for various materials.

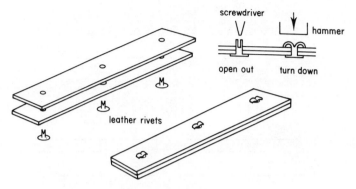

Fig. 5.5.3 Bimetallic strip

Table 5.5.3 Linear expansion of metals

Metal	Linear expansivity, $\alpha\,(\times 10^{-6})$
Aluminium	23
Brass	18
Copper	17
Iron, wrought	12
Steel, mild	15

The strips should be riveted or bolted together at three points along their length while at room temperature. Riveting the strips together can be done quite inexpensively by using 4 mm long leather rivets which are used by shoe repairers to fix leather straps on sandals and suitcases. These rivets are stocked by a few hardware merchants and by shoe repairers.

Line up the strips, one on top of the other, and drill a clearance hole for each rivet. You could also try punching a hole using a woodscrew as a punch and following through with a 4-inch nail.

5.5.4 Triangle and slot apparatus

Tools   : kits B and C
Materials: metal strip, nuts and bolts

Description

This is a variation of the ball-and-ring apparatus which is used to demonstrate the expansion of a body when heated. In this case the triangle, when heated, cannot slip through the slot.

Requirements

strip A	iron sheet, 18G	3–23	150 × 20	1
triangle B	iron sheet, 18G	3–23	60 mm side (equilateral)	1

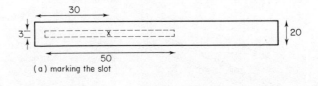

(a) marking the slot

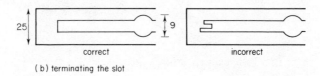

(b) terminating the slot

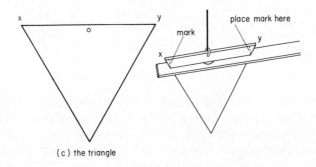

(c) the triangle

Procedure

With a hard pencil, mark out the position of a 50 mm by 3 mm slot as in Ins. (a). Using a centre-punch, mark the midpoint of the slot and drill a hole of 8 or 9 mm diameter at this spot, starting with a 2 mm hole and gradually increasing the size.

From this hole, the slot may now be cut. Use a junior hacksaw to enlarge the hole in the direction of the slot until you are able to insert a standard hacksaw blade.

Ensure that the ends of the slots are well defined and perfectly square (Ins. (b)). Use a small file to smooth the edges of the slot.

The triangle has the shape shown in Ins. (c). Drill a hole of 3 mm diameter as indicated and pass a wire ring through it. When the triangle is suspended from a string attached to this ring, the edge XY should be nearly horizontal. File away the ends X and Y until the triangle, held in this position, just passes through the slot (Ins. (c)).

When demonstrating the effects of thermal expansion, it will be shown that the triangle, if heated, cannot pass through the slot (Ins. (e)).

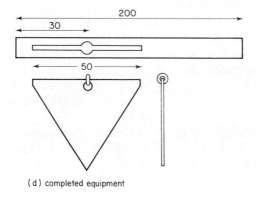

(d) completed equipment

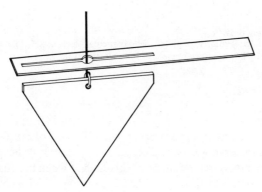

(e) when cold the triangle passes through the slot

Fig. 5.5.4 Triangle and slot apparatus

5.6 SOUND

5.6.1 The sonometer

Basic frame: box
Tools   : kit A, hole saw, hacksaw

Description

The sonometer consists of a resonance box measuring 1000 mm long by 120 mm wide and 60 mm deep with two metre rules arranged parallel to each other along its length. Steel or brass wires of 0.4 mm diameter or less are stretched above the metre sticks and held taut by weights attached to one end, the other being fixed to the box. The sonometer may be wall-mounted or used horizontally on a table.

Requirements

ends	timber, 40×20	1–04	95	2
sides	plywood, 12 mm or	1–13	1000×40	2
	timber, 40×20	1–04	1000	
top panel	plywood, 6 mm	1–14	1000×120	1
bottom	plywood, 6 mm	1–14	1000×120	1
post	timber, 40×20	1–04	25	1
bridges* A	timber, 25×25	see note†	50 (movable)	2
bridges* B	timber, 25×20	see note†	100 (fixed)	2
feet	timber, 25×12	1–03	120	2
ledge	strip, steel, 6 mm	3–30	100×30	1
wire	steel, 0.2 to 0.4 mm			
	diameter (see text)			4 m
	or brass, 0.2 to 0.4 mm			
	diameter (see text)			4 m

* for table mounting only.
† may be off-cuts of particularly tough hardwoods such as those used for laboratory furniture (see Table 1.2), or may be cuts from branches of certain thorn trees.

Procedure

(a) *The box*

Using a fretsaw, or employing any other method, make one or two holes of about 20 to 25 mm diameter in both side pieces. Assemble the box using glue and 1-inch by No. 8 screws but do not fit the top at this stage. Fasten the post to the centre of the floor of the box. Fix the feet at the extreme ends of the bottom of the box.

(b) *The bridges*

These may be made from hardwood but the top edge must be reinforced with a strip of metal to prevent the wood from being cut by the wire which passes over it. The metal is inserted in a slot cut along the edge (see Ins. (d)).

Other types of bridges may also be used and some of these are shown in Ins. (e).

The longer bridges (Ins. (b)) are screwed to the top panel, in the positions shown. After this is done, the top is fixed to the box. Remember to put a screw only through the centre of the lid into the post. Do not use glue with any of the fastening associated with the top.

(c) *The wire*

The wire must be of steel or brass which has a high breaking strength. Iron or copper wire cannot be used.

Guitar and piano wire are ideal but if this is not available then you resort, once again, to the usual source of steel odds and ends—the motor car. Solid cables

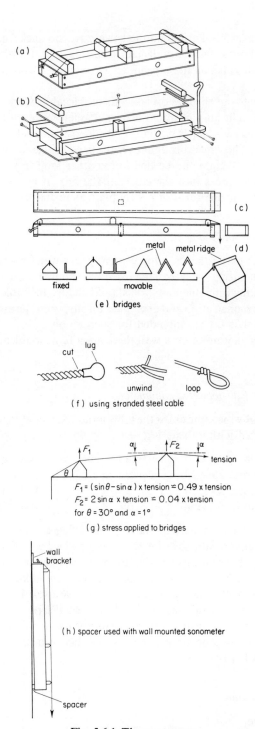

Fig. 5.6.1 The sonometer

used for hand-brakes, choke, and bonnet release are too thick for our purposes so look for stranded ones. These usually consist of 3, 5, or 7 strands of thinner wire. Avoid cables with kinks as these produce weak spots which could snap under tension.

Use a hacksaw to cut the lugs off the ends of the cable. Carefully separate the strands. Make a tight loop of about 10 mm diameter at each end. One loop is placed around a screw which is partially embedded at an angle in one of the ends of the sonometer. The wire is brought over the fixed bridges and dangles over the other end. A heavy weight can be tied to the other loop to keep the wire taut.

As the wire may press into the edges of the box, it is a good idea to add a reinforcing ledge in the form of a steel plate as in Ins.(c).

(d)   *Mounting the sonometer*

The complete unit may either be hung vertically on a wall (in which case it could be fixed permanently), or it can be used horizontally on a table. If you contemplate making only one unit, you should choose the table model which is suited for both demonstration and experimental purposes. the instructions which have been given thus far are intended for such a unit.

If you consider mounting on a wall there are a few modifications which you must make.

Requirements for wall-mounted sonometer

These are essentially the same as for the table mounted model except for the items which were marked with an asterisk.

bridges A	timber, 25 × 30	(see note on	50 (movable)	2
bridge B	timber, 25 × 20	previous list)	100 (upper)	1
bridge B	timber, 25 × 30		100 (lower)	1
bracket	strip iron, 3 mm	3–30	100 × 25	1

Choose a very hard timber for making the bridges. The fixed bridges are mounted in the same positions as before. The metal ledge is not needed. A wall bracket is made by bending an iron strip to form a right angle. This is fixed to the wall using plugs and screws. It may be necessary to get a builder or a carpenter to chisel a hole in the wall to fix this bracket. If you have a sturdy panelled wall or a suitable wooden beam or rail against a wall you could screw the bracket to it. If the sonometer is held vertically, the wire will not rest firmly against the lower bracket. To avoid this happening, place a spacer between the lower end and the wall as shown in Ins. (h).

5.6.2   Resonance tube

Basic frame: tube
Tools   : hacksaw

Requirements

See text.

Procedure

Usually a resonance tube consists of a glass tube of internal diameter between 15 and 50 mm, open at both ends. The tube is supported vertically with part of its length submerged in water. By raising or lowering the tube the column of air thus existing in the upper portion of the tube may be adjusted in length. If a tuning

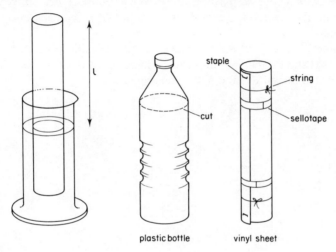

Fig. 5.6.2 Resonance tube

Table 5.6.2   Resonating air columns

Frequency of tuning fork (Stock No. 5-15-01)	Pitch notation	Resonant lengths† (mm)	
		Fundamental ($\lambda/4$)	Third harmonic ($3\lambda/4$)
*256	C	324	972
288	D	288	864
*320	E	259	777
341.3	F	243	729
*384	G	216	648
426.7	A′	194	582
480	B′	172	516
*512	C′	162	485

* more important frequencies.
† ignoring end-correction, with velocity
  of sound in air = 331.3 ms^{-1}.

fork is held near the upper end of the tube, then, for a certain length, the air column will resonate, causing a noticeable increase in the intensity of the sound.

If λ is the wavelength of sound in air at the frequency f of the tuning fork, then resonance occurs when the length l is an odd multiple of $\lambda/4$ (Fig. 5.6.2).

A convenient length of tube will be 500 mm. This would give resonance at all the usual frequencies from 256 hertz to 512 hertz, as well as a third harmonic resonance at 512 hertz (see Table 5.6.2).

Plastic or metal tubing may also be used. Many builders' merchants, especially those that deal with plumbing, will have some of these available.

For the outer vessel containing the water, a much more readily available substitute exists. This is the plastic bottle in which cooking oil or orange squash is sold. Cut off the tapered top end of the bottle either with a hacksaw or a sharp strong knife.

Of course it is always possible to make your own plastic tubes by rolling up a piece of vinyl sheet (500 × 80) to form a cylinder of 20 mm diameter. It may be fixed with staples and/or bound with sellotape.

CHAPTER 6

Chemistry

INTRODUCTION

Practical chemistry is usually classified as either analytical or physical. As the same basic equipment is often used in both areas, the classification of the simple apparatus described in this chapter cannot be arranged along the same lines. We have, instead, classified it according to the requirements of techniques and materials. In this way, the present chapter can be directly linked to Chapter 2. Therefore, before tackling any of these projects, you may find it profitable to read through the relevant sections of that chapter.

The presentation of the projects is the same as for the last chapter, insofar as this is feasible. Sometimes we have deviated from this approach because of the fact that we cannot now adhere to a few basic frames or to materials of standardized dimensions. Very often, in fact, we will be using scrap materials which cannot be specified beforehand for shape and size.

The tools required for these projects have a lower priority than before and so we will often suggest alternative ways in which the project may be tackled. You may therefore deviate from our suggestions much more widely and this places a burden on you to set your own standards of quality and reliability of the finished product.

6.1 WOOD AND METAL

6.1.1 Test-tube rack

Basic frame: platform
Tools   : kit A

Design No. 1

The rack, measuring 200 mm long by 100 mm high and 50 mm wide, when completed, should hold five test-tubes.

Requirements

back	timber, 100 × 12	1–01	200	1
ends A	timber, 40 × 20	1–04	200	1

ends B	timber, 40 × 20	1–04	200	1
ends C	timber, 75 × 12	1–02	200	1
pegs	wooden dowels, 9 mm	3–23	75 mm long	5
	or ball-pen sleeves	2–80		5
fixing	woodscrews, brass	4–28		4

Procedure

Give the back a coat or two of polyurethane varnish. Leave to dry. Using a fretsaw, cut holes of 25 mm diameter at intervals of 40 mm along the centre line of the ends A and B. Drill 9 mm diameter holes about 20 mm deep along a line 10 mm from the edge of C as shown in Ins. (c).

Assemble the rack using waterproof adhesive and 1-inch by No. 8 brass countersink screws to fasten A and C to the top and $\frac{3}{4}$ inch nails to pin B and C. Insert the dowels into the holes in C. When finished give it two or three coats of polyurethane varnish or polystyrene cement.

Design No. 2

If dowels are unobtainable, a good substitute is the outer tube of ballpoint pens. Ins. (d) shows a test-tube rack which is made from wood and ball-pen sleeves.

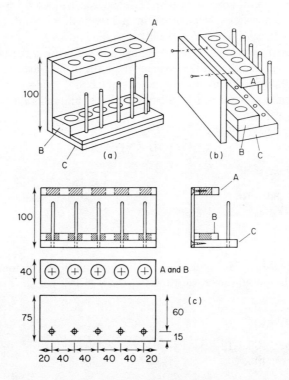

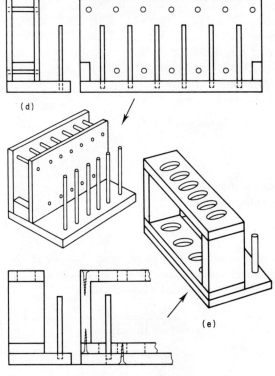

(d)

(e)

Fig. 6.1.1 Test-tube rack

Requirements

front	timber, 100 × 12	1–01	200	1
back	timber, 100 × 12	1–01	200	1
base	timber, 100 × 12	1–01	200	1
bracket	timber, 40 × 20	1–04	20	2
pegs	ball-pen sleeves	2–80		13
fixing	woodscrews, brass	4–28		
finish	polyurethane varnish	3–35		
	or polystyrene cement	1–51		

Design No. 3

This design has the advantage that the test-tubes may be viewed from two sides.

Requirements

sides	timber, 100 × 12	1–01	50	1
top A	timber, 50 × 12*	1–01	200	1

170

bottom B	timber, 50 × 12*	1–01	200	1
base C	timber, 100 × 12	1–01	200	1
pegs	dowels, 9 mm	3–23	75 mm	5
	or ball-pen sleeves	2–80		5
fixing	woodscrews, brass	4–28		
misc.	polyurethane varnish	3–35		
	or polystyrene cement	1–51		

*Stock number 1–01 cut lengthways.

6.1.2 Tripod

Tools   : kit A and C
Materials :   reinforcing rod

Description

Tripods have to be made from a metal which has the properties that it can withstand high temperatures (up to 500 °C) and also be strong enough to carry a load such as a 250 ml beaker filled with water.

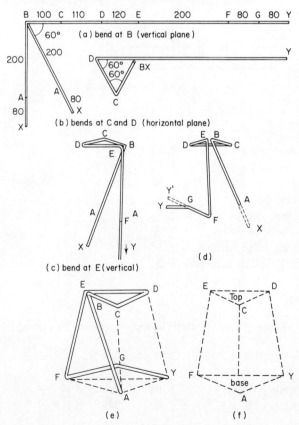

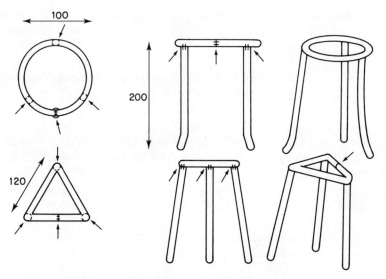

(g) arrows show position of welds

Fig. 6.1.2 Tripod

The project involves the use of the iron rods that are used for reinforcing concrete. This material is available in various diameters from builders merchants but can be obtained quite freely at building sites especially when demolition work has been carried out. As scrap, you may sometimes find it partly encased in concrete blocks which will have to be smashed or chipped off. The rod should then be straightened before it is put to use.

Rods of $\frac{1}{4}$-inch diameter can be very easily bent into the shape that is required, without the need for welding or brazing.

Requirements

Reinforcing rod,   6 mm ($\frac{1}{4}$-inch) diam.   3–25   1 metre

Procedure

Mark the spots at which the rod is to be bent (Ins. (a)). There are two planes in which the rod is to be bent. These planes are the vertical and the horizontal plane respectively.

Bend 1   This takes place at mark B. The arm BY is held horizontally and the angle YBX is exactly 60° in a vertical plane (Ins. (a)).

Bends 2 and 3   These are made in the horizontal plane at C and D with the angles BCD and CDY being 60° each. Marks B and E should be quite close together. The triangle BCD forms the upper platform of the tripod (Ins. (b)).

Bend 4   This is made at E at an angle of about 95° in the vertical plane below DE (Ins. (c)).

Bend 5 This is made at F and is probably the trickiest of the bends. It is required that, in the end, FY should lie almost parallel to DC and pointing slightly upward relative to the horizontal plane.

Bend 6 A slight bend or kink is made at G so that the free end of the rod, Y, returns to the horizontal plane (Ins. (d)).

The tripod may now be placed on a table to see how well it stands. It will be noted immediately that the leg BY appears to be too long. This is intentional. Your main task is to do the adjustments on leg EF and the prop FGY so that *when BX is shortened to the correct length BA*, the triangle BCD will be exactly horizontal and the legs of the tripod will splay out slightly to provide stability. The triangle formed by the points A, F, and Y should provide a firm base for the tripod to stand on.

It is suggested that you practise the bending procedure by using lengths of iron, copper, or aluminium wire about 1 or 2 mm in diameter before you attempt this project.

The triangular platform is relatively easy to make because the entire process then involves only the use of angular bends. These can be made fairly accurately by heating the rod strongly at the marks indicated. Provided you protect your hands against getting burned by the hot metal, these bends can be made manually. However, a machinist's vice will simplify the task. Furthermore, the use of a vice would also enable you to make a tripod with a circular platform. Make it with a diameter of between 80 and 150 mm.

In this project the tripod has been formed from a single length of rod and simple tools have been used.

If you have access to welding or brazing facilities the task of making these stands is made less complicated. In the design shown in Ins. (g), only four very simple welds are needed, each tripod again requiring about 1 metre of rod.

These reinforcing rods are usually supplied in 20 foot (6.1 metre) lengths. You should therefore be able to construct six tripods for the cost of one length of rod and 24 welds.

6.1.3 Retort stand

Tools: kit A

Description

A retort stand should have good stability, which it obtains from having a wide base and a low-placed centre of gravity. Fairly heavy objects can therefore be clamped to it without it toppling over. The stands may be made of wood or of metal.

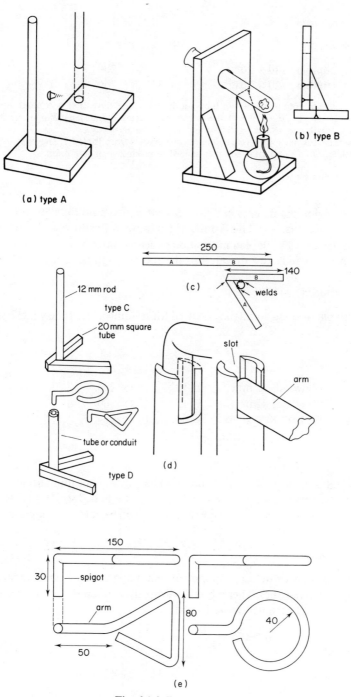

(a) type A

(b) type B

250

A · B

140

(c) welds

12 mm rod

type C

20 mm square tube

tube or conduit

type D

slot

arm

(d)

150

30

spigot

arm

80

40

50

(e)

Fig. 6.1.3 Retort stand

Type A (wooden)

Requirements

base	timber, 140 × 20*	3–32	200	1
post	timber, 20 × 20†	3–32	750	1

* For the base a 12-foot plank of 6-inch by 1-inch timber may have to be purchased. After being planed to 140 mm by 20 mm, it may then be cut into as many 200 mm lengths as are required. The remaining length may be cut lengthwise and used as standard stock.
† The post is made from a water resistant hardwood selected from Table 1.2. They may be rounded by whittling with a sharp knife and then sanded to produce a smooth finish.

Procedure

A hole of 16 mm diameter is cut with its centre not more than 30 mm from the edge of the base (Ins. (a)). This is done with a fretsaw. Ensure that the rod fits very tightly in the hole. Fix the rod in position by using water proof adhesive and a 1-inch by No. 8 woodscrew driven into the rod through the edge of the base.

Type B (wooden)

A very simple wooden stand may be used for holding a test-tube while it is being heated.

Requirements

base	plywood, 12 mm	1–13	150 × 100	1
hoarding	plywood, 12 mm	1–13	250 × 100	1
brackets	timber, 40 × 20	1–04	1	

Procedure

Using a fretsaw, cut a hole of 25 mm diameter in the hoarding about 200 mm from the lower end. Assemble the stand to form a L-shaped structure (Ins. b)). In use, the test-tube is inserted through the hole. It will be held at an angle as shown.

Type C (metal)

If you have access to welding equipment you may prefer to make metal stands rather than wooden ones. There should be very little difference in the cost and the final product will be much more robust.

Requirements

base	steel tube, square section 20 × 20	3–34	400 mm	1
post	reinforcing rod, 12 mm diameter.	3–25	750 mm	1

Procedure

The square tubing is cut, near its midpoint, at an angle of 60° (Ins. (c)). One piece should be 9 to 10 mm longer than the other. They are welded together at an angle of 60° to form the base. The rod is welded into place inside the angle of the base.

There is a bonus to be derived from this construction: you will find that the bases fit snugly inside each other and therefore these tripods are very easily stored.

Clean the tripod thoroughly by rubbing it down with sandpaper. It should then be rustproofed by giving it a coat of aluminium paint.

Type D (metal)

This is a variation of the above with a hollow tubular post taking the place of the conventional rod. It has the advantage that a selection of rings, triangles, etc. may be inserted into the tube so that boss heads are not needed.

Requirements

base	steel tube, square section 20 × 20	3–34	400 mm	1
post	steel tube, round section 9 mm bore	3–34	180 mm	1
accessories	reinforcing rod 6 mm diameter	3–25	350 mm	as needed

Procedure

Assemble the retort stand as is described for the type C. Cut a slot into the top end of the post as shown in Ins. (d).

The accessories such as triangles and rings are made from 300 to 350 mm lengths of reinforcing rod bent as shown in Ins. (e). The spigot enters the tube and the arm fits into the slot which keeps it fixed in position.

6.1.4 Scaffold

In physics, usually only one retort stand is used in a single experiment. In chemistry experiments, however, more than one is generally needed and therefore the tendency is to use a scaffold, that is, a framework of rods and clamps, rather than a single retort stand.

Once again, reinforcing rods of 12 mm diameter are used but now an overseas purchase of clamps or boss heads will have to be made. In this respect the multipurpose boss head (stock number 5–20–01, see Ins. (a)) is recommended. It can accommodate both round and square rods or tubes up to 16 mm across. It can also be used end-on as bases for the scaffold or clamped to the edge of a table

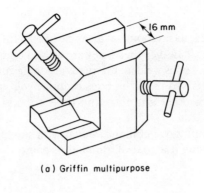

(a) Griffin multipurpose

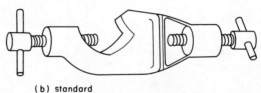

(b) standard

Fig. 6.1.4 Boss heads for scaffolds

or a wooden board up to 16 mm thick. The cheaper boss heads (Ins. (b)) cost half the price of the multipurpose ones and are also useful for clamping rods of up to 16 mm diameter at right angles to each other. Buy four to eight times as many standard boss heads as multipurpose ones.

6.1.5 Mercury tray

Frame :open box
Tools :kit A

Description

The tray measuring 500 mm by 500 mm and 28 mm high, is provided with a plugged outlet through which the mercury could be poured into a container.

Requirements

sides	timber, 25 × 12	1–03	500	2
ends	timber, 25 × 12	1–03	476	2
bottom	plywood, 3 mm	1–15	500 × 500	1
	or hardboard	1–18	500 × 500	
stopper	rubber, No. 4	5–29–01		1

Procedure

Drill a hole of 5 mm diameter through one of the side-pieces in position shown in Ins. (a).

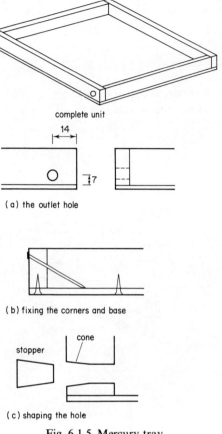

complete unit

(a) the outlet hole

(b) fixing the corners and base

(c) shaping the hole

Fig. 6.1.5 Mercury tray

Applying vinyl adhesive liberally to ensure that all joints are watertight, assemble the tray using $\frac{3}{4}$-inch by No. 6 woodscrews at 100 mm intervals to hold the bottom in place. Each corner is fixed with a single 40 mm nail driven into it at an angle (Ins. (b)).

The outlet hole is arranged close to the bottom of the tray. Using a triangular file, slightly enlarge the outer entrance of the hole so that hole is given a conical shape (Ins. (c)). The stopper, when pushed into it, should fit quite snugly and tightly.

Apply two or three coats of polyurethane varnish inside the tray.

6.1.6 Test-tube holders

(a) *Wire*

Tools: pliers

178

Requirements

iron wire, 2 mm diam.   2–21   400   1

Procedure

Wrap one end of the wire about two or three times around the test-tube (Ins. (a)).
The other end is bent to form a handle about 100 mm long.

(b)   *Terry clip holder*

Tools: kit A

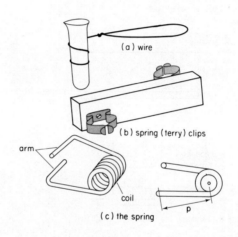

(a) wire

(b) spring (terry) clips

arm

coil

(c) the spring

p

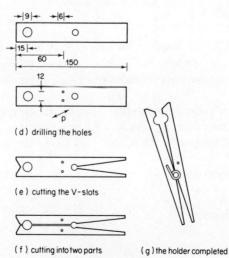

(d) drilling the holes

(e) cutting the V-slots

(f) cutting into two parts   (g) the holder completed

Fig. 6.1.6 Test-tube holders

Requirements

| handle | timber, 25 × 12 | 1–03 | | 150 | 1 |
| grip | terry clip, 12 mm | 3–36 and 5–10–03 | | | 1 |

Procedure

Use $\frac{3}{4}$-inch by No. 6 screws to fix the terry clip to one face of the handle as in Ins. (b). Fixing it to an end may also be done but, as the screw will be held in end-grain, it may not be secure. A second clip, of a different size, e.g. 25 mm, may be attached to other side to cope with larger test-tubes.

(c) *Wooden holder*

Tools: kit A

Description

Wooden clothes pegs may be used for smaller test-tubes. Unfortunately the strain on the arms may be too great to accept 12 mm tubes. The spring hinges of discarded pegs can be used to make robust holders for larger test-tubes.

Requirements

| arms | timber, 25 × 12 | 1–03 | 125 | 1 |
| hinges | clothes-peg springs | 2–08 | | 1 |

Procedure

Take the clothes-peg spring and measure the length, p, of the arm from the centre of the coil (Ins. (c)). This is about 16 or 17 mm for most of these types of wooden pegs. Drill holes of 6 mm and 9 mm diameter in the face side of the wooden piece at distances of 60 mm and 15 mm from one end. Drill two holes of 2 mm diameter, a distance, p, from the centre of the 6 mm hole, at the points shown in Ins. (d).

Using a tenon saw or a hacksaw, cut two V-slots, one in each end of the timber (Ins. (e)). Thereafter, cut the timber down the centre into two pieces (Ins. (f)).

Insert the spring (Ins. (g)) to complete the test-tube holder.

6.1.7 Molecular models

Tools: kit A

Description

The models are constructed of wooden balls held together with bonds made from short lengths of flexible curtain rod which may be purchased from most hardware shops. The rod may be bare or in a plastic sleeve, provided the sleeve fits tightly.

180

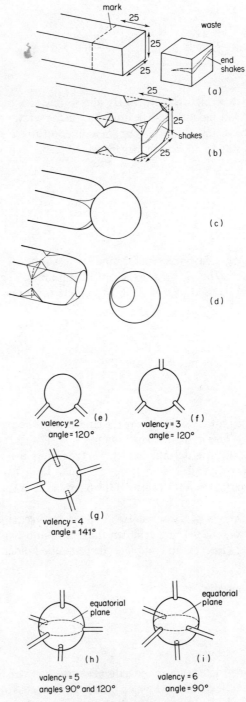

mark
25
25
25
waste
end shakes
(a)

25
25
shakes
25
(b)

(c)

(d)

valency = 2   (e)
angle = 120°

valency = 3   (f)
angle = 120°

valency = 4   (g)
angle = 141°

equatorial plane

valency = 5   (h)
angles 90° and 120°

equatorial plane

valency = 6   (i)
angle = 90°

spatial arrangement of holes and bonds

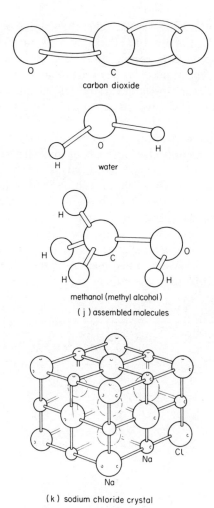

carbon dioxide

water

methanol (methyl alcohol)

(j) assembled molecules

(k) sodium chloride crystal

Fig. 6.1.7 Molecular models

Requirements

balls	timber, 10 × 10	3–32	500	as needed
	or timber, 25 × 25	3–32	500	as needed
bonds	curtain rod, flexible	3–26	25 or 50 mm	as needed

Procedure

To make balls of 25 mm diameter we start with a 500 mm length of moderately hard timber with a cross-section measuring 25 mm by 25 mm.

Avoid using wood which has cracks in the ends or along its lengths. These cracks, or 'shakes' as they are sometimes called, are caused by uneven drying of the wood. End shakes may be removed by cutting off the offending pieces (Ins. (a)). Then proceed as follows.

182

Mark off a length of 25 mm from the end of the wood. Do not cut off this piece just yet. Instead, use a tenon saw, or a coarse hacksaw, to cut notches in the edges of the timber and to remove the corners off the end of the piece (Ins. (b)). Using very coarse emery paper, sand away the remaining corners and edges until a spherical knob is produced (Ins. (c)). Cut this knob from the body of the wood and continue to smooth it with finer paper until a satisfactorily spherical shape is obtained (Ins. (d)).

The next ball is then marked off and, by repeating the notching, smoothing, and cutting sequence, ten or twelve balls may be made. In the same way, balls of other diameters (e.g. 10 mm) may be produced.

The balls should then be drilled to a depth of 8 mm with holes of the exact diameter of the rod, in various configurations depending on the oxidation number or valency of the particular atom which it is intended to represent. Table 6.1.7 gives a list of some elements, the recommended size ball and its valency. Ins. (e) to Ins. (i) show the spatial arrangements for 2, 3, 4, 5, and 6 holes. The remaining figures show assembled interesting molecules and crystals. The balls may be coloured by immersing them in an ink solution.

Table 6.1.7   Molecular models

Element	Ball diameter (mm)	Colour	Valency
Hydrogen	10	White	1
Sodium	10	Blue	1*
Magnesium	10	Green	2
Potassium	25	Blue	1
Chlorine	25	Green	1*
Fluorine	25	Orange	1
Calcium	25	Blue	2
Aluminium	25	White	3
Carbon	25	Black	4
Phosphorus	25	Purple	5
Nitrogen	25	Purple	5
Oxygen	25	Red	6
Sulphur	25	Yellow	6

* For crystal models, these atoms may have six bonds.

6.2   GLASS

6.2.1   Glass loop

Tools: kit C

Description

The glass loop is used in tests for the identification of certain gases, such as carbon dioxide, sulphur dioxide, hydrogen, etc. The loop is dipped in the solution of a suitable reagent. When it is withdrawn a film of the liquid will remain suspended in the eye of the loop. Normally this film would be clear. When the loop is then held in the gas, a reaction, involving a colour change, will occur depending on the gas and the reagent. The advantages of this test are:

1. simplicity, speed and efficiency;
2. economy in the use of reagents;
3. the gas is left unchanged and uncontaminated so that further test can be performed on the same sample.

The following is a list of some of the tests:

Gas	Reagent	Observed change
Carbon dioxide	Lime water	Clear to milky
Sulphur dioxide	Malachite green	Green to colourless
Hydrogen sulphide	Lead acetate solution	Clear to black
Chlorine	Iodine solution	Brown to clear

Requirements

rod   glass, 6 mm diameter   5–23–02   100   1

Procedure

Heat the glass rod at its midpoint over a short region covering not more than 10 mm. When this section has softened, draw it out to a length of 200 mm with the diameter reducing to about 1 mm. With a file make a scratch at the midpoint of this elongated portion and break in two pieces.

Using only the tip of the bunsen burner flame, momentarily heat the thin part at a point about 10 mm from the end as in Ins. (b). As soon as this spot softens, hold the rod vertically. The end should fold over and, if this is done quickly enough, could form a loop as in Ins. (c). With a little practice you could soon learn the correct wrist action to form a loop at the first try.

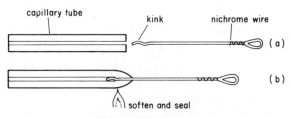

Fig. 6.2.1 Glass loop

184

It is not a good idea to make too many of these loops at a time. They are very fragile and most of them would probably be broken before you get around to using them. Therefore, make only four or six at a time just when you are about to require them. They should be stored between layers of cotton wool in a flat container. Rinse carefully in distilled water before and after use.

6.2.2   Wire loop

Tools: kit C

Description

Wire loops are used for performing flame tests to detect and identify certain metals such as sodium and potassium. A particle of salt containing the metal is held on the wire loop and placed in the hottest flame (type iv) of a bunsen burner. The excited atoms and ions of the metal will then impart a characteristic colour to the flame. For sodium this is yellow; for potassium, purple (lilac), and for calcium, brick-red.

Originally, platinum was used as the wire. This was because platinum could be heated to high temperatures without oxidizing and a short length of it could be embedded in a glass handle. Platinum and glass had the same coefficient of linear expansion and therefore there was very little danger of the wire either working loose or the glass cracking with repeated cycles of heating and cooling.

Nichrome is much cheaper than platinum and has the two essential properties: non-oxidation at high temperatures and the same coefficient of linear expansion as that of glass.

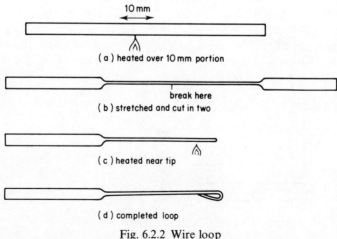

Fig. 6.2.2 Wire loop

185

Requirements

handle	tubing, glass, capillary	4–86	70 mm	1
	6 mm diam., 0.5 mm bore	5–23–06		
	or rod glass, 6 mm diam.	5–23–02	70 mm	1
wire	nichrome, 28G	5–10–08	100 mm	1

Procedure

Put a slight kink into one end of the wire (Ins. (a)). Soften one end of the rod over a length of about 20 mm. Heat the kinked end of the wire and push it into the soft end of the rod. The wire should penetrate to a depth of about 10 mm. Continue to heat strongly for a while then anneal in a cool flame. The kink grips the glass seal firmly and the wire will not be easily dislodged.

6.2.3. Droppers

Tools: kit C

Requirements (to make two droppers)

glass tubing	6 mm diam.	5–23–07	150	1
rubber tubing	5 mm bore, 1.5 mm wall	5–20–11	60	2
rubber solution		3–64		

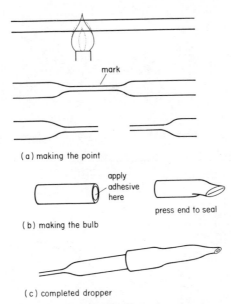

(a) making the point

(b) making the bulb

(c) completed dropper

Fig, 6.2.3 Dropper

Procedure

Heat a region of about 20 mm at the midpoint of the glass tube. When it has softened, pull the two ends of the tube apart until the heated part has narrowed to a diameter of about 2 mm. Mark the midpoint of this constriction and break, at this point, into two pieces (Ins.(a)).

Smear a thin film of rubber solution just inside one end of each of the rubber tubes. When the adhesive is dry, press the walls together at the other end so that an airtight seal is formed (Ins.(b)).

Finally, slip one rubber bulb over the wide end of each glass tube and the job is complete.

Droppers may also be made from ball-pen tubes (stock number 2–80).

6.2.4   Liebig's condenser

Tools: glass cutter, bunsen burner

Description

The condenser is made entirely of glass soda-lime tubing assembled with rubber stoppers.

Requirements

inner sleeve	glass tube, 6 mm diam.	5–23–07	500	1
outer tube	glass tube, 24 mm diam.	5–23–07	300	1
side tubes	glass tube, 6 mm diam.	5–23–07	100	2
stoppers	No. 23, two holes	5–29–01		2

Procedure

Pass the inner tube through a hole in one of the stoppers till a length of about 80 mm protrudes above the stopper. Pass the longer end of the tube through the larger outer tube and attach the second stopper to the other end. Insert the

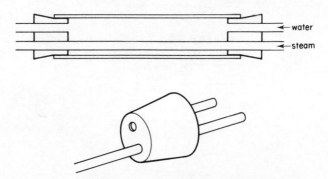

Fig. 6.2.4 Liebig's condenser

shorter side tubes through the second hole in each stopper. The tube should not protrude much below the narrow face of the stopper to avoid air being trapped in the condenser during use. Push the two stoppers toward each other until they fit tightly in each end of the outer tube. Ensure that the holes through which the outer tube passes are exactly aligned opposite each other so that the outer and inner tube run parallel. If this is not so, the inner tube may be under stress and could fracture. The ends of the glass tubes should be smoothed by heating (see Section 2.4.3) to ease the insertion of the tube into the stopper. Soap, or a few drops of detergent, smeared on the tube or in the hole will also help but must be completely washed off after the assembly is complete.

6.2.5   Test-tube

Tools: bunsen burner

Description and procedure

Test-tubes are one of the cheapest items required for a chemistry laboratory and it is probably unnecessary to have to make any yourself. However, they are fairly easy to make.

Start with a length of glass tubing, 12 mm diameter, about 250 mm long. Soften the midpoint and draw it out to a capillary. Heat the midpoint of the capillary to seal and thus divide the tube into two parts. Round the sealed end off as described in Section 2.4.4.

The open end of the test-tube is softened by heating and opened out with a brass reamer (Ins.(c)) to form a rim. When the test-tubes are annealed they can be used for heating liquids, etc. but, as is the case for all soda-lime glassware, not for heating dry solids.

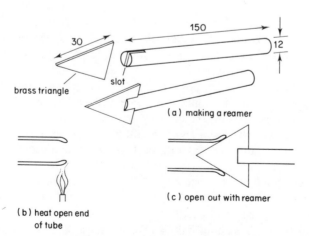

Fig. 6.2.5 Reaming a test-tube

188

6.2.6 Demonstration thermometer

Tools: kit C

Description

Manufactured thermometers have a very fine bore, often 0.2 mm or less and so require only a small bulb. In order to make a demonstration thermometer we will use the smallest bore available to us. This is 0.5 mm in diameter. If the mercury is to expand into the neck for a distance of 100 to 200 mm over the temperature range of 0 to 100 °C, we will require a spherical bulb of about 13 to 16 mm diameter.

With a wall thickness of 1 mm, the bulb will consist of 500 to 800 mm³ of glass. This is obtained by softening and then blowing out a length of the capillary tube of 20 to 30 mm. Within these limits, the bulb will hold between 14 and 28 grams of mercury.

Requirements

capillary	tubing glass, 6 mm diam. 0.5 mm bore	5–23–06	250 mm	1
mercury	clean and dry	4–82	40 g (only half will be used)	
tubing	rubber, 5 mm bore	5–20–11	70 mm	1
misc.	small funnel, to fit into rubber tube, retort stand and clamps, tripod, glass beaker with water			

Procedure

Seal one end of the tube and then, by the method described in Section 2.4.5 blow a bulb of about 14 mm outside diameter with a wall thickness of 1 mm. It has been shown that you will need to soften and blow up a 25 mm length of the tube at its sealed end. Anneal in a cool flame.

Clamp the tube in a vertical position with the bulb lowermost. Attach the funnel to the upper end of the capillary by means of the rubber tubing. Clamp the funnel. Pour the mercury into the funnel.

Because of the narrowness of the bore and the high surface tension of the mercury, none of the liquid will enter the neck of the thermometer. We therefore proceed as follows.

Gently heat the bulb of the thermometer. This will cause the air to expand and bubbles will pass up through the mercury. If the air is now allowed to cool, the mercury will be sucked through the capillary and into the bulb. Repeat if necessary until the bulb is about half-full. When this is achieved, heat the bulb quite strongly until the mercury starts to boil. The mercury vapour should drive

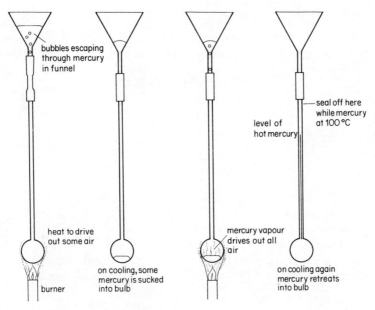

Fig. 6.2.6 Demonstration thermometer

all the remaining air out of the thermometer so that, if it is now allowed to cool, the bulb and the lower part of the neck should contain all the mercury without any trapped air bubbles. If there are any bubbles repeat the above until these are removed.

When you are satisfied that no air is still trapped in the mercury, immerse the thermometer and bulb completely in water in a glass beaker. Heat the water to boiling and note that the level of the mercury does not rise less than 180 mm or more than 220 mm up the neck. In the former case, add a drop more mercury. In the latter, heat the bulb in the flame until the mercury rises into the funnel or rubber tube. Suck out some of the mercury with a dropper. Do not use a pipette as there is a risk of swallowing this poisonous liquid.

Finally, while the bulb is kept in a beaker of boiling water, seal off the top end of the thermometer at a distance about halfway between the top of the tube and the top of the mercury (see Section 2.4.4). Some air may still be trapped in the space above the mercury but this will be at a very low pressure.

It should be mentioned that droplets of spilled mercury must not be left lying about as it could evaporate. Mercury vapour is toxic.

6.3 PLASTICS

6.3.1 Dishes and scoops

Tools: sharp knife or hacksaw

Description

The 4-litre or 1-gallon containers in which motor car engine oil is sold are so plentiful these days that we must include some project that uses them.

Requirements

| plastic containers | 2- or 4-litre capacity | 2–04 | as needed |

Procedure

Cut one of the containers in a vertical plane passing through the filler hole and just missing the handle (Ins.(a)). This results in the formation of two flat rectangular dishes both equipped with a lip for pouring. One would have a useful handle attached to it.

You may also cut a container diagonally and so produce a scoop with a handle and a hole through which the contents of the scoop can be poured (Ins.(b)).

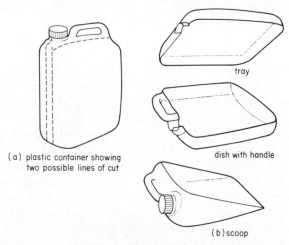

(a) plastic container showing two possible lines of cut

tray

dish with handle

(b) scoop

Fig. 6.3.1 Dishes and scoops

6.3.2 Stencils

Tools: knife

Description

Stencils are fast becoming one of the most useful teaching aids in science. They can be used for rapidly drawing outlines of animals, maps, ellipses, angles, lettering, laboratory equipment and so on. Many of these are available at bookshops but some may be fairly expensive especially if you require a wide selection. You can, of course, make them yourself by cutting the necessary shapes out of PVC sheet. Broken or even whole tiles are very often discarded as scrap. New ones may be purchased in small quantities.

Requirements

| tile, PVC | 2–22 or 3–31 |
| carbon paper | 2–81 or 3–80 |

Procedure

Draw an outline of the figure accurately on a sheet of paper, making any corrections that you need. Lay a sheet of carbon paper on the tile and over this place the drawing, face up. Pressing fairly hard with a ball-pen, trace the outline so that it is transferred to the tile through the carbon paper. Using a very sharp pointed knife such as a scalpel or a razor blade in a holder (see Section 2.2.4, Hints), firmly retrace the entire carbon outline on the tile. Do not use force but pay more attention to the accuracy of the cut. Repeat the retracing as often as necessary, gradually deepening the cut until it passes through the tile. When the outline has been completely cut out, any points or rough edges may be trimmed.

In the case of maps, the position of main towns may be indicated by holes of 1 or 2 mm diameter drilled in the tile or pierced with a hot one-inch nail.

Paint stencils are useful when you wish to paint an identification label on your equipment and furniture. Just lay the stencil on the surface to be painted. Using a brush or an old rag, dab the paint on the stencil. The letters will appear on the surface when the stencil is removed.

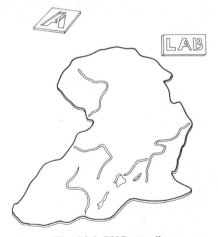

Fig. 6.3.2 PVC stencils

6.3.3 Lifeguards

Tools: knife, large needle

Description

Lifeguards are rubber sleeves that are slipped around measuring cylinders to protect them from damage if, by accident, they get knocked over.

Requirements

rubber tubing	5 mm bore, 4 mm wall	5–20–11	30 mm	1
plastic tubing	garden hosepipe, 12 mm bore	3–22		as needed
string		2–87		as needed

Procedure

Measure the circumference of the measuring cylinder. Cut a length of garden hose about 5% shorter than the circumference. Wet the rubber tubing and push it into one end of the hose until only half of it is exposed. Form the hose into a circle and push the exposed rubber tubing into the other end of the hose (Ins.(b)).

The rubber tubing should fit quite tightly in the hose but, to ensure that it does not slip out, it could be securely stitched into place with string using a long needle made from a sardine-can opener (see Section 2.6.1). Pass the needle and string a few times through each end of the hose and tubing and then, after wrapping the string several times around the hose, tie it tightly.

The lifeguard should fit snugly on the cylinder (Ins.(c)).

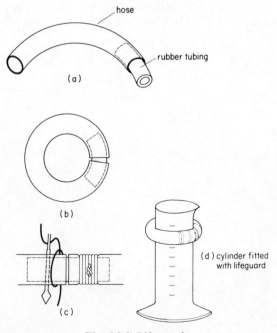

Fig. 6.3.3 Lifeguards

6.3.4 Displacement vessel

Tools: knife, soldering iron, razor blade

Requirements

See text.

Description and procedure

A displacement vessel is fitted with a spout or side tube which directs the overflow of the displaced liquid into a beaker for collection. For this project the vessel is constructed from a polythene or propylene container such as those used for dispensing washing-up liquid. The tapering upper section is cut off and may be used as an improvised funnel (Ins.(a)).

Make a second cut about 90 mm from the bottom. The lower section becomes the vessel. The upper section may be between 40 and 90 mm long depending on the original height of the container. It is used for making the spout or side tube. Cut a piece about 40 mm wide (Ins. (b)) and roll it into a tube of 10 mm diameter. Using a soldering iron, weld the edge of the overlap to close the side of the tube (Ins. (c)). With a very sharp knife, preferably a new razor blade, cut through the tube at an angle of 45° leaving a spout about 30 mm long.

In the wall of the vessel, about 70 mm from the bottom, make three intersecting incisions (Ins.(b)). When these cuts are opened out, there should be a hole,

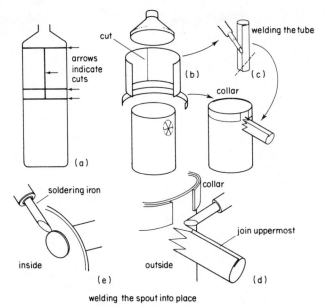

Fig. 6.3.4 Displacement vessel

roughly elliptical, just wide enough to admit the tube at an angle of 45°. You may find it easier to insert the tube through the hole from the inside of the container. About 3 or 4 mm of the tube should protrude into the vessel.

The six pointed flaps of the hole should rest quite tightly against the tube. Weld these in place (Ins.(d)). Then insert the soldering iron inside the vessel and weld the protruding end of the tube onto the edge of the hole (Ins.(e)). It is important that the weld around the lower edge of the hole should be watertight to prevent any loss of displaced liquid. The join along the tube need not be watertight provided that it is positioned along the uppermost surface of the tube.

We have already mentioned the need for cleanliness in welding. In this case the printing on the walls of the vessel should be removed around any area to be welded. Acetone is the best solvent for this type of ink but it may also be removed with petrol.

When the vessel contains water, you may find that it is difficult to pick it up as the walls tend to cave in under the pressure of your fingers. Part of the middle portion that was cut from the container is opened out with a longitudinal cut (Ins.(b)). It is then welded into place as a collar along the outside of the rim of the vessel. The gap caused by the cut is positioned just over the spout.

Further strengthening may be obtained by running the soldering iron around the rim. This will produce some thickening which can then be rubbed down with emery paper.

CHAPTER 7

Biology and Geography

7.1 BIOLOGY EQUIPMENT

7.1.1 Specimen box

Frame :box
Tools :kit A

Description

The box measures 300 mm by 200 mm, 60 mm deep and is covered with a single sheet of glass hinged with adhesive tape. Inside it is lined with a sheet of softboard or polystyrene to which the specimen may be attached.

Requirements

ends	A	timber, 75 × 12	1–02	170	2
	B	hardboard	1–18	194 × 85	2
sides	C	timber, 75 × 12	1–02	294	2
	D	hardboard	1–18	300 × 85	2
bottom	E	hardboard	1–18	294 × 194	1
top	F	glass plate, 3 mm	3–21	294 × 194	1
fixing		nails, sellotape			

Procedure

Assemble the box using pieces A, C, and E (Ins. (c)) and fixing them with 1-inch nails. Then add the hardboard pieces D and B (in that order) ensuring that these are square with the bottom and the sides. The top edges of the hardboard will rise higher than the timber strips (Ins. (d)). This provides a rebate in which the glass lid (f) can fit easily. This lid may be permanently taped in position, if you wish, but it would be more convenient if it could be raised and lowered as required. Sellotape, about 25 mm wide, attached along one edge of the glass plate and then, stuck to the outer face of the corresponding hardboard strip (Ins. (e)) can form a hinge. Better still, would be a 25 mm wide strip of nylon ribbon stuck on in the

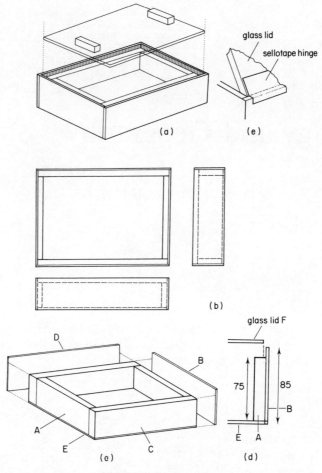

Fig. 7.1.1 Specimen box

same position. Use Bostik Clear Adhesive which makes good contact with glass.

A wooden or metal knob may also be attached to the glass with Bostik Clear Adhesive. This will provide a grip for raising and lowering the lid (Ins.(a)). A rectangle of styrofoam or softboard 276 mm by 175 mm and 12 mm thick lines the bottom of the box and to this you can pin specimens for display.

7.1.2 Mouse cage

Tools: kits A and C

Description

This is a large converted rectangular biscuit tin. It is provided with a see-through lid (Ins.(a)).

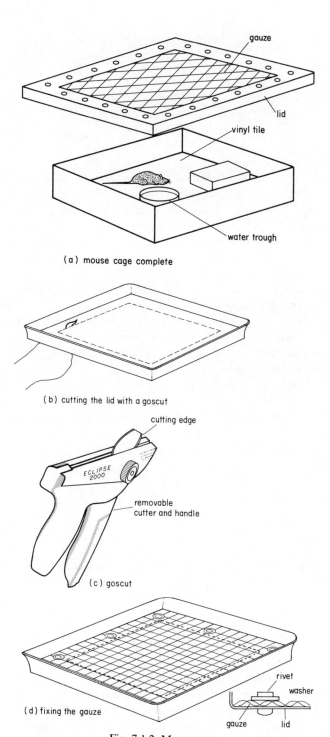

gauze

lid

vinyl tile

water trough

(a) mouse cage complete

(b) cutting the lid with a goscut

cutting edge

ECLIPSE 2000

removable cutter and handle

(c) goscut

rivet

washer

(d) fixing the gauze

gauze   lid

Fig. 7.1.2 Mouse cage

Requirements

box	biscuit tin	2–09
cover	expanded metal	3–39
fixings	leather rivets	3–40
	or nails, 100 mm	1–36

Procedure

Remove the lid of the container and turn it upside down. On the undersurface of the lid mark out a rectangle, the sides of which are about 20 to 30 mm from the edges of the lid. Cut out this rectangle (Ins. (b)) taking care not to damage the margin or the edges of the lid. A neat method for doing this is to use a goscut which is a nibbling tool with replaceable cutters (Ins. (c)). If you do not have access to this tool, use a hacksaw after drilling a starter hole in the lid. (Refer to Section 2.3.3 for drilling holes into thin metal sheet.) A hole of 6 or 9 mm diameter should admit a junior hacksaw blade which may be used to make an initial cut large enough to admit the standard hacksaw. Resting the lid on a piece of hardboard, cut through the metal and hardboard simultaneously. When this is done, flatten the cut edges and file away any irregularities.

Cut a piece of expanded metal or steel wire gauze large enough to fit inside the lid. Drill holes around the margin of the lid to admit the rivets and, with these, neatly fix the gauze to the lid. Washers help to increase the area of contact between the rivets and the gauze (Ins. (d)).

The floor of the cage should be lined with a piece of PVC floor-tiling for easy cleaning. It may be littered with two or three cigarette cartons or large matchboxes in which the mice may shelter.

7.1.3 Traps for small animals

Tools: kits A and C

The traps described here are intended for catching mice or lizards but could easily be increased in size for larger animals such as rats. The main difficulty is to contain the animal once it is caught. In both traps the animal drops into a large container and after which the trap is ready for a further catch.

(a)   *The see-saw trap*

Description

The trap is shown in Ins. (a). The bait is impaled on the end of a length of wire extending beyond the far edge of the see-saw. The animal, on trying to reach the bait, upsets the see-saw and tumbles into the container which could be a 18-litre (4-gallon) kerosene can. A piece of string attached to the see-saw returns it to its initial position and so the trap is automatically reset.

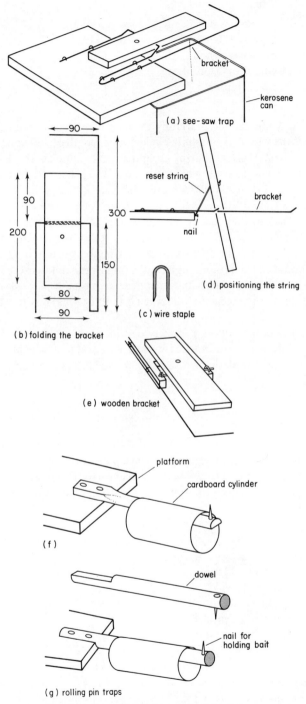

bracket

kerosene
can

(a) see-saw trap

90

90

200

90

80

90

(b) folding the bracket

300

150

(c) wire staple

reset string

bracket

nail

(d) positioning the string

(e) wooden bracket

platform

cardboard cylinder

(f)

dowel

nail for
holding bait

(g) rolling pin traps

Fig. 7.1.3 Traps for small animals

Requirements

base	plywood, 6 mm	1–14
see-saw	plywood, 6 mm	1–14
bracket	wire 2 or 3 mm diam.	2–21
fixings	wire, staples	1–37
	20 mm long	

Drill a hole of 3 mm diameter laterally through the see-saw about 90 mm from one end. Pass the wire A through this hole until a length of 120 mm protrudes at the other side. Bend this end sharply at right angles. Complete the bending of the remainder of the wire according to Ins. (b). The wire is fixed to the platform with wire staples (Ins. (c)) or nails which are bent over to clamp it. Ensure that the hinge is about 80 mm off the edge of the platform. The arms of the hinge may be turned up slightly so that the see-saw rests in a horizontal position.

When the trap is operated, the longer end should be prevented from swinging over the hinge by attaching a short piece of string between it and the platform. The string should be just long enough for the movement not to exceed an angle of 85° (Ins. (d)). The centre of gravity is therefore kept on the near side of the hinge and so the weight of the see-saw will return it to its original position and so reset the trap.

An alternative construction using wooden brackets is shown in Ins. (e). The pivot is a straight rod, held in place by two wire staples (or bent nails) driven underneath the see-saw platform and another two staples driven into the tops of the arms.

(b)   *The rolling pin trap*

This is a very simple trap and is recommended as a 'first try'. It consists of a rod or rounded beam protruding horizontally from a platform. A cardboard cylinder is slipped over the beam before the bait is attached to its free end. The cylinder, which is free to rotate, causes the animal to lose its balance and so it falls into the container.

Requirements

platform	plywood, 12 mm	1–13	300 × 100	1
beam	timber, 12 × 12	1–03	300	1
	or dowel, 12 mm diam.	3–23	300 mm long	1
roller	toilet roll cylinder	2–10		

Procedure

If a batten beam is used, round off two adjacent edges for a distance of about 200 mm from one end (Ins. (f)). Fix the square end to the platform, allowing the rounded portion to project over the edge. Slip the cylinder over the beam.

A 25 mm nail, for holding the bait, is driven upwards through the free end of the beam. To reduce the possibility of wood splitting, a hole of 1 or 1.5 mm diameter could be drilled to take the nail.

If a dowel beam is used, one end should be flattened either by sawing or filing, to make it easier to fix it firmly to the platform (Ins. (g)).

7.1.4 Auxanometer (growth-meter)

Frame: stand
Tools : kit A

Description

An auxanometer is a device for monitoring the growth of a plant. Usually the growth is magnified through a system of levers. Our design uses a single lever attached to the hoarding of a stand. In order that the hoarding should not obstruct the positioning and growth of the plant, it is cut to a wedged triangular shape with the pivot of the lever places at the apex (Ins. (a)).

Requirements

base	plywood, 12 mm	1–13	300 × 300	1
upright post	plywood, 12 mm	1–13	300 × 20	1
bracket	timber, 40 × 20	1–04	150 × 40	1
hoarding (triangle)	plywood	1–14	300 × 300	1
pivotal bracket	steel, 1 mm thick	3–30	140 × 20	1
lever arm	plywood, 12 mm	1–13	250 × 10	1
washers	hole 6 mm diam.	1–27		1

Procedure

The stand is assembled with the upright post placed as shown in Ins. (b). The triangular hoarding is slightly truncated, 200 mm from the hypotenuse (Ins. (c)) and is then screwed to the front of the post with its longest edge parallel to the post and 100 mm from it (Ins. (d)).

Bend the steel strip to the shape shown in Ins. (e) and drill clearance holes 10 mm from each end to accept the bolts and screws used to fix the pivotal bracket near the apex of the hoarding. If woodscrews are used drive them through the hoarding into a wooden batten. Drill an additional hole through the middle of this bracket. A 1-inch by No. 8 screw, inserted through this hole and driven into the hoarding, will serve as a pivot to hold the lever arm.

One end of the lever arm is cut to a point.

Starting at a distance of 10 mm from the other end, drill four holes, at 20 mm intervals, with a diameter of 5 mm. The fourth hole is used for the pivot.

Insert the screw through the hole in the pivotal bracket and then through the fourth hole in the arm. A washer may be placed on either side of the arm (Ins. (f)).

202

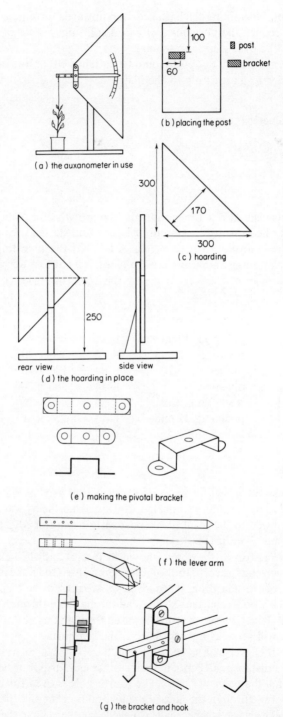

(b) placing the post

Ø post
▧ bracket

(a) the auxanometer in use

(c) hoarding

rear view   side view
(d) the hoarding in place

(e) making the pivotal bracket

(f) the lever arm

(g) the bracket and hook

Fig. 7.1.4 An auxanometer

A hook, made from stiff iron wire, is inserted into any of the other holes (depending on the degree of magnification required (Ins. (g)). Counting from the end towards the pivot, the holes should give magnifications of 3, 4.5 and 9 respectively if the longer arm of the lever is exactly 180 mm long.

In use, a potted plant may be placed on the base of the auxanometer directly under the hook. One end of a length of cotton is attached to the tip of the plant and the other is tied to the hook. The length of the string is adjusted till the lever points to the upper reaches of the scale. As the plant grows the pointer will tilt downward and its position may be recorded from time to time to obtain a record of the growth pattern.

7.1.5 Skeletons

Tools: sharp knife, old toothbrush

Description

This project describes an efficient method for removing traces of meat, fat, blood etc. from a carcass and so leaving a clean skeleton.

Requirements

container	plastic	2–04	4 litres	1
cover	glass plate, 3 mm	3–21	200 × 300	2
insulation	styrofoam	2–40		as needed
softening agent	(see text)			

Procedure

Remove the skin and all the entrails of the animal. If it is a large animal such as a dog, divide it up into manageable portions (e.g., head, neck, separate limbs etc.). Cut away as much of the meat as possible.

Each piece is then placed into a separate container of warm water containing a small quantity of washing soda. Allow the liquid to simmer (not boil) till the meat is quite soft and easily removed with a knife. It may be scrubbed with an old nylon toothbrush till clean.

A very efficient method of maceration (flesh removal) involves the use of papain powder (meat tenderizer) which is extracted from pawpaws. In fact, pawpaw skins and leaves may be used. They are placed with the specimen, in water and kept at a temperature of 37–45 ° C for two or three days, after which time all the flesh would have been digested away. In order to maintain this temperature for such a long time it is suggested to improvise a simple solar cooker using a plastic container. A cover is made from two panes of window-glass separated by a frame of polystyrene, 20 mm thick, and securely taped together (Ins. (a)). This is ideal for small specimens.

The rays of sun, entering through the glass, will heat up the interior. The heat

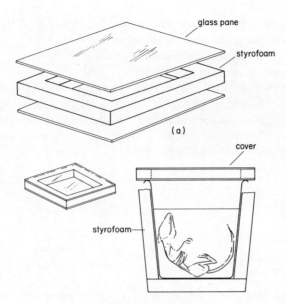

Fig. 7.1.5 Skeletons

will be prevented from escaping by the insulation and the double-glazed cover. Rinse the skeleton thoroughly. Empty the detergent solution from the cooker, fill it with 3 litres of clean water. Place the skeleton in the water and, with the glass cover in position, leave it in the sun for a further three days, changing the water at least twice a day. This will remove the blood from the bones. Some bones may still contain traces of fat. Dry them thoroughly and soak in petrol for a few days. It may be necessary to drill holes into the ends of the larger bones to facilitate the penetration of the solvent. The container for the solvent must be airtight or degreasing must be done in the open air.

The bones may be bleached with a preparation made from

> 50 ml hydrogen peroxide (20 volume solution),
> 250 ml water,
> a few drops of strong ammonium hydroxide.

Sprinkle a thin layer of bleaching powder (calcium hypochlorite) and allow this to dissolve slowly. Larger quantities of this solution may be prepared. Leave the bones in it for 24 hours. Then dry thoroughly.

The bones will be easier to keep clean if they are covered with a thin film of polystyrene cement. Dry and mount bones using adhesive and wire as needed.

7.2 GEOGRAPHY EQUIPMENT

7.2.1 Wet-and-dry hygrometer

Frame: stand
Tools : kit A

Description

Two thermometers are mounted next to each other on a stand. The bulb of the wet thermometer is kept moist by a wick immersed in water.

Requirements

base	plywood, 12 mm or	1–13	100 × 70	1
	blockboard, 12 mm	1–10	100 × 75	1
hoarding	plywood, 6 mm	1–14	250 × 100	1
brackets	timber, 75 × 12	1–02	100	2
clamps	timber, 14 × 12*	1–03	100	2
	timber, 8 × 12* or	1–03	100	2
	spring clips, 5 mm	3–36		4
thermometers	− 10°C to 50°C	5–14–02		2
tray	plastic container	2–04		1
wick	cloth	2–13	100 × 15	1

*timber of 25 mm by 12 mm section cut lengthwise.

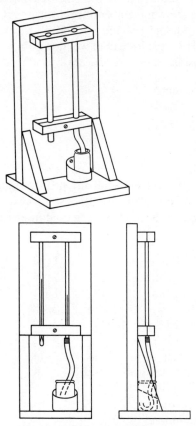

Fig. 7.2.1 Wet-and-dry hygrometer

206

Procedure

Construct the stand as shown. The clamps are intended to hold the thermometers in place without exerting any stress on the glass. They should be quite square and identical in every respect. Any remaining irregularities are taken up by placing pieces of rubber, plastic or cloth between the thermometers and the wood. The removable clamp is screwed to the fixed one. The clearance holes should be large so that the screws fit quite loosely.

The tray is cut from a plastic bottle (such as a washing-up dispenser). Cutting it diagonally, about 20 mm from the bottom, makes it easier to screw to the hoarding. A small bottle containing water is placed in the tray.

Mutton cloth probably makes the best wick. Wrap one end around the thermometer which is nearer to the container and tie it with cotton thread. Place the free end in water in the container.

A hole drilled near the top of the hoarding will allow the hygrometer to be hung from a nail in the wall.

The clamps are placed about 120 mm apart. They grip the topmost end of the thermometer and the part just above the bulb thus leaving visible the middle part of the thermometer and allowing temperatures from − 5 °C to 45 °C to be read. This temperature range should be sufficient for most tropical countries.

With spring-clips (terry clips) instead of wooden clamps, the full length of the thermometer will be visible.

7.2.2 Eclipse demonstration

Frame: bench
Tools : kit A

Description

The sun and the earth are fixed at the ends of a bench, 500 mm long. The sun is a frosted lightbulb; the earth, a tennis-ball on a peg. The moon, a ping-pong ball, is mounted on one end of a dowel or a length of stiff wire inserted into a length of timber which can be rotated around the peg holding the earth.

Requirements

base	plywood, 12 mm	1–13	1000 × 100	1
feet	plywood, 12 mm	1–13	100 × 20	2 or 3
arm	plywood, 12 mm	1–13	400 × 20	1
sun	lamp	3–48		1 each
	socket frosted lamp, 100 W	3–49		
	twin flexible lead	3–42		3 m
earth	old tennis ball, 60 mm diam.	2–14		1
moon	ping-pong ball (or other ball) 25 to 37 mm diam.	2–14		1
earth axis	dowel, tube or rod 6 to 12 mm diam.	3–23	150 mm long	
moon axis	dowel (6 mm), rod (3 mm) or thick wire	3–23	150 mm long	

Procedure

Assemble the bench, placing the feet 50 mm from the ends. Draw a centre line along the top surface of the bench. All fixtures are to be positioned along this line (Ins.(a)). The lamp-holder, complete with the twin-flexible lead, is mounted exactly over one of the feet.

Drill a hole, with the exact diameter of the Earth-axis dowel, along the centre line just 50 mm from one end. If the feet of the bench are correctly placed, this hole should pass through one of them and should therefore be 24 mm deep. Spread some vinyl adhesive inside the hole and insert the dowel until its end lies flush with the undersurface of the foot. The dowel may be fixed more securely by driving a small nail or pin into it through the side of the foot as shown in Ins. (b). Place a washer on the dowel.

A hole of the same diameter is also drilled at the exact midpoint of the arm. This hole should be slightly enlarged with sandpaper so that when it is placed on the dowel the arm can rotate freely around it.

Drill a smaller hole 20 mm from the end of the arm to take the moon axis dowel or rod. The heights of the axes should be adjusted so that, after the assembly is complete, the earth, moon and sun should be in line horizontally. You may adopt the same technique, described in Chapter 5, for the horizontal alignment of the components on an optical bench, i.e. measuring H, the height of the centre of the lamp from its base. However it may be easier, in this case to determine the heights of the axes by trial and error.

The simplest method for mounting the earth is to cut a circular hole in the ball, large enough to admit the dowel. When the ball is arranged squarely on the dowel, a small tack or pin should be driven through the top into the dowel (Ins. (c)). The moon should have a diameter appreciably less than that of the lamp bulb so that it would cast a discernible umbra and penumbra on the earth (Ins. (d)). A hollow table-tennis ball may be mounted in the same manner as the earth on a dowel. If a solid rubber ball, or, perhaps, a golf ball (which has an ideal cratered lunar-type surface) is used, then it could be drilled before being impaled on a rod or a length of stiff wire which is firmly embedded in the arm.

In use, the arm is rotated so that both solar and lunar eclipses may be demonstrated. Furthermore, if tropical and polar zones are painted on the earth, the apparatus may also be used to explain the seasons (Ins. (e)). The apparatus is rotated bodily about the sun while the geographical axis of rotation of the earth is kept pointing in the same direction (Ins. (f) and (g)).

7.2.3 Sundial

Frame: stand
Tools : kit A

Description

The sundial is about 100 mm high on a base measuring 400 mm by 200 mm (Ins. (a)). Ideally, it should be constructed of aluminium but steel sheet or waterproof timber may also be used. In the latter case, teak would be preferred as would any naturally waterproof timber mentioned in Table 1.2, but plywood or blockboard, if it is given a good covering of primer and paint, should be able to withstand the weather.

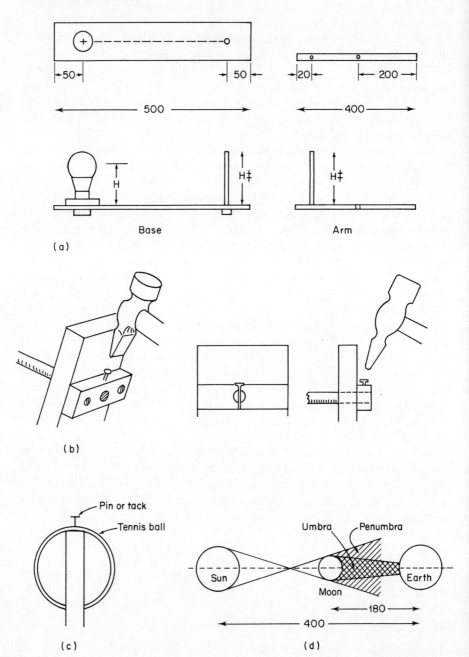

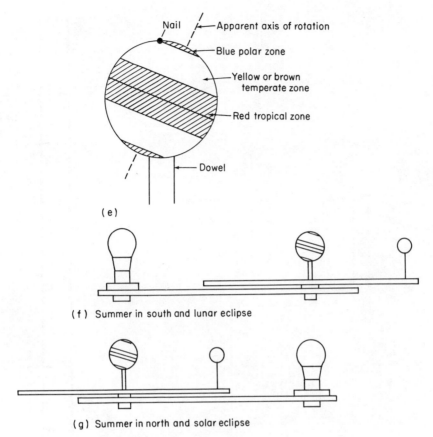

(e)

(f) Summer in south and lunar eclipse

(g) Summer in north and solar eclipse

Fig. 7.2.2 Demonstration eclipse apparatus

The instrument has a time scale which is correct for any location provided that the design of the fin is closely adhered to.

When the sun shines, the fin casts a shadow on the dial plate. The top edge gives a shadow line which indicates the time of day on the time scale. The seasonal shift of the sun to the north or south of the equator, is compensated for by setting this edge at an angle, λ, (see Ins. (a)) which is equal to the latitude of the place where it is to be located.

Requirements

(a) Metal model

dial base (B)	plate, 2 mm thick	3–20	400×200	1
fin (F)	plate, 2 mm thick	3–20	150×100	1
brackets	angle, 10 mm by 10 mm*	3–20	15 mm	4

210

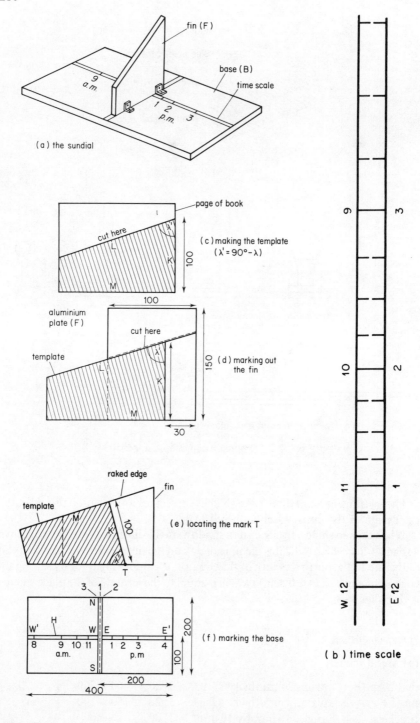

fin (F)

9
a.m.

base (B)
time scale

1 2
p.m. 3

(a) the sundial

page of book

cut here
λ'
L
100
K
M

(c) making the template
(λ' = 90° − λ)

100

aluminium
plate (F)

cut here
template
λ
L
150
K
M
30

(d) marking out
the fin

raked edge
fin
template
M
K
100
L
λ
T

(e) locating the mark T

3 1 2
N
H
W' W E E'
8 9 10 11 1 2 3 4
a.m. p.m
S
200
100
200
400

(f) marking the base

9   3
10   2
11   1
W 12   E 12

(b) time scale

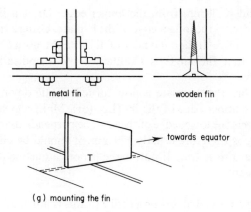

metal fin   wooden fin

towards equator

T

(g) mounting the fin

Fig. 7.2.3 The sundial

(b) Wooden model

| dial base (B) | blockboard, 12 mm | 1–10 | 400 × 200 | 1 |
| fin (F) | blockboard, 12 mm | 1–10 | 150 × 100 | 1 |

*made from 2 mm plate

Procedure

The purpose of the following design is to enable you to construct a sundial which is ready for use, i.e., it already has a time scale which is correct for your location. The time scale, shown in Ins. (b), is an exact replica of the scale which will be transferred to the dial plate. With the help of this you can inscribe the correct markings for the dial. None of the steps is complicated but it is important that you read each direction carefully to make certain that you understand what is required.

Step 1 Find out the exact latitude of your location. We will refer to this as λ.

Step 2 Making the template. A template, required for marking out the fin of the sundial, is made from a page of your exercise book. Make a mark exactly 100 mm along one of the shorter edges of the page (Ins. (c)). From this mark draw a line at an angle of $(90 - \lambda)$ degrees to the edge and cut along this line. The template is the shaded part. Mark the 100 mm side as K, the longest side as L, and the angle which they contain as λ' where

$$\lambda' = 90° - \lambda$$

Mark the side opposite L as M.

Step 3 Marking out the fin. Take the rectangular metal plate (F in the requirements list) and lay the template on it with M coinciding with the shorter edge (Ins. (d)) and K 30 mm from the longer edge. Draw a line along L and extend it until it reaches the longer edge of the F-plate. Using a hacksaw, cut very carefully along this edge. If the cut is not exactly straight, use a file to straighten it, ensuring always that the angle is maintained by periodically matching the template to the fin.

Having done this, the template is now turned upside down so that M now coincides with the upper edge of the fin (Ins. (e)). Make a clear mark T at the point where K meets the lower edge of the fin. The perpendicular distance from T to the raked edge is therefore exactly 100 mm. It should be checked, by direct measurement, that this is true. If not, make proper adjustments because it is a critical measurement.

Step 4 Marking out the dial. Using a scribe (if this is not available, a ballpoint pen or a hard pencil, 2H grade, with a fine point), draw a line (1) down the middle of the dial plate (Ins. (f)). Equally spaced on either side of this line, draw two more lines (2 and 3) running parallel to the first and separated by the thickness of the fin. That is to say, if the fin is made of material 6 mm thick, then these two lines should lie 3 mm on either side of the middle line.

Now draw a fourth line (4), along the middle of the plate in a direction at right angles to the other lines. This line will intersect lines 2 and 3 at the points E and W respectively. Line 4 will have two arms EE' and WW' respectively.

Table 7.2.3   Correction for solar mean time

Date		Correction (minutes)	Date		Correction (minutes)
Jan	1	+ 03	Jul	10	+ 05
	11	+ 08		20	+ 06
	21	+ 13		30	+ 06
	31	+ 14	Aug	9	+ 05
Feb	10	+ 14		19	+ 04
	20	+ 13		29	+ 01
Mar	2	+ 12	Sept	8	− 02
	12	+ 10		18	− 06
	22	+ 07		28	− 09
Apr	1	+ 04	Oct	8	− 12
	11	+ 01		18	− 15
	21	− 01		28	− 16
May	1	− 03	Nov	7	− 16
	11	− 04		17	− 15
	21	− 04		27	− 12
	31	− 02	Dec	7	− 09
June	10	− 01		17	− 04
	20	+ 01		27	+ 01
	30	+ 04		31	+ 03

+ to be added to your sundial reading.
− to be subtracted from your sundial reading.

Starting from E or W, inscribe the time scale marks according to the measurements given in Table 7.2.3. Alternatively, the time scale drawn in Ins. (b) may be reproduced on tracing on airmail paper and then transposed onto EE′ and WW′.

These measurements are based on the assumption that K, the vertical edge of the template, is 100 mm long. If any other value is used, the scale may be recalculated according to the equation

$$ED = K.\tan(3.75x)$$

where ED is the calculated distance from E (or W) to the time-mark and x is the time, in quarter-hours, before and after 12 noon. For example, the value of x is 11 at 2.45 p.m. and also at 9.15 a.m.

Step 5 Mounting the fin. The dial is held horizontally with the lines EE′ and WW′ pointing east and west respectively. Place the fin vertically with the lower edge fitting into the space between lines 2 and 3 on the dial plate. Position the fin so that:

(a) the shorter vertical edge points towards the equator, i.e. if you are in the northern hemisphere, it should point south and vice versa;
(b) the mark T made in step 3 should coincide with E or W so that the time scale lies perpendicular to the plane of the fin *at this point* (Ins. (g)).

With these conditions satisfied, secure the plate in a vertical position to the dial plate.

If the sundial is to be made of metal, then it should be fixed with metal brackets. Welding or brazing may cause distortion.

If wood is used, drive two or more screws from beneath the dial plate into the bottom edge of the fins, provided that the fin is thick enough (at least 9 mm) to take the screws. Wood should be waterproofed with two coats of polyurethane varnish.

Step 6 Orienting the sundial. Place the sundial on a horizontal surface with the fin pointing along the true or geographical north–south line. True north differs from magnetic north which is obtained from a compass. In Section 9.4 a method for locating true north is described.

Step 7 Correction for standard time. The time is indicated by the edge of the shadow cast on the time scale. When the sundial has been set up according to the above instructions, it indicates local time. This is not the same as standard time as indicated on your watch. Standard time is fixed by law for all places in your country or time zone. You may compensate for the difference by tilting to the east or the west depending on whether your local time is behind or ahead of standard time. The amount of tilt is discussed in Section 9.5.

214

Step 8 Correcting for solar mean time. A further complication is introduced by
the fact that the length of the solar day is not constant, but varies periodically
throughout the year. Your sundial time will be correct only four times in the year
around the following dates:

April 16
June 13
September 1
December 25

At other days it may be as much as 16 minutes fast or slow. This variation shown
in Table 7.2.3 is called the 'equation of time' and allows you to correct your
reading to solar mean time. If positive, the correction should be added to your
sundial reading.

7.2.4 Shadow clock

Frame: stand
Tools : kit A

Description

The shadow clock is a simplified version of the sundial described in Project 7.2.3
and incorporates most of the basic design featured for that instrument. It is,
however, only intended for demonstration. It is portable so that the teacher may
explain its function inside the class and then carry it to the school grounds for the
demonstration in the sun. It need not therefore be waterproofed.

Requirements

base A	plywood, 12 mm	1–13	1000 × 100	1
Upright post B	timber, 75 × 12	1–02	200	1
cross beam C	timber, 25 × 12	1–03	300	1
fasteners	plywood, 3 mm	1–15	100 × 100	1
	or hardboard	1–18		
brackets	timber, 40 × 20	1–04	100	2
feet	timber, 25 × 12	1–03	100	2

Procedure

Cut the post B, near its top edge, at an angle equal to $(90° - \lambda)$ where λ is the
angle of latitude of the location of your school. (λ is obtained from an atlas.)
    Lay the post on the worktable and place the cross-piece against the top edge.
Adjust the cross-piece so that the line through its midpoint (Ins. (b)) intersects
the bottom edge of the post (not necessarily at its midpoint). Spread some
adhesive over the join and on one face of each fastener plate. Arrange a fastener

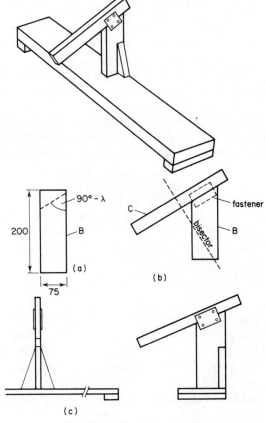

Fig. 7.2.4 The shadow clock

plate over the join and fix with half-inch nails or screws. Turn the assembly over and fix a plate on the other side as well. Using the brackets, the post may now be mounted vertically at the centre of the base with the cross-piece lying in a plane exactly perpendicular to the length of the base (Ins. (c)). Position the post over to one edge of the base to counteract the asymmetrical arrangement of the cross-piece. If you do not allow this, the structure will tend to topple over very easily.

This design ensures that the shadow of the cross-piece will always fall on the base provided that the base is aligned in an east–west direction with the cross-piece slopping down *towards the equator*, i.e. towards the south, if you are in the northern hemisphere and vice-versa, if in the southern hemisphere.

A simple method for locating true north (as distinct from magnetic north, which is obtained with a compass) is given in Section 9.4.

7.2.5 Sextant

Tools: kit A

Description

The sextant is an instrument for determining the elevation of the sun. If this measurement is taken at noon, it may be used to calculate the local angle of latitude.

The horizon is viewed through an eyepiece and seen in the horizon sight. The sextant is pointed directly south, if you are in the northern hemisphere, and vice versa. The swivel arm is adjusted till the sun, as seen in the reflector, is in line with the horizon. At this position the arm is clamped and the reading taken. This reading, E, is the elevation of the sun above the horizon. If, D, the position of the sun relative to the equator is known, the latitude, L, may be calculated as follows:

$$L = 90 + D - E$$

The angle, D, varies during the year and is a maximum of $23\frac{1}{2}$ degrees north or south of the equator when the sun lies over the Tropics of Cancer and Capricorn respectively, i.e. on the 21st of June and 22nd of December each year. At other times of the year it varies between these limits. Table 7.2.5 shows the variation of D during the year.

Requirements

board	plywood, 6 mm	1–14	200 × 200	1
arm	timber, 25 × 12	1–03	140	1
eyepiece A	tin plate*	2–06	30 × 20	1
horizon sight B	tin plate*	2–06	30 × 20	1
reflector	glass slide	4–91 or 5–33–01		1
pivot	machine bolt, 6 mm	1–27	25 mm length	1
	washers, 6 mm	or 3–65		2
	wingnut	3–65		1
pointer C	tin plate*	2–06	30 × 20	1

*the tin plate may be cut from tin cans.

Procedure

(a) *Marking out the board* Draw a line parallel to, and 30 mm from, the top edge of the board. Mark a point, A on this line at a distance of 30 mm from the left edge (Ins. (b)). With A as centre, draw an arch of radius 140 mm across the lower section of the board. At A, drill a tight-fitting hole for the bolt. Insert the bolt through this hole with the head to the rear of the board. Fix it with adhesive. It is important that the bolt should be truly perpendicular to the board.

(b) *The swivel arm* Drill a clearance hole for the bolt about 10 mm from one end of the arm. Once again, this hole should be truly perpendicular to the plane of the arm so that when it is placed on the bolt (with a washer above and below it), it should be able to rotate freely without scraping the board.

Table 7.2.5 The declination of the sun

Declination D (degrees)	Dates		Declination D (degrees)	Dates	
0	19 Mar to 21 Mar	22 Sept to 24 Sept	0	22 Sept to 24 Sept	19 Mar to 21 Mar
1	22 Mar to 23 Mar	20 Sept to 21 Sept	−1	25 Sept to 26 Sept	17 Mar to 18 Mar
2	24 Mar to 26 Mar	17 Sept to 19 Sept	−2	27 Sept to 29 Sept	14 Mar to 16 Mar
3	27 Mar to 28 Mar	15 Sept to 16 Sept	−3	30 Sept to 1 Oct	12 Mar to 13 Mar
4	29 Mar to 31 Mar	12 Sept to 14 Sept	−4	2 Oct to 4 Oct	9 Mar to 11 Mar
5	1 Apr to 2 Apr	10 Sept to 11 Sept	−5	5 Oct to 6 Oct	7 Mar to 8 Mar
6	3 Apr to 5 Apr	7 Sept to 9 Sept	−6	7 Oct to 9 Oct	4 Mar to 6 Mar
7	6 Apr to 8 Apr	4 Sept to 6 Sept	−7	10 Oct to 12 Oct	1 Mar to 3 Mar
8	9 Apr to 10 Apr	2 Sept to 3 Sept	−8	13 Oct to 14 Oct	27 Feb to 28 Feb
9	11 Apr to 13 Apr	30 Aug to 1 Sept	−9	15 Oct to 17 Oct	24 Feb to 26 Feb
10	14 Apr to 16 Apr	27 Aug to 29 Aug	−10	18 Oct to 19 Oct	22 Feb to 23 Feb
11	17 Apr to 19 Apr	24 Aug to 26 Aug	−11	20 Oct to 22 Oct	19 Feb to 21 Feb
12	20 Apr to 22 Apr	21 Aug to 23 Aug	−12	23 Oct to 25 Oct	16 Feb to 18 Feb
13	23 Apr to 25 Apr	18 Aug to 20 Aug	−13	26 Oct to 28 Oct	13 Feb to 15 Feb
14	26 Apr to 28 Apr	15 Aug to 17 Aug	−14	29 Oct to 31 Oct	10 Feb to 12 Feb
15	29 Apr to 1 May	12 Aug to 14 Aug	−15	1 Nov to 3 Nov	7 Feb to 9 Feb
16	2 May to 4 May	9 Aug to 11 Aug	−16	4 Nov to 6 Nov	4 Feb to 6 Feb
17	5 May to 8 May	5 Aug to 8 Aug	−17	7 Nov to 10 Nov	31 Jan to 3 Feb
18	9 May to 12 May	1 Aug to 4 Aug	−18	11 Nov to 14 Nov	27 Jan to 30 Jan
19	13 May to 17 May	27 July to 31 July	−19	15 Nov to 19 Nov	22 Jan to 26 Jan
20	18 May to 21 May	23 July to 26 July	−20	20 Nov to 23 Nov	18 Jan to 21 Jan
21	22 May to 27 May	17 July to 22 July	−21	24 Nov to 28 Nov	13 Jan to 17 Jan
22	28 May to 3 June	10 July to 16 July	−22	29 Nov to 5 Dec	6 Jan to 12 Jan
23	4 June to 13 June	30 June to 9 July	−23	6 Dec to 14 Dec	28 Dec to 5 Jan
23½	14 June to 29 June		−23½	15 Dec to 27 Dec	

positive values: sun in northern hemisphere
negative values: sun in southern hemisphere

218

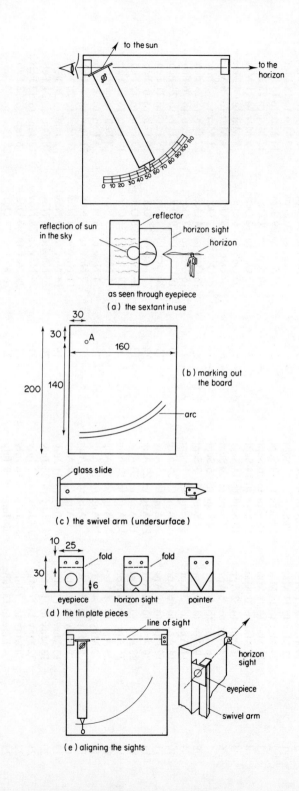

to the sun

to the
horizon

reflector

reflection of sun
in the sky

horizon sight

horizon

as seen through eyepiece
(a) the sextant in use

30

30

A

160

200

140

arc

(b) marking out
the board

glass slide

(c) the swivel arm (undersurface)

10
25

fold

fold

30

6

eyepiece   horizon sight   pointer
(d) the tin plate pieces

line of sight

horizon
sight

eyepiece

swivel arm

(e) aligning the sights

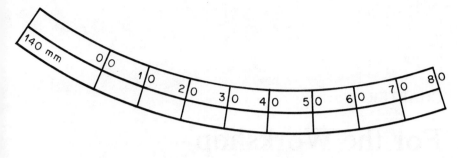

(f) the scale

Fig. 7.2.5 The sextant

Remove the arm and, using strong adhesive, attach the slide glass to the end near the hole (Ins. (c)) ensuring that this, too, will not scrape against the board when the arm is rotated.

(c) *The tin plate pieces* These are shaped according to Ins. (d):

(i)   the eyepiece. Drill a hole, 6 mm diameter, exactly 10 mm from a shorter edge.
(ii) the horizon sight. Drill a hole, 6 mm diameter, as for the eye piece, then using a hacksaw cut a neat V-shaped notch.
(iii) the pointer. Cut this piece to a V-shaped point. This piece is attached to the undersurface of the free end of the arm. The arm is then replaced on the bolt with the washers and the wing-nut.

(d) *Aligning the sights* Clamp the arm in such a position that the glass plate lies parallel to the upper edge of the board. This setting is made easier by placing a ruler with its edge against the glass plate. With the ruler in this position draw a line across the board (Ins. (e)). This is the line of sight at the ends of which the eye piece and the horizon sight should be fixed with panel pins.

(e) *Fixing the scale* Reproduce, as accurately as possible, the scale shown in Ins. (f). The centre line of this scale lies on an arc of 140 mm radius. Align this along the pencilled arc which has already been drawn on the board.

With the arm in the position described in (d), above, the zero on the scale should be directly under the pointer (see Ins. (e)). Fix the scale in this position with adhesive. It will be noticed that the pointer indicates exactly twice the angle through which the arm is rotated. For example, the arm rotates through an angle of 30° to indicate an elevation of 60°.

The sextant will be easier to use if a suitable handle is attached to the rear of the board.

Finally, the instrument may be given one or two coats of polyurethane varnish (optional).

CHAPTER 8:

For the Workshop

8.1 WORKBENCH

Tools: kits A and B

Description

This stout and robust workbench is 850 mm high, 820 mm deep (front-to-rear) and 1200 mm long. It has a worktop of 50 mm thick timber and legs of 75 mm by 75 mm posts. A well in the table-top and a shelf under it allows tools and workpieces to be kept while a job is in progress. Provision is made for mounting a carpenter vice.

Requirements

legs	timber, 75 × 75	3–32	800	4
top	timber, 150 × 50	3–32	1200	2
front board	timber, 150 × 50	3–32	1200	1
rear board	plywood, 12 mm	1–13	1200 × 200	1
end rails	timber, 100 × 40	3–32	750	4
front rail	timber, 100 × 40	3–32	1080	1
rear rail	timber, 100 × 40	3–32	1080	1
well board	plywood, 12 mm	1–13	1200 × 500	1
shelf	plywood, 12 mm	1–13	1100 × 820	1

Procedure

Fixing may, in all cases, be done with 100 mm round nails, hammered in at an angle to the surface to improve the grip (refer to Fig. 1.22). If you can afford the additional expense and time you may, instead, use 9 mm diameter dowels or 4-inch by No. 12 woodscrews or a combination of all three types.

Making the ends Lay two of the legs parallel to each other and fix the end rails (Ins. (c)). Repeat for the other two legs. These end-frames should be quite square. This is tested by measuring the diagonals and ensuring that they are equal.

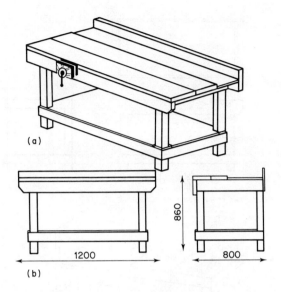

(a)

(b)

1200

800

860

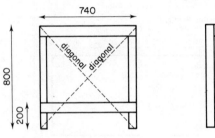

740

800

200

diagonal diagonal

(c) assembling the end-frames

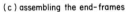

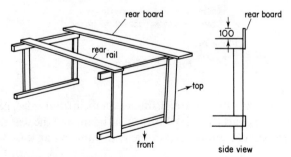

rear board

rear rail

top

front

(d) fixing the rear board and rail

rear board

100

side view

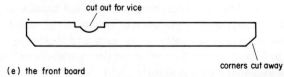

cut out for vice

corners cut away

(e) the front board

222

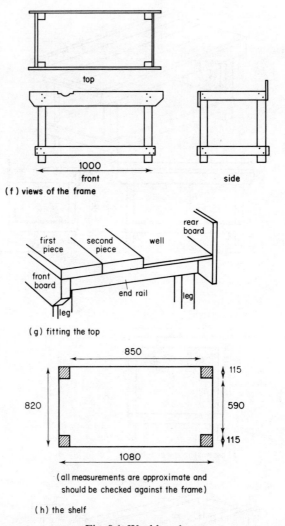

top

1000

front

side

(f) views of the frame

rear
board

first
piece

second
piece

well

front
board

end rail

leg

leg

(g) fitting the top

850

115

820

590

115

1080

(all measurements are approximate and
should be checked against the frame)

(h) the shelf

Fig. 8.1 Workbench

Fixing the rear pieces Place the end-frames on their front sides, parallel to each other and 1000 mm apart (Ins.(d)). Fix the rear board and the rear rail in position. The rear board should project above the end-frame by at least 100 mm.

Fixing the front pieces Cut away the lower corners of the front board to a distance of 50 mm. This is a safety measure to avoid bruises to your legs (and your back, if you happen to work on the floor near the table).

If you intend to install a carpenter's vice, now is the best time to cut the slot in which this is to fit under the table-top. Read the manufacturer's instructions for the exact size and shape of this slot (Ins.(e)).

Get someone to help you turn the frame completely over onto its rear face. The front board and front rail are now fixed in position. The front rail will fit over the ends of the end rails and should be fixed with nails to the end rails.

Fitting the top Having checked that the frame is square, the two top pieces are now fixed into position starting with the frontmost piece which should be flush with the front board. The well board is cut to fit exactly into the space between the second board and the rear board. Avoid leaving any gaps in the table top. Ideally the pieces should, of course, be rebated, but if care is taken this may not be necessary.

Fitting the shelf The piece of 12 mm plywood measuring 1100 mm by 820 mm should be cut to fit exactly in the space between the legs. It should fit on the rails so that it can be nailed in place along its edges. The measurements given in Ins. (h) are approximate.

8.2 A HAND-OPERATED DUPLICATOR

Description

Electrically operated duplicating machines are quite expensive and the dye-line duplicators can only produce a limited number of copies. A compromise is reached with this machine which uses ordinary office stencils and duplicating ink to produce as many copies as are required. The stencils may, of course, be filed away and re-used for further copies at a later date.

The machine consists of two parts: a base on which the paper is placed and an inking frame which holds the stencil firmly against a screen on which the ink is spread. A squeegee is used to push the ink, through the cuts in the stencil, onto the paper. The method may be compared to that of a silk-screen printing.

Requirements

base	blockboard, 12 mm	1–10	400 × 290	1
frame	blockboard, 12 mm	1–10	400 × 290	2
screen	organza or organdie	3–94	500 × 330	1

Procedure

Mark out on both B and C, a rectangle as shown in Ins. (a). Drill a 3 mm hole at one corner of each rectangle and, insert the blade of a fretsaw through it. Using the fretsaw carefully cut out these rectangular pieces so that two rigid frames are obtained (Ins. (b)). Use sandpaper to smooth the cut edges of the frame.

Align the frames accurately with each other and drill a 6.5 mm hole in each corner. Pass a bolt through each hole to ensure that the two frames can be firmly clamped together.

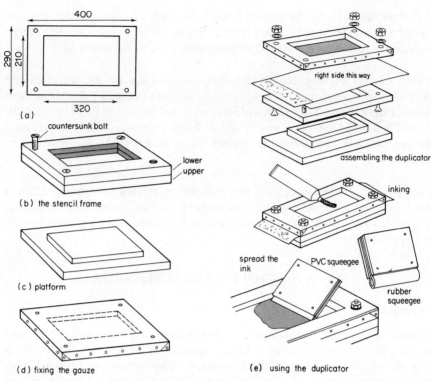

Fig. 8.2 Duplicator

One of the rectangular pieces, which were cut out of the frames, is fixed to the base. This provides a raised platform which is just accommodated by the frames when they are placed on the base (Ins. (c)).

At this stage the base platform and the two frames, after a thorough smoothing with sandpaper, should be given one or two coats of polyurethane varnish.

Remove the upper frame, using tacks or office staples, attach the organza to its lower surface (i.e. to the surface which is brought into contact with the lower frame). The organza must be stretched slightly and uniformly so that no creases or wrinkles are formed. Tacks or staples are driven into the edges of the frame instead of the undersurface, so that they do not interfere with the flush fitting of the two frames (Ins. (d)).

Use of the duplicator

Separate the two parts of the frame. Turn the upper frame with the gauze-side facing up. Remove the backing and carbon from the stencil and place the stencil, reverse side up, on the gauze, positioning it centrally. Place the lower frame over the stencil and clamp the two frames together tightly.

Place a sheet of paper on the platform. turn the frames upside down (with the gauze above the stencil) and place it over the platform so that the stencil is in contact with the paper.

Extrude some duplicating ink on the gauze and spread it with the squeegee until a uniform layer is obtained.

Lift up the frame and reject the first sheet of paper. Place a second sheet on the platform and reposition the frame assembly. Using a single sweep, draw the squeegee across the gauze.

Lift up the frame and inspect the copy to determine if (a) it is correctly positioned with respect to the stencil and (b) that the ink has been applied uniformly. Adjust for (a) and (b) if necessary. Do a second test copy, this time moving the squeegee in the opposite direction.

When you are satisfied with the copies obtained, you may proceed to produce as many as you require. In each case use only a single sweep of the squeegee, in alternating directions, trying to keep the film of ink as uniform as possible.

The squeegee

The simplest squeegee is a piece of PVC tile about 200 mm by 100 mm. The two longer edges should be rubbed down with fine emery paper to reduce wear on the organza. The PVC may be supported between two pieces of plywood or hardboard, 200 mm by 80 mm, leaving a projection of 20 mm with which the ink is spread.

Another method is to use a sheet of rubber, 200 mm by 150 mm cut from an old inner tube of a car. The sheet is folded lengthwise to produce a perfectly straight edge and then mounted between two pieces of plywood as before. This squeegee is longer-lasting and causes less wear to the organza.

8.3 BATTERY CHARGER

Basic frame: box
Tools   : kits A, C and D

Description

This unit can provide a charging current of 2 amperes. A number of accumulators, connected in series, with a combined voltage of up to 12 volts, may be charged in this way. It can therefore also be used for automobile batteries. The charger may, if necessary, be housed in a large powdered milk can.

Requirements

| transformer | 240 V, 60 VA | 5–16–13 | secondary 0–9–18 V at 2 A | 1 |
| | | or 5–16–12 | secondary 0–4.5–9V at 2.2A | 1 |

rectifier	bridge type 40 V min/			
	2 A min	5–17–04	200 V, 6 A	1
switch on–off	double pole			
	on–off	5–16–09		1
switch selector	single pole,			
	2-way	5–16–09	1 A	1
fuse holder	open type	5–16–03		1
fuse	glass	5–16–01		1
		or 3–67		
chassis	timber, 100 × 12	1–01		1
wire	insulated, solid core/	1–40	100 mm	3
cable	3-core flexible 5 A	1–43	2 metres	1
grommet	6 mm diameter	5–10–09		1
case	powdered milk can	2–06	900 g size	1
	or box, wooden	—	constructed	1
	300 × 250 × 200			

Procedure

The circuit is shown, in schematic form (Ins. (a)) and again, with actual components (Ins. (b)).

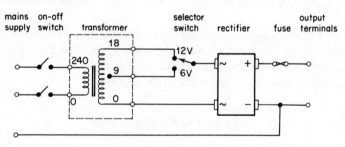

(a) schematic diagram

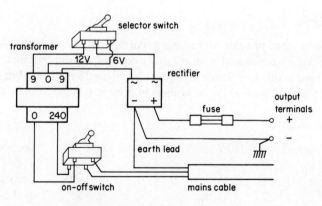

(b) component diagram

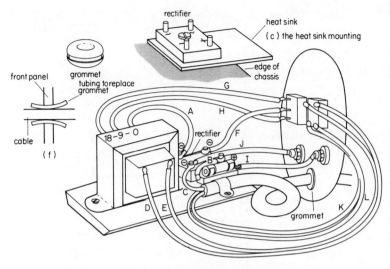

rectifier

heat sink

(c) the heat sink mounting

edge of chassis

front panel

grommet

tubing to replace grommet

cable

(f)

18-9-0

rectifier

A   H

G

F

J

B   I

C

D   E

grommet

K

L

(d) the interconnections and layout

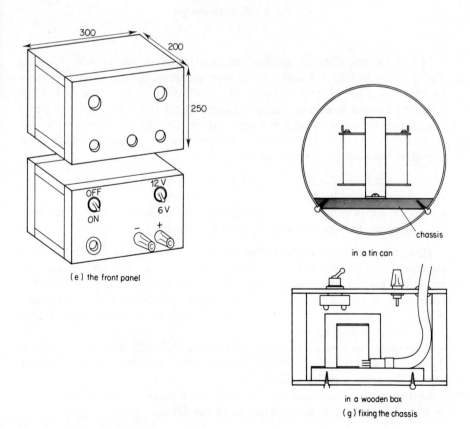

300

200

250

OFF
ON

12 V
6 V

−   +

(e) the front panel

chassis

in a tin can

in a wooden box

(g) fixing the chassis

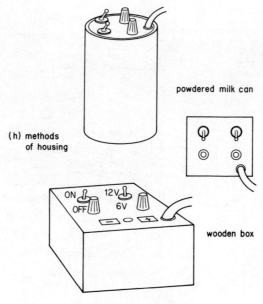

Fig. 8.3 Battery charger

Mount the transformer, rectifier and fuse holder on the chassis or circuit board. Place the heat sink under the rectifier and let it extend beyond the chassis by 25 mm (Ins. (c)). A margin about 10 mm around the edge of the board will allow for fixing it to the case. Strip the outer sheath from the mains cable to a distance of 200 mm from one end. Fix the cable to the chassis with a clamp across the end of the sheath. The interconnections between the rectifier and the chassis-mounted components are now made:

A.   from the transformer secondary to the first rectifier input terminal.
B.   from the fuse holder to the rectifier positive terminal.
C.   The mains cable earth (shortened to 50 mm) to the rectifier negative terminal. (All connections are shown in Ins. (d).)

Holes for mounting the switches and terminals are drilled or cut into the lid of the case (Ins. (e)). These components are inserted and firmly fixed in place. The entry hole for the mains supply cable should be lined with a grommet of the correct size. If this is not available, rubber tubing, or rubber sheet rolled to form a tube, may be inserted in the hole before the wire is drawn through it. Ensure that the fit is very tight (Ins. (f)).

If necessary tie a tight knot in the cable on the inner side of the grommet hole. This will prevent the cable from slipping and will remove the strain on the solder joint if the cable is pulled accidently.

Clearly mark the terminals as positive (+) and negative (−), the selector switch as 6 V or 12 V and the mains switch as ON or OFF.

Use flexible insulated cable, about 150 mm long for the following connections between the chassis-mounted components and those on the front panel:

D, E. from the on–off switch output terminals to the transformer secondary.

F.   from the selector switch common to the second rectifier input.

G.   from the upper terminal of the selector switch to the transformer 18 V secondary terminal.

H.   from the lower terminal of the selector switch to the transformer 9 V (middle) terminal.

I.   from the fuse holder to the charger positive output terminal.

J.   from the rectifier negative terminal (earth) to the character negative output terminal.

K, L. connect the 200 mm long live and neutral leads from the mains cable to the on–off switch input terminals. Pass the free end of the cable through the grommet and fix a three-pin plug to it.

Place the chassis in the box and screw it down. If a tin can is used, screws should be driven through the walls of the can into the wooden chassis (Ins. (g)).

Place the front panel in position. Label the switches and terminals clearly. Ins. (h) shows two ways in which the charger may finally be housed.

Further remarks on this project

In this project the transformer will be the most expensive item and we have chosen one which may just be available locally. It is possible that you may have placed an overseas order for one. If so, you may just as well order the correct type. Charger transformers are available with the following secondary voltages:

    for 3-volt batteries—5-volt supply
    for 6-volt batteries—9-volt supply
    for 12-volt batteries—17-volt supply

In size, you can expect that a 17-volt, 2-ampere transformer will measure about 70 mm by 70 mm by 80 mm. If you only intend to recharge the usual laboratory-type accumulators, you may economize by purchasing a transformer with only a 6-volt secondary supply. With this, two alkali cells (2 volts each) may be recharged together. A further economy to be considered is to use a low-power cassette recorder transformer. These are usually rated at 6 volts and 0.3 ampere, and are available from electronic repair shops. Use such a transformer in a trickle charger (i.e. a charger which supplies current at a very low rate). It will take two or three days to recharge your cells but if you have only a few and you only require them once a week, such a charger will be quite adequate and may cost less than a tenth of the price of an 18-volt, 2-ampere, unit.

Lastly it should be mentioned that chargers for use with car batteries are often produced much more cheaply than it would cost anyone to make from standard components. If you cannot get one from dealers of car supplies in large towns, it may be well worth your while to get one through a friend living or travelling

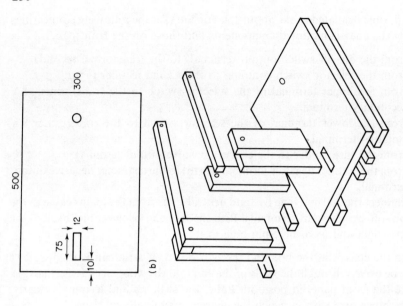

(b)

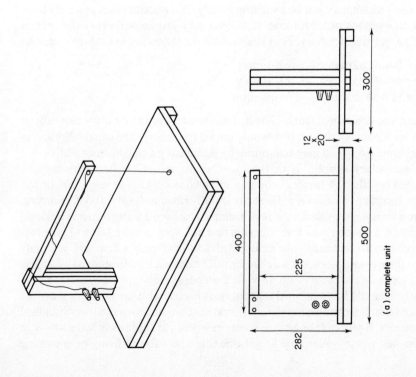

(a) complete unit

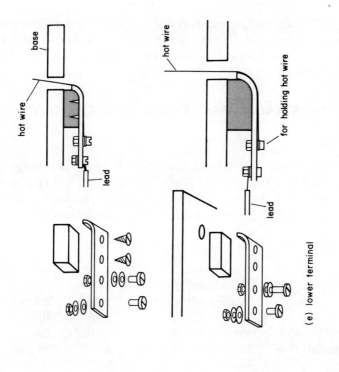

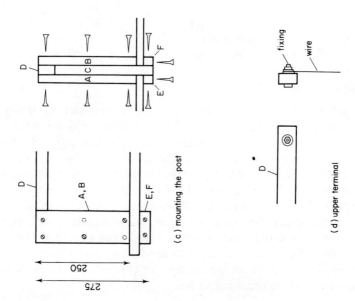

Fig. 8.4 Polystyrene cutter

(c) mounting the post

(d) upper terminal

(e) lower terminal

overseas. In Britain, dealers such as Halford's and Universal Car Supplies (the latter found in Surrey) usually have one or two types on offer. Your friend may obtain the addresses of the nearest branch of these firms from the appropriate telephone directory.

8.4 STYROFOAM CUTTER (HOT-WIRE CUTTER)

Description

This is a very useful teaching accessory and is being increasingly used in preparing displays, relief maps, etc. The model described here may be operated directly from a 12 V battery charger such as that described in Project 8.3. Styrofoam blocks up to 220 mm thick may be cut with this unit (Ins. (a)).

Requirements

base	blockboard, 12 mm	1–10	500 × 300	1
post A, B	blockboard, 12 mm	1–10	250 × 75	2
C	blockboard, 12 mm	1–10	250 × 75	1
arm D	timber, 25 × 12	1–03	400	1
feet	timber, 40 × 20	1–04	500	2
lower terminal	brass strip, 3 mm	4–22	50 × 12	1
	brass nuts and bolts, 2.5 mm diam.	3–27	10 mm long	2
	timber, 25 × 12	1–03	20	1
upper terminal	brass nut and bolt 2.5 mm diam.	3–27	49 mm long	1
input terminals		5–16–11		2
leads	twin flexible cable 5 A	3–42	600 mm	1
wire	constantan, 26G	5–10–05	320 mm	1

Procedure

Two holes are cut into the base (Ins. (b)). One is rectangular, 12 mm by 75 mm, and is made using a fretsaw. A second hole, is drilled with a 6 mm bit.

The post is constructed of three pieces of 12 mm blockboard (or plywood, if the former is not available), (Ins. (c)). The middle piece passes through the rectangular hole and is held firmly by the two brackets which are screwed to it and to the undersurface of the base. The fixed end of the arm rests on top of the middle piece and is firmly clamped, with woodscrews, between the outer pieces. It therefore projects at right angles to the post. The constantan wire is attached to the free end of the arm by means of a bolt and screw (Ins. (d)). The wire then passes through the round hole and is clamped firmly, underneath the base, to a metal strip. This strip curves toward the hole (Ins. (e)) and provides a smooth surface around which the wire can pass.

The strip is mounted on a small block of wood. This leaves one end free for the attachment of the electric lead wire and the constantan hot-wire. The hot-wire passes around the curve of the brass strip and up into the hole in the base. Do not allow the brass strip to project into the hole because it will cool down this end of the wire. Such uneven heating makes it difficult to control the cutting of the styrofoam.

Before the wire is fixed, the arm should be pushed down 20 mm below its horizontal level. This gives tension and compensates for the expension of the wire when it is heated.

A lead is attached to each end of the heater wire. After passing along the arm, in one instance, and underneath the base, in order, they may be brought to a pair of terminal posts fixed to the pillar. Another pair of flexible leads, attached to the terminals, will carry current from the accumulator or 12-volt transformer. Alternatively the heater leads may themselves be flexible and terminate in battery clips which can be attached to the accumulator.

The wire will draw about 2 amperes. This should make it hot enough to cut blocks of polystyrene foam up to 220 mm thick at a rate of about 10 mm per second.

8.5   CONTINUITY TESTER

Frame: box
Tools : kits A and B

Description

The tester is contained in a box. Contact is made through crocodile clips and continuity is indicated when a pilot lamp lights up. A size C dry-cell battery supplies the voltage.

Requirements

ends	timber, 25 × 12	1–03	50	2
side	plywood, 6 mm	1–14	80 × 25	2
top	hardboard	1–18	62 × 80	1
bottom	hardboard	1–18	62 × 80	1
indicator	lamp, 3 V, 0.3 W	3–55		1
battery	size C (HP11)	3–41		1
	25 mm diam.			
	48 mm length			
battery terminals	toothpaste	2–15		1
	tube (85 ml size)			
terminals	crocodile	4–45 or		
	clips	5–10–02		2

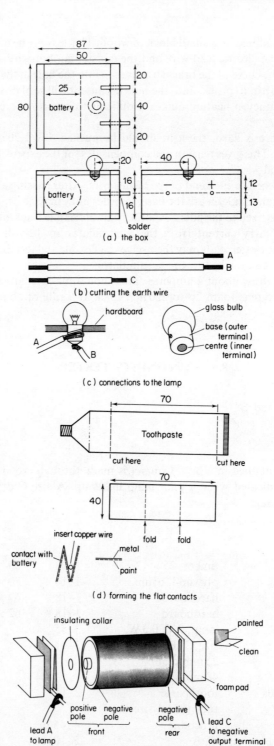

(a) the box

(b) cutting the earth wire

(c) connections to the lamp

(d) forming the flat contacts

(e) the battery assembly

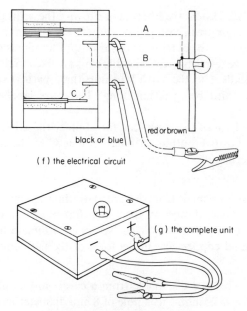

(f) the electrical circuit

red or brown

black or blue

(g) the complete unit

Fig. 8.5 Continuity tester

leads	copper wire,			
	1.5 mm² solid*	1–40	50 mm	2
	copper wire,			
	1.5 mm² solid*	1–40	25 mm	2
	three-core cable,†			
	flexible, 15 A	1–42	300 mm	1

* start with 30 mm of twin-and-earth cable, strip off all the insulation and cut into required lengths.
† strip off outer sheath only.

Procedure

Assemble the box (Ins. (a)) but do not fix the top. Drill a hole in the top just large enough to accommodate the base of the lamp. Insert the lamp in this hole. Prepare the following pieces.

Solid copper wire   Strip all the insulation off the twin-and-earth cable, leaving three lengths of wire of 1.5 mm² cross-sectional area (1.5 mm diameter), each 50 mm long. Cut one of these in two pieces of 25 mm length.

Drill two holes of 1.5 mm diameter in one end of the box as shown in Ins. (a). Push the wires of 25 mm length through the holes and apply spots of solder at each end to hold the pieces in place. These are the output terminals. The two long pieces of wire are to be used with the flat contacts as described below.

Flexible leads   Strip the outer sheath from the three-core flexible cable thus leaving three insulated leads: the live (red or brown), the neutral (black or blue), and the earth (green or green with yellow stripes), each 300 mm long. Solder the live and neutral leads to the outer ends of the output terminals marking these as positive and negative respectively. Crocodile clips are fixed to the free ends of the live and neutral leads. Cut the earth lead into three parts, two of these being 120 mm long, the third being 60 mm long. These are labelled A, B, and C respectively (Ins. (b)).

Solder A to the base of the lamp (Ins. (c)). Solder the other end of B to the inside end of the positive output terminal. Solder C to the inside end of the negative output terminal.

Flat contacts　These are made from discarded toothpaste tubes. Cut the ends off the tube and slit it lengthways to form two flat pieces of metal measuring approximately 70 mm by 40 mm. Fold each piece according to Ins. (d). Insert the longer pieces of solid copper wire in the folds of the flat contact as shown.

Insulating collar　This is a disc made from a cardboard or plastic sheet. The diameter of the disc is 25 mm. Cut a hole of 8 mm diameter in the centre of the disc. The disc fits over the positive end of the dry cell with the positive terminal protruding through the hole (Ins. (e)).

The battery assembly　The battery is to be installed in the box in the position shown in Ins. (a). Place the foam pads and the flat contacts in position. Sandwich the battery between the flat contacts with the insulating collar and the solid wires in place (Ins. (e)). Solder the free end of A and C to the solid copper wires in contact with the positive and the negative ends of the battery respectively.

The circuit should now be complete. Check the interconnections against those shown in Ins. (f). The unit may now be tested by bringing the crocodile clips into contact with each other. The lamp should light up. Finally, place the top in position and fix with $\frac{3}{4}$-inch by No. 6 woodscrews.

8.6　BUNSEN BURNER

Tools: kit A, file (round file is preferred), soldering iron.

Description:

The burner (Ins. (a)) is designed, in the first instance (Model A), for operation with coal gas or with the gas generated by the cracking of diesel oil. The basic design may be modified (Model B) for operation with bottled gas, i.e. butane, which is more widely available. Butane has a much higher calorific content so that a low gas-to-air ratio is required. A gas jet with a hole diameter of 0.25 mm or less is required. Methods of providing such a small hole are discussed.

Model A. Coal-gas burner

Requirements:

flame tube	tube, metal, 12 mm diameter	2–67	100	1
jet	nipple from ballpoint pen	2–80		1
gas tubes	outer tubes of ballpoint pens	2–80		2
block	timber, 40 × 20	1–04	40	1
base	timber, 75 × 12	1–02	75	1
vent flap	tin plate (from tin cans)	2–06	25 × 30	1
adhesive,				
fixings				

Procedure:

The flame tube   This may be made of copper tubing and is available from hardware stores or plumbers' merchants. On the other hand, the metal tube may be obtained as scrap. Many light-frame mobile structures such as bicycles, perambulators, baby-buggies, etc., are made from metal tubing. Choose a tube with an internal diameter of 10 to 15 mm (5/16 to 7/16 inch), the smaller being preferred.

Cut off a length of 100 mm using a hacksaw and carefully debur (remove any metallic projections left after sawing), using a file. Then file a hole for the air vent at a distance of 20 mm from the lower end of the flame tube (Ins. (b)). Stop when the hole has a diameter of about 6 mm.

The vent control flap is made from a flat piece of tin plate cut from a tin can. It is wrapped tightly and smoothly around a tube slightly narrower than the flame tube. When it is slipped over the flame tube it should therefore fit quite snugly. The gap between the ends of the control should be nearly equal to the width of the vent. If not the ends of the flap may be folded up. This fold will provide a grip which will simplify the adjustment of the air intake (Ins. (c)).

The gas tubes   The ballpoint pens used for this project should be those with round (not hexagonal) outer tubes, which will fit more tightly in the holes drilled into the body of the burner. Two lengths of tube are required, both being cut from the tapering end: one being 20 mm long and the other being 40 mm long.

The ink-nipple of a ballpoint pen consists of two parts: a plastic conical adaptor and the metal point which holds the ball which gives this pen its name. Remove the point (Ins. (d)) using a pair of pliers. The cone is used as the jet of the Bunsen burner. It has a hole with a diameter of 1 to 1.5 mm (about 1/16 inch) which is just about the correct size for coal gas.

The block   Various holes are to be drilled in the wooden block (Ins. (e)). Drill a central hole, about 8 mm deep, with a diameter just large enough to provide a very tight fit to the flame tube. If a large enough bit is not available, use the

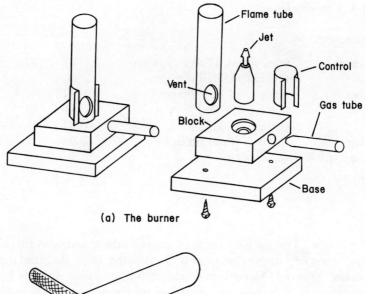

(a) The burner

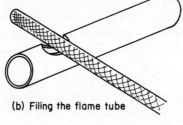

(b) Filing the flame tube

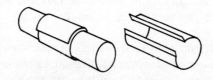

(c) Making the vent control

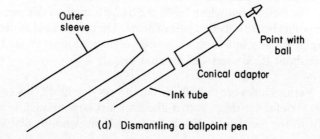

(d) Dismantling a ballpoint pen

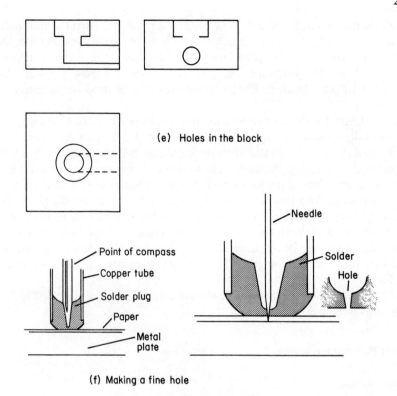

(e) Holes in the block

(f) Making a fine hole

Fig. 8.6 Making a Bunsen burner

smallest bit to drill a cluster of holes which may then be enlarged with a knife and sand-paper to the desired diameter.

In the centre of this hole, drill a smaller hole, 12 to 16 mm deep, of a diameter to accept the shorter gas tube with the taper pointing outwards. Fix the jet cone in position with adhesive.

In one end of the body drill a second hole, just deep enough to break through to the central hole. Insert the longer gas tube into this hole. In this case the taper points inward and so makes it easier to insert. Fix the body of the burner to the base with 1-inch No. 8 woodscrews.

With both tubes in position, it should be easy to blow air through without encountering any obstruction. Eventually (but not now) the tubes will be sealed into the body with vinyl adhesive so that no air can leak out past the sides of the tubes. Fit the flame tube in position in the large central hole with the lower edge of the vent just level with the top of the jet.

Testing and adjusting the burner   When gas issues from the jet, it is blown up the flame tube. The principle of operation of the Bunsen burner depends on the fact that this upward draught creates a region of low pressure near the bottom of the tube and so draws air in through the vent. The mixture of air and gas reaches the top of the tube where it is ignited. The first test is to ensure is that the air is indeed drawn into the tube. Connect a length of flexible tubing to the gas inlet tube. Blow through it while holding a lighted match near the vent. If the flame is sucked in, all is well. If not, the position of the jet should be adjusted, usually upward, till a proper draught is obtained. The gas tubes may then be fixed permanently with adhesive.

The richness, i.e. the gas-to-air ratio, of the mixture should now be tested with the vent fully open or the flap completely removed. A rich mixture will produce a smoky flame and indicates that the vent should be enlarged with the file. A thin mixture may not sustain the flame at all so that it may retreat down the tube and burn at the jet. Turn off the gas immediately if this happens. It indicates that the vent is too large. An adjustment could be made by increasing the diameter of the jet hole. In severe cases it may be necessary to make a new flame tube with a smaller initial vent. With the flap fully open, the gas should burn with a clear flame, the blue zone being much reduced. The flap may then be adjusted to ascertain that the full range of flame types described in Section 2 can be produced.

The gas tubes and the flame tube should now be permanently fixed in place with vinyl adhesive.

Model B.   Butane burner

Requirements:

As for the Model A burner, except for the following:

gas tube	copper	tubing,	6 mm		
	diam		2–68	60 mm	1
gas tube	copper	tubing,	6 mm		
	diam		2–68	20 mm	1
jet	solder				

Procedure

Cut and file the flame tube as before. Drill holes in the body to accommodate the flame and gas tubes.

Making the jet   One end of the shorter gas tube should be plugged up with solder. The plug should extend about 5 mm into the tube and should protrude about 2 mm above it. Heat the point of a pair of compasses (from a mathematical set). Holding the tube, plug downmost, on a hard flat surface, push the point of the compass to within 2 mm of penetrating through the solder. The tube is now held, plug downmost again, on a sheet of exercise-book paper lying on a metal plate. A large sewing needle is now pushed down the hole made by the compass until it is stopped by the metal plate (Ins. (f)). the tiny hole produced in this way should have a diameter of about 0.25 mm or so.

A second method, by which even smaller holes may be obtained, is to push the needle into the solder without penetrating through it. The end of the solder is then carefully smoothed away using fine emery paper until a hole just appears. The advantage in using solder for making the jet is that, if the hole is made too large, it is easily closed up again by touching it with a hot soldering iron.

Brass jets may also be obtained from the suppliers of bottled gas. They have a screw fitting with which they may be turned into a slightly narrower hole drilled the wooden block.

The testing and adjusting of the burner is carried out in much the same way as for Model A. The vent may have to be substantially larger than was the case for Model A.

PRECAUTION

The tests on the burner must be carried out in a well ventilated room. Never allow the gas to flow for more than a few seconds without being ignited. The accumulation of gas in a small enclosed room forms a dangerously explosive mixture with air.

CHAPTER 9

Appendix

9.1 STOCK LISTS

Stock list 1: basic stock

Priority rating: it is recommended that as many as possible of these items be kept in permanent stock. A, essential; B, supplementary; C, only as required

Stock number	Description	Quantity	Priority
1–01	timber, 100 mm × 12 mm section	3.6 m (12 feet)	A
1–02	timber, 75 mm × 12 mm section	3.6 m (12 feet)	A
1–03	timber, 25 mm × 12 mm section	3.6 m (12 feet)	A
1–04	timber, 40 mm × 20 mm section	3.6 m (12 feet)	A
1–10	blockboard, 12 mm thick	1 board (8 feet × 4 feet)	A
1–13	plywood, 12 mm thick	(8 feet × 4 feet)	A
1–14	plywood, 6 mm thick	(8 feet × 4 feet)	C
1–15	plywood, 3 mm thick	(8 feet × 4 feet)	C
1–18	hardboard, medium grade	(8 feet × 4 feet)	A
1–20	woodscrews, 1-inch by No. 8	1 gross	A
1–24	woodscrews, $\frac{3}{4}$-inch by No. 6	1 gross	A
1–27	machine bolts, with nuts and washers 6 mm diameter, 25 mm long	10	A
1–31	nails, round, 20 mm ($\frac{3}{4}$-inch)	500 g	A
1–32	nails, round, 25 mm (1-inch)	100 g	A
1–33	nails, round, 40 mm ($1\frac{1}{2}$-inch)	100 g	B
1–34	nails, round, 50 mm (2-inch)	200 g	C
1–35	nails, round, 75 mm (3-inch)	200 g	C
1–36	nails, round, 100 mm (4-inch)	500 g	C

Stock list 1 (*contd.*)

Stock number	Description	Quantity	Priority
1–37	wire staples, 20 mm	100 g	C
	cable, PVC covered, as below:		
1–40	cable twin-and-earth, 1.5 mm² solid-core		A
1–41	cable twin-and-earth, 2.5 mm² solid-core		C
1–42	cable three-core flexible, 15 ampere		C
1–43	cable three-core flexible, 5 ampere		A
1–50	adhesive, vinyl	500 g	A
1–51	adhesive, polystyrene cement	as required	A
1–53	sellotape, 25 mm wide		A
1–56	paint, aluminium	250 g	C
1–60	kit A		A
1–61	sandpaper, medium		A
1–70	kit B		C
1–80	kit C		B
1–90	kit D		B
1–91	solder, electrician		B

Stock list 2: scrap or borrowed materials

Priority rating: A to be collected and stored whenever available; B a minimum stock to be maintained; C not normally stocked but should be collected when and as required.

Stock number	Description	Source	Priority
2–01	eye-droppers	medicine bottles	A
2–02	leather	old shoes	B
2–03	plastic bags		C
2–04	plastic containers		C
2–05	thread: cotton, nylon		C
2–06	tin cans		C
2–07	wheels, castors	old prams, toys	A
2–08	clothes pegs		C
2–09	biscuit or cake tins		A

Stock list 2 (*contd.*)

Stock number	Description	Source	Priority
2–10	toilet roll cylinders		
2–11	powder detergent		C
2–12	tooth brushes		A
2–13	cloths, rags		C
2–14	balls, tennis or ping-pong		A
2–15	toothpaste tubes		B
2–16	nichrome wire	electric heaters	A
2–20	iron rods (reinforcing rods)		A
2–21	iron wire 2 or 3 mm diameter		C
2–22	tiles PVC		B
2–40	expanded polystyrene (styrofoam)	packing	B
2–60	cable, steel		A
2–61	lamp holders, 12 V		A
2–62	plate, steel, glass		B
2–63	rods, steel		B
2–64	seat covers, plastic		B
2–65	sockets		A
2–66	switches		A
2–67	tubing, aluminium		A
2–68	tubing, copper		A
2–69	tubing, plastic		A
2–70	wiring, electrical		A
2–80	ballpoint pens (ball-pens)		A
2–81	carbon		C
2–82	duplicating paper		C
2–83	paper clips		C
2–84	rubber bands		C
2–85	sellotape		B
2–86	straight pins		B
2–87	string		B
2–90	wire, guitar or piano	from miscellaneous	
2–91	syringes, disposable	clinics	
2–92	can-opener keys		C

Stock list 3: local purchases

Priority rating: all items to be purchased as required

Stock number	Description
3–01	adhesive, Bostik
3–02	buckets, enamel or galvanized
3–03	buckets, plastic
3–04	candles
3–05	cotton wool
3–06	gas lighter
3–07	lamp bulbs 12 V
3–08	polythene bags
3–09	polythene containers
3–10	polythene gloves
3–11	PVC, sheets
3–12	thread: cotton, nylon
3–20	metal plate
3–21	glass plate
3–22	garden hose
3–23	dowels, wooden
3–24	hinge, piano
3–25	rods, reinforcing iron
3–26	rod, flexible curtain
3–27	screws, nuts and bolts
3–28	sheet, galvanized iron
3–29	solder, Tinman's
3–30	strip, iron or steel
3–31	tiles, PVC
3–32	timber
3–33	tubing, cast-iron, copper
3–34	tubing, steel
3–35	varnish, polyurethane
3–36	spring-clip (terry clips)
3–37	wire, staples
3–38	screw hooks (cup-hooks)
3–39	expanded metal
3–40	leather rivets
3–41	batteries, dry-cell
3–42	cable, twin flexible, 5 A (lighting flex)
3–43	cable, three-core flexible, 1 A
3–44	cable, solid core twin-and-earth 1.5 mm^2 section
3–45	cable, solid core twin-and-earth 2.5 mm^2 section

Stock list 3 (*contd.*)

Stock number	Description
3–46	capacitors
3–47	fuses
3–48	lamp bulbs 240 V
3–49	lamp socket, surface mounted
3–50	plug, 3-pin, 13 A (rectangular pins)
3–51	resistors
3–52	socket, 3-pin, 13 A (surface-mounted with switch)
3–53	solder, rosin-cored
3–54	transformer
3–55	lamp, 3 V, 0.3 W
3–61	batteries, accumulators
3–62	tape, insulating PVC
3–63	tubing polythene
3–64	adhesive, rubber solution
3–65	machine bolts, nuts and washers
3–66	elastic luggage strap (bicycle-type)
3–67	glass fuses
3–80	carbon paper
3–81	chinagraph pencils
3–82	felt pens
3–83	plasticine
3–84	sellotape
3–85	string
3–86	ruler, 300 mm
3–91	balloons
3–92	wire, steel (guitar wire)
3–94	organza, organdie

Stock list 4: personal overseas purchases

Sometimes the items listed here may be available in the capital or chief
commerical centre at a reasonable price. However they may be very expensive. In
that case, make use of any personal contacts overseas.

Priority rating: All items listed here should be purchased whenever possible.

Stock number	Description
4–01	adhesive, epoxy-resin
4–20	boss heads
4–21	brass rod, 4 mm diameter
4–22	brass strip
4–23	copper strip
4–24	nuts, bolts, washers, BA sizes
4–25	wire, brass 0.4 mm diameter
4–26	wire, constantan, 26G or 18G
4–27	wire, nichrome, 28G (electric heaters)
4–28	woodscrews, brass 1-inch by No. 8
4–29	electric drill (power tool), 9 mm chuck
4–30	accessories for electric drill
4–41	capacitors (as required)
4–42	circuit boards, group panels
4–43	circuit board, strip boards
4–44	circuit board, solder boards
4–45	clips, crocodile
4–46	clips, terry: 6, 12, 24 mm
4–47	diodes, IN4148
4–48	fuses, household: 3 A, 13 A
4–49	fuses, glass $1\frac{1}{4}$-inch: 1 A, 5 A
4–50	fuses, glass 20 mm: 250, 500 mA
4–51	fuse holders, open-type 20 mm
4–52	fuse holders, panel-mounted 20 mm
4–53	lamps, neon bulbs
4–54	lamp holders, panel-mounted, 12 V
4–55	multimeter, 20 kilohm per volt
4–56	rectifiers, 200 V at 2 A, 6 A
4–57	resistors (as required)
4–58	switches, toggle DPDT 240 V, 2 A
4–82	mercury
4–91	glass-slides.

Stock list 5: overseas purchases

GG: Griffin International Ltd, PO Box 14, Wembley, Middlesex, HAQ 1HJ, England.
PH: Philip Harris (International) Ltd, Lynn Lane, Shepstone, Staffordshire WS14 OEE, England.
RS: RS Components Ltd, Head Office, National Distribution Centre and Trade Counter, PO Box 427, 13–17 Epworth, London EC2P 2HA, England.

Note: The items listed here are those which are needed for the construction of equipment mentioned in this book or for use with such equipment after construction. Substitutes may be allowed in some cases.

Stock number	Description Source Catalogue number	Specification (where necessary)
5–10–01	Boxes, for housing circuits, plastic	
	RS 508–942	190 mm by 110 mm by 60 mm
5–10–02	Clips, crocodile	
	GG ECD–290–R	
	PH P71900/1	
	RS 423–021	
5–10–03	Clips, spring (terry clips)	
	GG CNK–720–010R	5 mm to 6 mm nom
	GG CNK–720–050F	12 mm to 13 mm nom
	GG CNK–720–110N	24 mm to 25 mm nom
	PH C28620/8	5 mm to 6 mm nom
	PH C28660/9	12 mm to 13 mm nom
	PH C28720/1	24 mm to 25 mm nom
5–10–04	Clips, worm-drive, for hose-clamping (jubilee clips)	
	GG CNK–600–010Q	13–19 mm
	GG CNK–600–050E	25–35 mm
	PH C28540/9	13–19 mm
	PH C28580/0	25–35 mm
5–10–05	Wire, constantan, 26G	
	GG ECW–280–190K	bare
	GG ECW–300–190M	dcc
	PH P74210/2	bare
	PH P74530/9	dcc
	(dcc = double cotton-covered)	

Stock list 5 (*contd.*)

Stock number	Description Source Catalogue number	Specification (where necessary)
5–10–06	Wire, constantan (for primary standard resistors)	
	GG ECW–280–130F	20G, bare (1375 mm/ohm)
	GG ECW–300–150B	22G, dcc (786 mm/ohm)
	PH P74050/6	18G, bare (2445 mm/ohm)
	PH P74450/0	22G, dcc (786 mm/ohm)
5–10–07	Wire, copper, enamelled, 24G	
	GG ECW–220–170M	
	PH P72630/3	
	RS 357–750	
5–10–08	Wire, nichrome, bare, 28G,	
	GG ECW–440–210T	
	PH P73900/0	
5–10–09	Grommet	
	RS 543–204	6 mm cable, 9.5 mm panel hole
5–11–01	Rule, metre, horizontal reading, single scale	
	PH C48762/7	
	GG RUL–380–T	
5–11–02	Rule, meter, vertical reading double scale	
	GG RUL–320–P	figures along edge
	PH C48880/2	figures along centre
5–11–03	Stopclock, inexpensive, general purpose	
	GG TKL–400–P	
	PH C80860/2	
5–13–01	Balance, sliding mass, double pan	
	GG BCJ–200–K	cap 2 kg, 0.1 g divisions
	PH C12890/1	as above
5–13–02	Balance, spring	
	GG BAW–620–R	5 kg max, 25 g divisions
	PH P11040/7	as above
5–13–03	Masses, with hanger, slotted, 10 g	
	GG BGT–650–G	hanger with 9 masses
	PH P12220/3	as above
5–13–04	Pulley, board mounting, screw-on	
	GG XBD–720	
	PH P13750/4	

Stock list 5 (*contd.*)

Stock number	Description Source Catalogue number	Specification (where necessary)
5–13–05	Pulley, set	
	GG XBD–480–V	single, plastic
	GG XBD–510–Q	double, plastic
	GG XBD–540–S	triple, plastic
	PH P13550/7	single, aluminium
	PH P13570/2	double, aluminium
	PH P13590/8	triple, aluminium
5–14–01	Thermometers, maximum and minimum, horizontal	
	GG THR–630–U	
	PH C79782/3	
5–14–02	Thermometers, stirring	
	GG THL–340–030T	$- 10$ to $50\,°C$, $150\,mm$
	GG THL–340–050N	$- 10$ to $110\,°C$, $150\,mm$
	GG THL–360–090K	$- 10$ to $360\,°C$, $300\,mm$
	PH C79480/9	$- 10$ to $50\,°C$, $150\,mm$
	PH C79500/0	$- 10$ to $100\,°C$, $150\,mm$
	PH C79440/8	$- 10$ to $360\,°C$, $304\,mm$
5–15–01	Tuning forks, set of four (256, 320, 384, and 512 Hz)	
	PH P44565/9	
5–16–01	Fuses, glass, 20 mm length	
	GG ECF–630–090D	200 mA
	GG ECF–630–130R	500 mA
	GG ECF–630–170F	1 A
	PH P76320/8	250 mA
	PH P76340/3	500 mA
	PH P76360/9	1 A
	RS 412–122	250 mA
	RS 412–138	500 mA
	RS 412–144	1 A
5–16–02	Fuses, glass, 1.25 inch length	
	GG ECF–570–330M	5 A
	GG ECF–570–390R	15 A
	RS 412–302	5 A
	RS 412–330	15 A
5–16–03	Fuse holders, chassis-mounting, open type	
	GG ECF–710–090J	for 20 mm fuses
	GG ECF–710–030E	for 1.25 inch fuses
	PH P76541/2	for 20 mm fuses
	RS 412–661	for 20 mm fuses
	RS 412–677	for 1.25 inch fuses

Stock list 5 (*contd.*)

Stock number	Description Source Catalogue number	Specification (where necessary)
5–16–04	Group panels, miniature RS 433–703	
5–16–05	Lamps, filament RS 586–302	6 V, 0.36 W
5–16–06	Lamp holders, LES, single hole, panel-mounting RS 565–131	clear
5–16–07	Plugs, 4 mm, with side-entry hole GG ECD–370–A GG ECD–400–030J GG ECD–400–070U PH P71180/4 PH P71200/6 RS 444–797, etc.	 red, stackable black, stackable black red various colours
5–16–08	Strip boards (Veroboard type) RS 433–826 RS 433–832	 95 mm by 292 mm, 2.5 mm pitch 95 mm by 291 mm, 3.8 mm pitch
5–16–09	Switches, 240 V a.c., 1 A min, toggle GG ECK–840–050L RS 316–591	 single-pole, two-way (SPDT) 2 A double-pole, two-way (DPDT) 1 A
5–16–10	Terminal post, brass PH P70715/1 RS 423–093	
5–16–11	Terminal post, for tags and 4 mm plugs (slimline) GG ECD–760–030M GG ECD–760–070A PH P71010/1 PH P70990/1 RS 423–201, etc.	 red black red black various colours
5–16–12	Transformer, charger (for 3 V and 6 V combinations) RS 207–122 RS 207–239	 0–4.5–9 V, 2.2 A 0–4.5–9 V, 5.5 A
5–16–13	Transformer, power supply RS 207–560 RS 207–576	 0–9 V, 0–9 V, 2.7A, 50 VA 0–9 V, 0–9 V, 5.5 A, 100 VA

Stock list 5 (*contd.*)

Stock number	Description		Specification (where necessary)
	Source	Catalogue number	
5–16–14	Battery charger, with meter		
	GG	BMV–220–T	2, 6, and 12 V, 1.5 A
	GG	BMV–260–X	2, 6, and 12 V, 2 A
	GG	BMV–280–A	as above, but tropicalized
	GG	BMV–330–E	2, 6, and 12 V, 4 A
	PH	P68622/6	6 and 12 V, 6 A
	PH	P68680/9	2, 6, and 12 V, 1 A
	PH	P68685/8	as above, but tropicalized
5–16–15	Charger-inverter (to supply 240 V a.c. from 12 V battery and vice versa)		
	GG	EKP–200–K	150 W output at 240 V a.c.
5–17–01	Capacitors, electrolytic, axial leads		
	RS	103–654	2.2 μF 63 V
	RS	103–660	4.7 μF 63 V
	RS	103–553	10 μF 25 V
5–17–02	Capacitors, polyester, 250 V d.c. working (160 V a.c.)		
	RS	112–850	0.1 μF
	RS	112–901	1 μF
	RS	113–263, etc.	100 pF to 0.01 μF (E3 values)
	RS	113–904, etc.	0.1 μF to 0.47 μF (E3 values)
5–17–03	Rectifiers, single diodes		
	RS	261–823	200 V, 6 A
	RS	261–299	100 V, 3 A (1N5401)
	RS	261–176	400 V, 1 A (1N4004)
5–17–04	Rectifiers, bridge type		
	RS	262–078	200 V, 6 A
	RS	261–592	200 V, 2 A
5–17–05	Resistors, carbon, 0.5 W		
	RS	142–097, etc.	10 to 10 Mohms (E24 values)
	RS	955–332	set containing 10 of each of the above values
5–17–06	Resistors, carbon, 1 W		
	RS	143–090, etc.	10 to 10 Mohms (E12 values)
	RS	955–348	set containing 10 of each of the above values
5–17–07	Resistors, carbon, 2 W, high stability		
	RS	134–513, etc.	10 to 10 Mohms (E12 values)
	RS	955–310	set containing 10 of each of the above values

Stock list 5 (*contd.*)

Stock number	Description Source Catalogue number	Specification (where necessary)
5–17–08	Resistors, wire-wound, 2.5 W	
	RS 151–518, etc.	0.22 to 270 ohms (E12 values)
	RS 955–382	set containing 5 of each of the above values
5–18–01	Spheres, expanded polystyrene (for molecular models)	
	GG MTC–210–030V	12.5 mm diam.
	GG MTC–210–050P	19 mm diam.
	GG MTC–210–090D	32 mm diam.
	PH C50600/2	13 mm diam.
	PH C50620/8	19 mm diam.
	PH C50660/9	32 mm diam.
5–20–01	Boss heads, multipurpose, 16 mm opening	
	GG STE–410–X	
	PH C69725/7	
5–20–02	Boss heads, standard	
	GG STE–330–070F	
	PH C69680/0	
5–20–03	Burner, bunsen, butane (bottled gas)	
	GG BYD–404–S	
	PH C23020/3	
5–20–04	Burner, meker, butane (for higher temperatures)	
	GG BYD–805–D	
	PH C23300/9	
5–20–05	Crucible tongs, iron	
	GG TNS–380–C	
	PH C81160/1	
5–20–06	Gauze, iron, with circular ceramic centre	
	GG GMX–310–010E	125 mm by 125 mm
	PH C42500/2	as above
5–20–07	Clamps, retort stand	
	GG STE–300–010D	
	PH C69660/5	
5–20–08	Clips, Mohr	
	GG CNK–300–010R	11 mm opening
	PH C28400/5	as above
5–20–09	Cork borers	
	GG CSD–550–010E	set of 6, 4 mm to 10 mm diam.
	PH C73720/6	set of 6, 5 mm to 11 mm diam.

Stock list 5 (*contd.*)

Stock number	Description Source Catalogue number	Specification (where necessary)
5–20–10	Cork borer sharpener GG CSD–570–Q PH C73760/6	
5–20–11	Tubing, rubber GG TWR–250–130V GG TWR–250–170J GG TWR–460–130V PH C86620/1 PH C86660/2 PH C86941/9	5 mm bore, 1.5 mm wall (size N5) 8 mm bore, 2 mm wall (size N8) 5 mm bore, 4 mm wall (size H5) 5 mm bore, 1.5 mm wall 8 mm bore, 2 mm wall 5 mm bore, 4 mm wall
5–20–12	Test-tube brush GG BUR–550–010P PH C21340/0	15 mm diam. 15 mm diam.
5–22–01	Eye shields, simple form GG SAP–210–X PH 64540/3	
5–23–01	Absorption tubes, glass plain (U-tubes) GG ABL–400–030L PH C10300/9	15 mm bore, 125 mm long 13 mm bore, 105 mm long
5–23–02	Rod, soda-lime glass, 6 mm outside diam	
5–23–03	T-tubes GG ADF–710–030S PH C40420/5	polypropylene, 7 to 8 mm diam. glass
5–23–04	Test-tubes, borosilicate glass (Pyrex), with rim GG TES–630–070W GG TES–600–150 W PH C77120/2 PH C77260/7	100 mm long by 12 mm diam. 150 mm long by 25 mm diam. 100 mm long by 12 mm diam. 150 mm long by 25 mm diam.
5–23–05	Test-tubes, soda-lime glass, with rim GG TES–200–110U PH C76700/4	100 mm long by 12 mm diam. as above

Stock list 5 (*contd.*)

Stock number	Description Source Catalogue number	Specification (where necessary)
5–23–06	Tubing, soda-lime glass, capillary	
	GG TWL–380–070V	6 mm diam. by 0.5 mm bore
	PH C85940/3	5 mm diam. by 0.5 mm bore
5–23–07	Tubing, soda-lime glass, normal wall	
	GG TWL–300–060L	6 mm diam.
	GG TWL–300–120T	12 mm diam.
	GG TWL–300–260D	24 mm diam.
	PH C85500/8	6 mm diam.
	PH C85580/9	13 mm diam.
	PH C85660/8	25 mm diam.
5–27–01	Mercury	
	PH S54000/0	1 kg pack
5–29–01	Stoppers, rubber	
	GG SYH–530–110P	for 12 mm opening, one hole (No11)
	GG SYH–580–170Y	for 25 mm opening, two holes (No23)
	GG SYH–580–190C	for 29 mm opening, two holes (No27)
	PH C72260/4	for 12 mm opening, one hole (No11)
	PH C72780/8	for 25 mm opening, two holes (No23)
	PH C72820/5	for 29 mm opening, two holes (No27)
5–29–02	Stoppers, cork, to fit soft drink bottles with 16 mm openings (always very useful)	
	GG CSD–460–130S	diam: 18 mm top, 15 mm bottom
	PH C73220/8	diam: 19 mm top, 16 mm bottom
5–33–01	Glass slides, 76 mm long by 26 mm wide	
	PH B38123/4	1.0 to 1.2 mm thick
5–79–01	Graph paper, isometric (for technical drawing)	
	GG PBH–330–F	
	PH C48060/8	
5–93–01	Adhesive, epoxy-resin	
	GG AES–300–R	Araldite rapid
	PH C10820/3	Epoxy-resin, quickset
	RS 554–850	Quickset epoxy adhesive

9.2 THE CORONA EXPERIMENT

Apparatus: optical bench, corona apparatus, sodium-light source

Theory

Small spherical particles will cause light waves to be diffracted through an angle θ given by

$$d\sin\theta = m\lambda$$

where d is the diameter of the particles and λ is the wavelength of the light. For spherical particles, m takes the values 1.22, 2.23, etc. If a point source of light is viewed through a suspension of these particles, e.g. dust particles floating in air, a series of concentric rings will appear to surround the light source. These rings

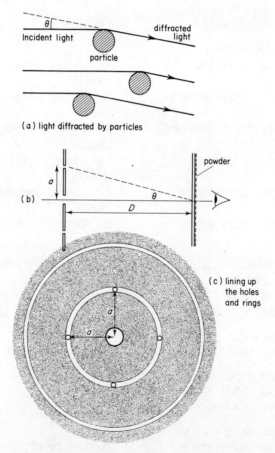

Fig. 9.1 The Corona experiment

form the corona, and they may be used experimentally in two ways:

1. to determine the mean diameter of the particles if the wavelength of the light is known; and
2. to determine the wavelength of the light if the diameter of the particles is known.

The diameter of the particles may be determined by direct measurement using a graticule in the eyepiece of a microscope.

Method

Sprinkle the lycopodium powder on the glass plate. Gently shake the plate from side to side to spread the powder uniformly. Carefully remove any excess by holding the glass vertically and giving it a single gentle tap.

Mount the plate on a lens holder. View the centre hole of the screen through the plate. Rings of light appear to be encircling the hole (Fig. 9.1(c)). The angular radius of these rings is measured by adjusting the distance D, between the plate and the screen, until one of the rings coincides with a set of four arranged symmetrically around the central hole. If the angular radius of the ring is θ, then $\tan \theta = a/D$ where a is the distance between the smaller holes and the central hole.

9.3 CHEMICAL INDICATORS

Indicators are substances which change colour when transferred from an acid medium to an alkaline one. The most common indicator is litmus which is red when acidic and blue when alkaline.

Many plants contain pigments called anthocyanins which may be used as

Table 9.1 Natural indicators from plants

Plant	Part	Colour acid to alkali	pH
Red cabbage	Leaves	Red to blue	6 to 7
Karkadeh	Petals	Red to blue	6 to 7
Prickly pear (*Opuntia* species)	Berries	Red to yellow/green	6.6
Rhododendron	Petals	Red at	3
		Pink at	4
		Violet at	5 to 8
		Blue at	9
		Green–blue at	10
		Green at	11
Field poppy (*Papaver* species)	Petals	Vermilion at	3 to 4
		Pink at	5 to 6
		Orange–brown at	7 to 8
Verbena	Berries	Red to yellow/green	6.6
Mulberries	Berries	Red to blue	6 to 7
Bougainvillaea	Petals	Red to yellow/green	6.6

indicators. They change colour at a specific pH value depending on the type of anthocyanins contained in the pigment. Colour variations may be from vermilion through purple to bright green.

Red cabbage is a very common source of indicator. In Sudan and other parts of North Africa, the petals of a particular variety of rose are used to prepare a drink called karkadeh (or carcade) which show the same colour changes as litmus. Mulberries and similar fruits also have this litmus-like pigment.

Table 9.1 lists a number of plants which contain anthocyanins. The possible colour changes are also shown but these may vary from place to place depending on the soil constituents in which the plant is grown.

The pigment may be extracted either by boiling in water or by crushing.

9.4   FINDING TRUE NORTH

True, or geographic, north may be obtained by using an ordinary wrist watch or alarm clock provided that it is of the analogue type, i.e. it is of the traditional kind with an hour hand and a shorter minute hand. (Most people today have taken to wearing the new digital electronic watches which unfortunately, cannot be used for the present purpose.)

In the northern hemisphere

Holding the watch face horizontally, orientate it so that the *hour hand* points towards the sun. To check that this is so, hold a matchstick vertically at the point of this hand. If the shadow of the match falls along the length of the hour hand and crosses directly over the centre of the watch (Fig. 9.2(a)) then this hand is pointing towards the sun. If you bisected the angle *between the hour hand and the figure '12'*, the bisector will lie in the direction of *true south*.

True north, of course, lies in the opposite direction.

In the southern hemisphere

Holding the watch face horizontally, orientate it so that the *figure '12'* points towards the sun (Fig. 9.2(b)). Check this by holding a matchstick vertically over the "12". If the shadow of the matchstick falls across that of the watch face, then the '12' is pointing directly at the sun. Bisect the angle between *the '12' and the hour hand*, as above. The bisector will lie in the direction of *true north*.

Correction for standard time

The above methods assume that your watch is indicating local time, i.e. the correct time for the longitude of your particular location. This is not necessarily the same as standard time which is usually determined by legislation for the entire country or state in which you are living. For example, Nigeria takes its standard time from the meridian of 15 degrees east of Greenwich; Sudan, East Africa and

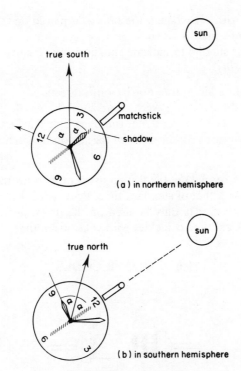

Fig. 9.2 Using the watch

Zimbabwe take it from 30 °C east of Greenwich, etc. If your local meridian is appreciably different from your country's standard then an adjustment to the direction obtained for the true north has to be made.

The general rule is: rotate the bisector by an amount and in the direction in which your local meridian differs from the standard.

For example, Lagos, Nigeria, has a longitude of 3° 27' east of Greenwich. Lagos therefore lies $11\frac{1}{2}°$ west of the Nigerian standard meridian (which, in fact, passes through Ndjamena, Chad). The bisector, indicating true south, should therefore be rotated by $11\frac{1}{2}°$ toward the west.

On the other hand, Bulawayo, Zimbabwe, has a longitude of 28° 30' east of Greenwich. The bisector, indicating true north, should be rotated by 1° 30' to the west.

The situation is further complicated if your country, besides having standard time, also has summer time. If this is the case, the bisector has to be rotated an additional *15° toward the west* while summer time is in force.

9.5   LOCAL SOLAR TIME AND STANDARD TIME

A sundial, if it is mounted with the fin vertical and pointing exactly north or south, will indicate the solar local time. This means that the dial will indicate twelve noon when the sun is directly overhead. Standard time, on the other hand, will only coincide with solar time if the sundial is placed on the exact meridian from which standard time is taken.

If you want your sundial to indicate standard time then you must make the following adjustments:

1. set the fin pointing along true north–south direction.
2. determine the difference between your local longitude and that of the meridian from which your national standard time is taken.
3. tilt the sundial towards the direction of the standard meridian by exactly this difference.

A simple method of making the last adjustment is to tilt the sundial till the reading coincides with that of standard time. Because of the 'equation of time' variations, this method may only be used on the dates, mentioned in Project 7.2.3, when solar local time coincides with solar mean time.

9.6   COLOUR CODES

Resistors

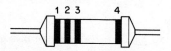

Band 1 is the first figure of the value in ohms.
Band 2 is the second figure of the value in ohms.
Band 3 is the number of zeros following the first and second figures of the value (gold and silver are exception).
Band 4 is the tolerance, i.e. the permitted error in the stated value.

Colour	Band 1 1st figure	Band 2 2nd figure	Band 3 multiplier	Band 4 tolerance
Black	0	0	× 1	—
Brown	1	1	× 10	1%
Red	2	2	× 100	2%
Orange	3	3	× 1000	
Yellow	4	4	× 10000	
Green	5	5	× 100000	
Blue	6	6	× 1000000	
Violet	7	7		
Grey	8	8		
White	9	9		
Gold			× 0.1	5%
Silver			× 0.01	10%

Examples

Band 1	Band 2	Band 3	Band 4	
Brown	Black	Black	Gold	$= 10 \times 1 = 10$ ohms at 5%
Red	Violet	Gold	Gold	$= 27 \times 0.1 = 2.7$ ohms at 5%
Green	Blue	Yellow	Red	$= 56 \times 10\,000 = 560$ kohms at 2%
Grey	Red	Green	Silver	$= 82 \times 100\,000 = 8.2$ Mohms at 10%

Polyester film capacitors

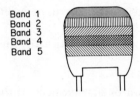

Band 1
Band 2
Band 3
Band 4
Band 5

Band 1 is the first figure of the value in picofarads.

Band 2 is the second figure of the value in picofarads.

Band 3 is the number of zeros following the first and second figures of the value (no exceptions).

Band 4 is the tolerance: black $= \pm 20\%$; white $- \pm 10\%$.

Band 5 is the working d.c. voltage: Red $= 250$ V d.c. working; Yellow $= 400$ V d.c. working.

The colour interpretation of Bands 1, 2, and 3 is the same as that for resistors. Gold and silver bands are not used.

Examples

Band 1	Band 2	Band 3	Band 4	Band 5	
Brown	Black	Orange	Black	Red	$= 0.01\,\mu$F, 250V d.c. working, at 20%
Red	Red	Green	White	Yellow	$= 2.2\,\mu$F, 400 V d.c. working, at 10%

Three-core mains cable (domestic, single phase)

	Former UK	European Common Market preferred
Live	Red	Brown
Neutral	Black	Blue
Earth	Green	Green/Yellow

9.7 GLOSSARY

The following is a list of timber and woodworking terms which are used in this book or which you may come across when purchasing timber.

arris intersection of two plane or curved surfaces (see Fig. 9.3(a)).

batten a thin piece of timber, usually about 50 mm by 25 mm; in the construction of crates, used for reinforcing the sides, tops and bottoms.

bevel a sloping surface.

chamfer the surface produced by bevelling the intersection of two or more plane surfaces (see Fig. 9.3(b)).

dowel a cylindrical piece of hardwood used for joining two pieces of timber. Dowels are sometimes grooved (keyed) to facilitate gluing (cf. dowel joints, Fig. 9.3(d)).

deal a piece of square-sawn softwood (usually pine).

end see Fig. 9.3(a).

face see Fig. 9.3(a).

grain the general direction or arrangement of the wood elements or fibres (cf. growth rings).

grained,
    coarse- having relatively large wood elements or unusually wide growth rings.
    distorted- due to presence of knots.
    end- wood elements on cross-section.

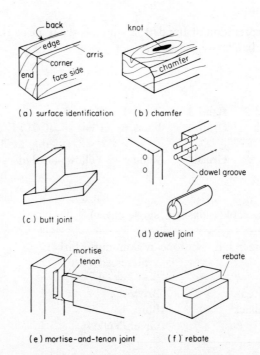

(a) surface identification

(b) chamfer

(c) butt joint

(d) dowel joint

(e) mortise-and-tenon joint

(f) rebate

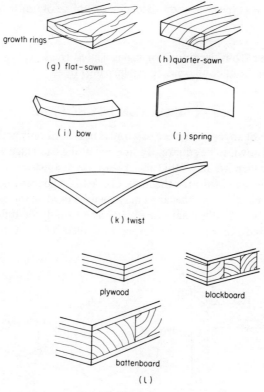

growth rings

(g) flat-sawn

(h) quarter-sawn

(i) bow

(j) spring

(k) twist

plywood

blockboard

battenboard

(l)

Fig. 9.3 Timber terms

even- little variation in grain.

fine- narrow growth rings, sometimes referred to as fine textured.

growth rings a layer of wood produced by the growth of one year, also referred to as annual rings

hardness the ability of the wood to resist indentation

joint,

butt see Fig. 9.3(c)

dowel see Fig. 9.3(d)

mortise and-tenon see Fig. 9.3(e)

knots that part of a branch embedded in the wood by the annual growth of the tree (see Fig. 9.3(b))

rebate a stepped or step-shaped reduction formed on an arris or end or face of a piece of wood (see Fig. 9.3(f))

sawn,

flat- wood sawn with the rings running almost parallel to a face (see Fig. 9.3(g))

quarter- wood sawn with the rings running almost perpendicular to a face (see Fig. 9.3(h))

264

warp for various types warps or distortion of a piece of timber see Fig. 9.3 (i) to
(k)
wood
hard- timber from deciduous or broad-leafed trees
soft- timber from coniferous (cone-bearing) trees

9.8 USE OF THE TRY-SQUARE

Marking out right angles on a piece of wood is best done only with reference to an
arris which is known to be square. By sighting along each face and edge, find an
adjacent pair which are flat. Hold the try-square against the arris, as shown in
Fig. 9.4a and, looking towards the light, check that the face and the edge are at
right angles to each other. This arris may then be used as the reference straight
edge against which all other marks are made. It is usually identified by marking it
with a circle-and-tail on the corresponding face and a cross on the edge
(Fig. 9.4b).

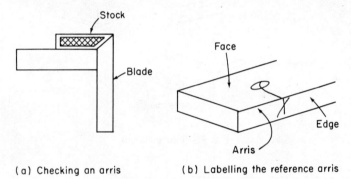

(a) Checking an arris   (b) Labelling the reference arris

Fig. 9.4 Fixing a reference

It is important to check that the try square itself is accurate. This is done by
drawing overlapping lines to an arris with the stock pointing in opposing
directions (Fig. 9.5).

More often than not, you will be required to cut strips of wood to the required
length. If the cut is to be exactly square, lines should be made right around the
piece. A line must therefore be drawn on each of the four sides. To ensure that
these lines coincide at every arris, each of them must be squared against the

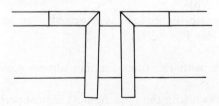

Fig. 9.5 Testing the try-square

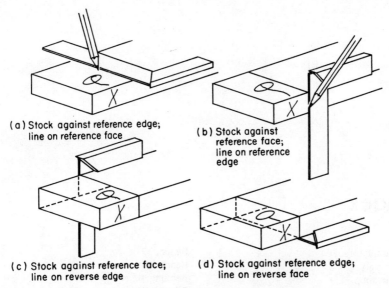

(a) Stock against reference edge;
line on reference face

(b) Stock against
reference face;
line on reference
edge

(c) Stock against reference face;
line on reverse edge

(d) Stock against reference edge;
line on reverse face

Fig. 9.6 Marking a batten

reference arris, face or edge. Make such marks in the sequence shown in Fig. 9.6. They should meet at the arris diagonally opposite to the reference. If the stock is always made to point in the same direction, the marks will almost certainly coincide even if the trysquare is slightly inaccurate.

Accurate marking may be spoiled by inaccurate sawing, very often due to the saw not being held vertically. You can check that you are holding the saw vertically by standing the square on the wood and holding the saw against it (Fig. 9.7).

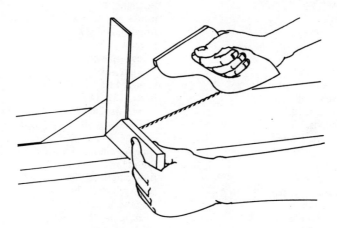

Fig. 9.7 Controlling a saw cut

Index